Upper Space Security and Information Warfare

Upper Space Security and Information Warfare

Col. Retd. S.C. Narang

PRASHANT PUBLISHING HOUSE
DELHI-110094

Published by :
Prashant Publishing House
C-34, 28 Foota Road, Gali-3,
West Karwal Nagar, Delhi-110094
Phone : 011-22963970, Mob. : 9810396373
e-mail.: prashantpublishinghouse@gmail.com

Upper Space Security and Information Warfare

First Published 2018

ISBN 978-81-938012-2-2

PRINTED IN INDIA
Published by Mr. R.K. Jha M/s Prashant Publishing House and Published at H.S. Offset House Press, Delhi.

Contents

Preface

Space warfare will be an integrated part of battle planning by the Chinese People's Liberation Army in any future conflict with the United States. The People's Liberation Army has carefully absorbed and is reacting to what the American armed forces have published on space warfare and counter-space operations. Chinese strategists and legal scholars are engaged in an internal debate on how traditional ideas of sovereignty and the laws of war apply in space.

Space power is the capability to exploit space forces to support national security strategy and achieve national security objectives. Used effectively, space power enhances America's opportunities to succeed across the broad range of military operations. Space warfare is combat that takes place in outer space, i.e. outside the atmosphere. Technically, as a distinct classification, it refers to battles where the targets themselves are in space. Space warfare therefore includes ground-to-space warfare, such as attacking satellites from the Earth, as well as space-to-space warfare, such as satellites attacking satellites.

The use of the space medium and systems that operate in space are of critical importance to the Air Force and its ability to provide our nation with global reach, power, and awareness. Each Air Force core competency relies on the attributes of space systems to meet stringent requirements for navigation, weather, command and control, surveillance, reconnaissance, and other essential capabilities. The Air Force is unique in its ability to capitalize on the attributes of space systems by being able to respond with rapid mobility and firepower to the near-real-time information afforded by systems operating in space. As an operational medium, space and the systems that operate in space, offer several useful attributes.

Information warfare is the tactical and strategic use of information to gain an advantage. It includes multiple types of operations and has been pursued in radically different ways during different eras. Information warfare is also known as cyberwarfare, electronic warfare and cyberattack.

Space warfare is combat that takes place in outer space, i.e. outside the atmosphere. Technically, as a distinct classification, it refers to battles where the targets themselves are in space. Space warfare therefore includes ground-to-space warfare, such as attacking satellites from the Earth, as well as space-to-space warfare, such as satellites attacking satellites.

This is a reference book. All the matter is just compiled and edited in nature, taken from the various sources which are in public domain.

The aim of this book is to evaluate and differentiate between the phenomena of cyberwarfare and information warfare, as manifestations of what we perceive as postmodern warfare. We describe and analyse the current examples of the use the postmodern warfare and the reactions of states and international bodies to these phenomena. The subject matter of this paper is the relationship between new types of postmodern conflicts and the law of armed conflicts (law of war).

—*Editor*

1

Space Power

The term space power is found in writing as early as 1964, but appears without a definition. Concerted efforts to define space power did not occur until much later. In 1988, Lt Col David Lupton, in his publication, *On Space Warfare, A Space Power Doctrine*, presented the first formal definition. Lupton suggested that respected definitions of land, sea and air power offered by Mahan, Mitchell, Arnold and others included three characteristics: 1) elements of national power, 2) purposes that are military and non-military, and 3) systems that are military and civilian. With this in mind, Lupton offered this definition:

Space power is the ability of a nation to exploit the space environment in pursuit of national goals and purposes and includes the entire astronautical capabilities of the nation.

Lupton adds that a nation with such capabilities is also called a *space power*. Col Robert Larned, former Deputy Director for Operations, AFSPACECOM, presented the following definition at the 1994 Air & Space Doctrine Symposium:

Spacepower is the ability to exploit the civil, commercial and national security space systems and associated infrastructure in support of national security strategy.

He further defined space systems as, "distributed systems consisting of three elements: a space element, a terrestrial element, and a link element."

In 1995, the authors of Space Power 2010 offered another definition of space power.

Their idea was to define the individual terms space and power, and then marry them together to form the full concept. They defined space as "the area above the Earth's atmosphere extending out to infinity in all directions, beginning approximately 62 miles (or 100 kilometers) above the Earth's surface."

They defined power as "the ability of a state or non-state actor to achieve its goals and objectives in the presence of other actors on the world stage." Their overall definition then looked like this:

Space power is the ability of a state or non-state actor to achieve its goals and objectives in the presence of other actors on the world stage through control and exploitation of the space environment.

More recently, Colin Gray offered yet another definition in his 1996 article, "The Influence of Space Power upon History." Gray said, Space power may be defined as the ability to use space while denying reliable use to any foe.

Finally, the authors of the February 1997 draft of *AFDD 2-2, Space Operations*, defined space power as:

The capability to exploit space forces to support national security strategy and achieve national security objectives.

The authors also provide categories of space power. First, they suggest that the subparts to space power can be seen as national, DOD, civil and commercial space systems and their associated infrastructures. Secondly, these parts can be further subdivided as follows: space-based systems, ground-based systems, and launch systems.

Predictions of Space Power

Predictions of space power are a valid part of space power theory. Some predictions are derived from explanations of space power like those discussed above. Many of these explanations carry with them an ability to predict "more of the same" (or a variation of it) in the future. Yet some predictions are stand-alone and do not enjoy an accompanying explanation. These stand-alone predictions of space power cause us to look (and hopefully plan) ahead in the same way that Giulio Douhet's *Command of the Air* assisted air power. Nevertheless, the major predictive theories have strengths and weaknesses. Mantz' theory looked at firepower in space. His publication predicted space power to progress in much the same manner that air power has—to the point of being a decisive force by applying long range, strategic firepower (including bombardment) through the sky. Mantz' respectful discussion of space strike operations gives amplification to the idea of decisive space power as a potential war winner. It also gives specific details to accomplish space control in a weaponized space environment. Disappointingly, Mantz intentionally chose to limit his theory to fire power and thus makes no statement on the significance of information systems to the future of warfighting. Nor does he address but scant information on joint operations. Thus, Mantz' theory is not a space power theory; it is a space *combat* theory. Nevertheless, with the exception of his omission of force enhancement roles from space, Mantz' theory remains one of the most scholarly works on space power that actually claims to be a theory.

Other discussions about the weaponization of space add to space power theory. Predictions that use scenarios help to create a believable picture of the future with (or without) appropriate space capabilities. These "what if" scenarios raise awareness of the importance of space-based information and weapon systems. If there is value in fiction literature to the body of space power theory, this may be an area of possible contribution.

There are, however, some concerns with the idea of space weaponization. First, authors discussing space weaponization generally assume that space weaponization is inevitable and thus focus on weapons in space giving little attention to the use of groundbased or air weapons to target space-based assets. Additionally, given the lack of history to describe, some of these theories take on a how-to flavor thus departing conservative descriptive theory.

Without thorough explanations, prescriptive approaches run the risk of being less than theory (probably strategy or doctrine regarding the functions of space weapons). A complete theory of why weapons in space are important (as opposed to "how-to") may be more valuable at this point in history.

Several other predictive theories exist. The Air Force studies cause the reader to imagine more future details than one might envision on his or her own. On the other hand, it is possible that the Air Force studies are simply not free enough from political "guidance" to "sell" to a wide audience of space "high ground" enthusiasts, "infowarriors" and advocates of joint operations. Furthermore, like explanations of space power, a coherent prediction of integrated air and space power is missing from Air Force libraries. This theoretical foundation must be laid in order to pave the way for future Air Force operations.

Lack of Comprehensive Theories of Space Power

The body of space power literature currently lacks a single comprehensive theory. No one theory thoroughly defines, explains and predicts the nature, significance and functioning of space power. Space power theory lacks the exhaustive treatment of military theory comparable to Clausewitz' work. Nevertheless, an examination of the closest candidates to a comprehensive theory is illuminating.

The closest candidates to a comprehensive theory were trailblazing efforts, but lacked the scope and sense of thoroughness associated with comprehensive theories. These three works were: 1) the gravity well theory; 2) Lupton's *On Space Warfare*; and 3) Mantz' space combat theory. Writers referred to these three theories more often than any other space power theory. Each of these theories served as a baseline or starting point for other theories.

Each theory made a unique and significant contribution. The gravity well theory raised the importance of space power to that of other types of military power. Through a respectable scientific discussion of space as the high ground of modern war, Stine and others placed space power on an equal level with air, land and sea power. Stine's "geographic" approach to space power established it as a member to the joint warfighting team as well as a potentially decisive war winner. Likewise, Lupton's theory helped to advance a solid definition of space power. Also, Lupton's four philosophical schools of thought concerning the military use of space is referenced more than any other work in the body of space power theory. His explanation of the space control school was not only illuminating, it has heightened awareness of this important subject. Finally, Mantz' theory represented a first in space power theory. Mantz is the first to capture a theory of the nature, importance and uses of firepower from space. He is one of the first theorists to formally explain why space combat power may require an independent branch of service to organize, train and equip armed forces for a separate combat arena. As beneficial as three theories were to space power theory, each one fell short of a comprehensive theory.

The gravity well theory lacked a single author, which made it difficult to capture its full explanation in a single document. The theory, however, was embraced in 1958 when Air Force Gen Homer A. Boushey, Director of Space Flight Research and Development proposed putting missiles on the moon; the idea, however, met political and economic resistance. This theory's time has simply not arrived.

Additionally, this theory did not define space power, and it lacked sufficient discussion on space power used in a force enhancement or treaty verification role. Likewise, Mantz' theory offered no explanation of current space operations; it was fundamentally a prediction. More importantly, all three theories lacked historical examples of space power from the Persian Gulf War and, therefore, failed to draw conclusions about the importance of space power to information warfare.

Each theory ultimately lacked a sense of thoroughness found in those theories recognized as complete and comprehensive works. Furthermore, none of these theories claimed to be a comprehensive theory. Proponents of the gravity well theory did not claim they have a complete theory. Lupton described his work as "doctrine" not theory. And Mantz' theory was not a space power theory, but a theory of space *combat* power. Even in his excellent article "The Influence of Space Power upon History," (which sounds remarkably like an attempt at a Mahaniantype space theory), Colin Gray stated that "Despite its growing importance, no comprehensive theory of space power has been formulated."

SPACE CHARACTERISTICS

The space operating environment is different from that of terrestrial-based forces. Space is the largest operating medium and surrounds all other operating media. Space offers the highest possible positioning above land, sea, air, and special operations forces. This affords a commanding view of operations and provides an important military advantage. Space-based forces operate in accordance with the laws of astrodynamics, while terrestrial-based air and space forces operate in accordance with the laws of aerodynamics.

Although there are no international agreements delineating a boundary between air and space, terrestrial-based forces generally operate below an altitude of 100 kilometers; whereas space-based forces operate above this altitude, where the effects of lift and drag are negligible.

Space-based forces operate in an environment characterized by high-energy particles and fluctuating magnetic fields and temperatures, while terrestrial forces operate in the Earth's atmosphere, with its temperature, moisture, wind, precipitation, and pressure differences. Airmen must understand both environments as they create an integrated air and space operation. Space and terrestrial forces complement each other. Used properly, space forces are a significant force multiplier for terrestrial forces—space forces facilitate more efficient and coherent terrestrial operations.

Space Systems

Space systems consist of three elements: a space element, a terrestrial element, and a link element. The space element consists of the platform in which astrodynamics is the primary principle governing its movement through its environment. The terrestrial element consists of the land, sea, or airborne equipment and personnel used to receive, transmit, and process data from, or to control, the space element. The link element is the communication used to convey data and information between the space element and the terrestrial element. All three elements can be key factors in military operations. Just as stealth technology and precision munitions permitted new operational approaches to airpower, the recent additional emphasis placed on operational and tactical exploitation of space capabilities offers a new operational horizon from which military forces can increase their situational awareness, operations tempo, information dominance, and overall responsiveness and effectiveness.

Recommendations

In view of the above analysis of space power definitions, explanations and predictions, this chapter proposes the following recommendations for future space power theorists. Future approaches should discuss definitions, explanations and predictions of space power more thoroughly. Serious theorists should aspire to pen a single comprehensive theory of space power. In addition, this chapter submits the following list of topics for more complete exploration:

1) The contributions of the four groups of space power theorists intentionally omitted from this chapter.
2) A thorough descriptive approach to space power (using space power in the Gulf War which can be further assessed and reassessed as further historical examples of space power become available)
3) An updated and complete definition of space power
4) The influence of the space environment on space strategy
5) What makes space power unique from other forms of military operations
6) Hot topic one: space control
7) Space superiority (Why? What is it? How?)

8) Hot topic two: space power organization (Douhet, Mitchell, and Trenchard all said a nation needs centralized control of air power—how does this apply to space power?)
9) Limitations of space power
10) The integration of space power theory with air power theory to clearly shape the future of US air and space forces (integration of air and space environments, common attributes, superiority, common roles, operations such as using a spaceplane, and common themes such as exploiting the third dimension)
11) The operational use of space to enhance terrestrial operations in a comprehensive understanding of war as a total phenomena
12) The independent use of space power to win wars
13) Force application from and through space
14) The need for, nature, significance and uses of human beings in space (why a manned space program)
15) Training space crews (ground and space-based)
16) Space power as an extension of policy
17) Probable courses of action in response to friendly use of space power (making use of Clausewitz' idea that an enemy is someone you wrestle with, not someone you do something to)
18) Fog and friction (war on paper vs. war in reality: real world problems/space debris) in space operations (expanding on Baucom's work)
19) Space power's tie to technology and need to keep up with technology (short vignettes would help)
20) Asteroids and space power (the use of orbiting asteroids, the threat of natural or man-made disasters)
21) The contribution of science fiction (H. G. Wells, Buck Rogers, Star Wars, Star Trek, Battlestar Galactica, Babylon 5) to space power theory
22) Overcoming enormous distances in space
23) Undersea power as an analogy for space power

24) Currents and winds as an analogy for gravity
25) Unforeseen technology that may "revolutionize" warfare (like the steam engine, or nuclear weapons)
26) Defense of space launch facilities
27) Enemy use of our information systems (such as GPS)
28) Space weaponization (realistic discussion of the important of weapons in space)
29) Transitioning from space as functional support for terrestrial regions to space as an Area of Responsibility
30) Centers of Gravity in space power (satellites = COGs?)
31) Protection vs. prevention (treaties)
32) Denying space to an adversary
33) Access to space
34) Investments, interests and dependence on space power (a la Space Day panel)
35) Protecting the space lines of communication (SPLOCs)

A comprehensive theory would cover a majority, and ideally all of the above topics. In the interim, a separate and deeper treatment of each subject is needed.

SPACE TREATIES

Treaties are agreed to when all parties perceive a benefit from becoming a signatory participant in the treaty. As mutually assured destruction (MAD) became the deterrent strategy between the two superpowers in the Cold War, many countries worked together to avoid extending the threat of nuclear weapons to space based launchers.

Outer Space Treaty

The Outer Space Treaty, considered by the Legal Subcommittee in 1966. Later that year, agreement was reached in the General Assembly. The treaty included the following principles:

- the exploration and use of outer space shall be carried out for the benefit and in the interests of all countries and shall be the province of all mankind;

- outer space shall be free for exploration and use by all States;
- outer space is not subject to national appropriation by claim of sovereignty, by means of use or occupation, or by any other means;
- States shall not place nuclear weapons or other weapons of mass destruction in orbit or on celestial bodies or station them in outer space in any other manner;
- the Moon and other celestial bodies shall be used exclusively for peaceful purposes;
- Astronauts shall be regarded as the envoys of mankind;
- States shall be responsible for national space activities whether carried out by governmental or non-governmental activities;
- States shall be liable for damage caused by their space objects; and
- States shall avoid harmful contamination of space and celestial bodies.

In summary, the treaty initiated the banning of signatories' placing of nuclear weapons or any other weapons of mass destruction in orbit ofEarth, installing them on the moon or any other celestial body, or to otherwise station them in outer space. The United States, the United Kingdom, and the Soviet Union signed the treaty and it entered into effect on October 10, 1967. As of January 1, 2005, 98 States have ratified, and an additional 27 have signed the Outer Space Treaty.

Note that this treaty does not ban the placement of weapons in space in general, only nuclear weapons and WMD.

Space Preservation Treaty

The Space Preservation Treaty was a proposed 2006 UN General Assembly resolution against all space weapons. Only the United States of America voted against the treaty, with Israel abstaining.

In February 2008, China and Russia together submitted a draft to the UN known as the *Treaty on Prevention of the*

Placement of Weapons in Outer Space and of the Threat or Use of Force against Outer Space Objects (PPWT). The US opposed the draft treaty due to security concerns over its space assets despite the treaty explicitly affirming a State's inherent right of self-defense. On December 4th, 2014, the General Assembly of the UN passed two resolutions on preventing an arms race in outer space.

The first resolution, *Prevention of an arms race in outer space*, "call[s] on all States, in particular those with major space capabilities, to contribute actively to the peaceful use of outer space, prevent an arms race there, and refrain from actions contrary to that objective." There were 178 countries that voted in favor to none against, with 2 abstentions (Israel, United States).

The second resolution, *No first placement of weapons in outer space*, which emphasizes the prevention of an arms race in space and that "other measures could contribute to ensuring that weapons were not placed in outer space." 126 countries voted in favor to 4 against (Georgia, Israel, Ukraine, United States), with 46 abstentions (EU member States abstained on the resolution).

National Missile Defense (NMD)

With the fall of the Soviet Union and the end of the Cold War defense spending was reduced and space research was chiefly focused on peaceful research. American military research is focused on a more modest goal of preventing the United States from being subject to nuclear blackmail or nuclear terrorism by a rogue state.

On 16 December 2002, US President George W. Bush signed National Security Presidential Directive which outlined a plan to begin deployment of operational ballistic missile defense systems by 2004.

The following day the US formally requested from the UK and Denmark use of facilities in RAF Fylingdales, England and Thule, Greenland, respectively, as a part of the NMD Program.

The administration continued to push the program, despite highly publicised but not unexpected trial-and-error technical failures during development and over the objections of some scientists who opposed it. The projected cost of the program for the years 2004 to 2009 was 53 billion US dollars, making it the largest single line in The Pentagon's budget.

Missile Defense does not station weapons in space, but is designed to intercept incoming warheads at a very high altitude which requires the interceptor to travel into space to achieve the intercept. These missiles are both land based and sea based.

Ballistic Warfare

In the late 1970s and through the 1980s the Soviet Union and the United States theorized, designed and in some cases even tested an astonishing variety of bizarre and exotic weaponry designed for warfare in outer space. Space warfare was seen primarily as an extension of nuclear warfare, and so many theoretical systems were based around the destruction or defence of ground and sea-based missiles. Space-based missiles were not a target due to the Outer Space Treaty, which banned the use, testing or storage of nuclear weapons outside the Earth's atmosphere. Systems proposed ranged from measures as simple as ground and space-based anti-missiles to railguns, space based lasers, orbital mines and other such futuristic weaponry. Deployment of these systems was seriously considered in the mid-1980s under the banner of the Strategic Defence Initiative (popularly known as Star Wars). If the Cold War had continued, then many of these systems could have seen deployment: the United States got as far as developing working railguns, and a laser that could destroy missiles at range, though the power requirements of both were phenomenal, and the ranges and firing cycles utterly impractical.

Electronic warfare

With the end of the Cold War and continued development of satellite and electronics technology, attention was focused on space as a supporting theatre for conventional warfare. Currently, military operations in space primarily concern either the vast tactical advantages of satellite-based surveillance, communications, and positioning systems or mechanisms used to deprive an opponent of said tactical advantages.

Accordingly, most space-borne proposals which would traditionally be considered "weapons" (a communications or reconnaissance satellite may be useful in warfare but isn't generally classified as a weapon) are designed to jam, sabotage, and outright destroy enemy satellites, and conversely to protect friendly satellites against such attacks. To this end, the US (and presumably other countries) is researching groups of small, highly mobile satellites called "microsats" (about the size of a refrigerator) and "picosats" (approximately 1 cubic foot (H"27 litres) in volume) nimble enough to manoeuvre around and interact with other orbiting objects to repair, sabotage, hijack, or simply collide with them.

Kinetic bombardment

Another theorized use involves the extension of conventional weaponry into orbit for deployment against ground targets. Though international treaties bar the deployment of nuclear missiles outside the atmosphere, other categories of weapons are largely unregulated. Traditional ground-based weapons are generally not useful in orbital environments, and few if any would survive re-entry even if they were, but as early as the 1950s, the United States has toyed with kinetic bombardment, i.e. orbiting magazines of non-explosive projectiles to be dropped onto hardened targets from low-earth orbit.

Kinetic weapons have always been widespread in conventional warfare—bullets, arrows, swords, clubs, etc.—but the energy a projectile would gain while falling from orbit would make such a weapon rival all but the most powerful explosives. A direct hit would presumably destroy all but the most hardened targets without the need for nuclear weapons.

Such a system would involve a 'spotter' satellite, which would identify targets from orbit with high-power sensors, and a nearby 'magazine' satellite to de-orbit a long, needle-like tungsten dart onto it with a small rocket motor or just dropping a very big rock from orbit (such as an asteroid). This would be more useful against a larger but less hardened target (such as a city). Though a common device in science fiction, there is no publicly-available evidence that any such systems have actually been deployed by any nation.

Directed-Energy Weapons

Weapon systems that fall under this category include lasers, linear particle accelerators or particle-beam based weaponry, microwaves and plasma-based weaponry. Particle beams involve the acceleration of charged or neutral particles in a stream towards a target at extremely high velocities, the impact of which creates a reaction causing immense damage. Most of these weapons are theoretical or impractical to implement currently, aside from lasers which are starting to be used in terrestrial warfare. That said, directed-energy weapons are more practical and more effective in a vacuum (i.e. space) than in the Earth's atmosphere, as in the atmosphere the particles of air interfere with and disperse the directed energy. Obviously, that problem would not occur in space.

Practical Considerations

Space warfare is likely to be conducted at far greater distances and speeds than terrestrial combat. The vast distances involved pose difficult challenges for targeting and tracking, as even light requires a few seconds to traverse ranges measured in hundreds of thousands of kilometres. For example, if attempting to fire upon a target at the distance of the Moon from the Earth, the image one sees reflects the position of the target slightly more than a second earlier.

A projectile from a railgun recently tested by the US Navy would take over eighteen hours to cross that distance (making the simplifying and optimistic assumption that it will travel in a straight line at a constant velocity of 5.8 km/s along its entire trajectory). Even a laser will need approximately 1.28 seconds, meaning a laser-based weapon system would need to lead a target's apparent position by 1.28×2 = 2.56 seconds.

Three factors conspire to make engaging targets in space very difficult. First, the vast distances involved mean that an error of even a fraction of a degree in the firing solution could result in a miss by thousands of kilometres. Second, space travel involves tremendous speeds by terrestrial standards—a geostationary satellite moves at a speed of 3.07 km/s whereas objects in low earth orbit can move at up to 8 km/s.

Third, though distances are large, targets remain relatively small. The International Space Station, currently the largest artificial object in Earth orbit, measures slightly over 100m at its largest span. Other satellites can be orders of magnitude smaller, e.g. Quickbird measures a mere 3.04m. External ballistics for stationary terrestrial targets is enormously complicated—some of the earliest analog computers were used to calculate firing solutions for naval artillery, as the problems were already beyond manual solutions in any reasonable time—and the issues in targeting objects in space make a difficult problem even harder. Additionally, though not a problem for orbital kinetic weapons, any directed energy weapon would require large amounts of electricity. So far the most practical batteries are lithium batteries, and the most practical method of generating electricity in space is through photovoltaic modules, which are currently only 5-18% efficient, and fuel cells, which have limited fuel. Current technology might not be practical for powering effective lasers, particle beams, and railguns in space.

Regardless of one's reasons for going to war, at present those reasons are not likely to suggest major targets located in space. Most of the main theories which attempt to explain human proclivity for warfare—psychological, sociological, demographic, economic, political, or otherwise—would not indicate space as a likely location of conflict until a significant population is engaged in large-scale activity there. Until then, space warfare is likely to take a supporting role to conventional, terrestrial warfare. Aside from applications such as communications, reconnaissance, GPS, and the like, which would be difficult or impossible without satellites, there do not appear to be any major advantages to basing weapons systems in space. The main reason is simply cost. Space warfare that involves humans being deployed in space to fight each other is not currently practical because of the difficulty and cost of sustaining human life in space, especially over long periods of time.

Additionally, there are few things that could be accomplished by space warfare that any nation wealthy enough to finance them cannot accomplish far more cheaply through conventional means. Raising any significant mass beyond Earth's gravity will always require a large amount of energy, and the cost increases with mass. For example, though kinetic bombardment potentially offers the ability to strike any target anywhere in the world within minutes, both the United States and Russia, possibly the only nations with the resources and facilities necessary to implement such a system, have sufficiently long-range supersonic bombers that the same target could already be deployed in a matter of hours at a mere fraction of the cost.

The Evolution of Information Based Warfare

Therefore, at times of revolution, when the normal-scientific tradition changes, the scientist's perception of his environment must be re-educated-in some familiar situations he must learn to see a new gestalt.

The Structure of Scientific Revolutions

Whereas we had available for immediate purpose one hundred and forty-nine first-class warships, we now have two, these two being the Warrior and her sister Ironside. There is not now a ship in the English navy apart from these two that it would not be madness to trust in an engagement with that little [American] Monitor.. -The Times (London), 1862.

The most recent steps in that evolution can be found in the Military Technical Revolution (MTR) which may be attributed to Soviet Military thinkers; and, a recurrence of what is called the Revolution in Military Affairs (RMA).

In the early 1980's the Soviets noted that "the emergence of advanced non-nuclear technologies was engendering a new revolution in military affairs. They were particularly interested in the "incorporation of information sciences into the military sphere" and in the idea of a "reconnaissance-strike complex. The events in the Gulf War convinced them of their hypothesis (comparative strategies). RMAs matter principally for two reasons. First, being second best may lead to catastrophic loss in future wars. Since the only objective benchmark for determining the relative effectiveness of forces (that is, success in combat) is unavailable in long periods of peace, there is great potential for asymmetries in combat effectiveness between militaries, observable only when the next war occurs. Secondly, as equipment life cycles, especially for platforms, steadily grow to encompass decades, many of the principal weapons systems of 2025 will likely be designed and built in the next few years. Since militaries are stuck with force structures they choose for long periods, it is more crucial than ever to think about them now, in peacetime, about the revolutionary changes in the nature of war and the about what will matter in winning wars in twenty or thirty years.

Today with the United States arguably the only superpower for the foreseeable future, one might ask why this issue is especially pressing. Replicating the US force structure is clearly beyond the reach of all but a few other nations, even in the long term.

This may not be relevant. Even small-to medium sized powers may be able to exploit specific technologies for significant military leverage in certain areas.

The current rate of change suggests that state of the art in any technological context will be an extremely short-lived phenomenon, particularly with respect to the technologies that were key to the success of Desert Storm: space systems, telecommunication systems, computer architecture's, global information distribution networks, and navigation systems. Future revolutions will occur much more rapidly, offering far less time for adaptation to new methods of warfare. The growing imperative in the business world for rapid response to changing conditions in order to survive in an intensely competitive environment is surely instructive for military affairs.

The present RMA entails a fundamental change in who, how, and, perhaps even why wars are fought. It is driven not only by new technologies but by new operational concepts, new tactics, and new organizational structures. The impact of the current confluence of social, political, economic, and technological forces on American society and armed forces may equal-or exceed-what occurred during the 1960's and 1970's during the turmoil associated with the war in Vietnam.

The question that must be asked as we attempt to understand this RMA, is what were the results of change wrought by past Revolutions in Military Affairs? It has been suggested that accelerated interservice rivalries and over-reliance on management systems marked the last RMA, driven by the advent of atomic weapons at the end of WW II and the relatively stable and sparse defense budgets of the 1950's.

The current RMA is characterized by four types of changes:

- extremely precise;
- stand-off strikes;
- dramatically improved command, control, and intelligence;
- information warfare; and
- nonlethality.

Many analysts see a number of benefits from harnessing the current revolution in military affairs and using it to build 21st century US armed forces:

- rejuvenating the political utility of military power;
- delaying the emergence of a peer competition;
- providing a blueprint for technology acquisition and force reorganization;
- and inspiring conceptual, forward-looking thinking.

Looking ahead, many believe that the current RMA will have at least two stages. The first is based on stand-off platforms, stealth, precision, information domination, improved communications, computers, global positioning systems, digitization, "smart" weapons systems, jointness, and use of ad hoc coalitions.

The second may be based on robotics, nonlethality, pyscho-technology, cyberdefense, nanotechnology, "brilliant" weapons systems, hyperflexible organizations, and "fire ant warfare." Steven Metz and James Kievit of the Strategic Studies Institute argue that a cost /benefit analysis of the present RMA needs to be pursued. One the one hand, they argue that a case can be made that costs and risks of vigorous pursuit of the current RMA outweigh the expected benefits. These include the risk that:

- the current RMA will not generate increased combat effectiveness against the most likely or most dangerous future opponents;
- American pursuit of the RMA will encourage opponents or potential opponents to seek countermeasures;
- the current RMA might lead the United States toward over reliance on military power; and, vigorous pursuit of the current RMA might increase problems with friends and allies.

On the other hand, they argue that there are very pressing reasons for supporting the current RMA: it should bring significant increase in combat effectiveness against some mid-level opponents; a force built around stand-off, precision weapons and disruptive information warfare capabilities would be more politically usable than a traditional force-projection military; the RMA could augment deterrence; and, the United States may need to pursue the current RMA to avoid stumbling into strategic inferiority.

Lastly, they posit-and we strongly agree-that if policymakers decide to pursue the present revolution in military affairs, strategy, rather than technological capability should guide force development. The key question is: What do we want the future US military to be able to do? Unfortunately one finds little discussion of the foregoing ideas in the DOD's recently completed

"Bottom-Up" Review. Former Secretary of Defense Aspin initiated the review with the laudable goal of rethink the basis for US defense planning. It placed emphasis in many of the right areas: readiness, keeping forces for more than one regional war, acquisition reform. This review built a substantial consensus in the Pentagon behind the new force structure. Nonetheless, the review offers a classic example of military leaders planning to fight the last war. The report's proposed force for a single regional contingency-four to five Army divisions, four to five Marine brigades, 10 Air Force fighter wings, 100 heavy bombers, and four to five carriers-mirrors almost exactly the forces deployed in Operation Desert Storm. The review offers few thoughts on new technologies or techniques that might change the nature of war in coming decades. Clearly, the challenge is to move beyond the last war-an undertaking that is fraught with peril and promise.

SPACE POWER FOR THE THEATER CAMPAIGN

Commanders must integrate and optimize all available space forces to effectively employ space power. Space operations use terrestrial- and space-based assets to gain space superiority, ensuring the ability to exploit space capabilities during all phases of terrestrial operations and to support the theater commander in chief's (CINC) campaign objectives.

Counterspace Planning Factors

The theater CINC can direct the employment of air, land, sea, space, and special operations forces against the adversary's space forces by targeting enemy terrestrial and link elements. Adversary space forces to be targeted include data links, launch sites, booster storage facilities, communications links, TT&C nodes, and launch vehicles. These targets are coordinated with all elements of the joint campaign plan to ensure control of the activities conducted in space.

Theater Planning And Operations Support

Theater planners need to understand the enabling and supporting capabilities that reside in space forces. They must ensure their requirements are clearly identified so space forces can be effectively, efficiently, and coherently focused on theater planning and mission execution.

Planners may require access to national system information and other space-related data. Joint Pub 3-14, *Joint Doctrine; Tactics, Techniques and Procedures for Space Operations*, and the *Joint Service Tactical Exploitation of National Systems Manual* provide further guidance on the use of space forces.

Peacetime Planning

In peacetime, planners ensure that when a crisis erupts in any theater, forces are fully prepared to use all space systems efficiently. Space systems should be used to full advantage and tailored to the unique situation in that theater.

Planners ensure sufficient and appropriate user equipment is available to provide access to space capabilities and to support the full range of military operations.

Education and Training

Space power must be integrated into professional military education and combat training.

As space forces are incorporated into training scenarios, war games, and exercises, airmen and commanders will gain confidence and experience that will allow them to exploit space's full potential during the planning and execution of a theater campaign. Commanders should encourage attendance at the space education courses offered by Air Education and Training Command.

Additionally, planners should attend one or more of the courses offered by the Space Warfare Center.

Interested personnel should contact the Space Warfare Center, Falcon AFB, Colorado, for course attendance. Space planning courses are available to assist air components with exploiting established unit type codes available to the AFSST to supplement the warfighting CINCs or their component.

War Games

Air Force Space Command provides the modeling and simulation capability to permit interactive war games with the Army, Navy, and joint war-gaming centers.

War games help the Space Warfare Center develop concepts, doctrine, and tactics that can be implemented in future operations plans.

By exploiting war games, new tactics, techniques, and procedures are identified and developed that will integrate space power into all facets of joint warfighting.

Exercises

During major exercises, Air Force Space Support Teams are deployed to Air Force components and, when established, to joint air force components to ensure space capabilities are integrated into all facets of warfighting. These teams provide strategy and concept development planning and execution assistance to all service, joint, and multinational exercises. Participation by all commands and agencies associated with space systems is required to ensure accurate assessment of performance, to identify new applications of space power, and to identify areas of improvement in current operations.

ATTRIBUTES OF SPACE POWER

The use of the space medium and systems that operate in space are of critical importance to the Air Force and its ability to provide our nation with global reach, power, and awareness. Each Air Force core competency relies on the attributes of space systems to meet stringent requirements for navigation, weather, command and control, surveillance, reconnaissance, and other essential capabilities. The Air Force is unique in its ability to capitalize on the attributes of space systems by being able to respond with rapid mobility and firepower to the near-real-time information afforded by systems operating in space. As an operational medium, space and the systems that operate in space, offer several useful attributes.

Global Coverage

Space-based systems in appropriate orbital deployments provide worldwide coverage and frequent access to specific earth locations, including those denied to terrestrial forces, on a recurring basis. Unconstrained by political boundaries, satellites deployed in specific orbits and in sufficient numbers maintain a continuous presence over enemy territory. For example, three surveillance satellites in geostationary orbit provide surveillance of almost the entire Earth's surface.

Twenty-four navigation satellites placed in semi-synchronous orbit enable terrestrial forces anywhere on the earth to be within line of sight of the necessary three satellites to obtain three dimensional precision navigation. Space systems provide an instantaneous presence not available from terrestrial forces, permitting the US to leverage information to influence, deter, or compel an adversary or affect a situation.

Global coverage and utilization of multiple space platforms permits warfighters to exploit the various sensors, providing a synergistic battlespace perspective that reduces the fog of war. Although space systems provide global coverage, some can be focused to provide information on specific areas of interest, which can improve situational awareness, planning tempo, and enable information dominance for all friendly military forces. By exploiting comprehensive space capabilities, space forces can focus on and provide detailed services for a specific geographic area and support regional planning requirements.

The attribute of global coverage offers significant advantage to Air Force battle management. Properly positioned in sufficient numbers, space-based systems may provide a global capability for much of the information currently provided by airborne platforms such as the joint surveillance, target attack radar system (JSTARS) and the Airborne Warning and Control System (AWACS).

Flexibility

Space systems provide flexibility in meeting requirements for timely, accurate, and reliable space-derived information, data products, and services. For example, today's satellite systems perform continuous tasks such as navigation, communications, and surveillance. Operationally, they can adapt to new situations through on-orbit, real-time reprogramming; modifying terrestrial processing operations; and by modifying replacement satellites being readied for sustainment launches. The Air Force has concluded that in the near future autonomous space system operations, from peace through all levels of conflict, are cost-effective, operationally responsive, and less complicated. As one looks further out, inhabited transatmospheric vehicles may provide additional flexibility in performing complex missions.

Economy

Some functions are performed more economically from space. For example, global communications are generally more economical when operated from space. Similarly, global weather forecasting would require numerous ground-based or aerially deployed weather sensors around the world if weather data was not available from space.

Effectiveness

Some activities such as global weather monitoring and forecasting and wide area surveillance are more effective when they are conducted from space. The absence of atmosphere and attenuation provides an optimum operating medium for future directed energy weapons such as lasers and particle beams that travel at the speed of light with great range. Absence of atmospheric drag also enables objects to obtain high velocities that provide tremendous kinetic energy which could be used for space- to-space and space-to-earth weapons.

Robustness

Functions accomplished both in space and in the terrestrial environment provide mutual backup and complicate hostile attempts to neutralize our overall military capability. However, an adversary's ability to conduct counterspace missions precludes the space medium from being a sanctuary for our space systems. The current threat against our space systems focuses on attacks against the terrestrial and link elements of a space system. Attacks could include both lethal and non-lethal means such as attacks against ground nodes or jamming communications satellite links. Therefore, the defense of our space systems is critical in order to sustain space operations and maintain redundancy among terrestrial and space systems.

HISTORIC RISE OF SPACE ORGANIZATIONS IN THE FIRST AND SECOND BATTLES

Both the first and second battles in space were driven by an organizational renaissance within the national security space realm. By the turn of the century, much of that organizational momentum had stalled. Space has become increasingly more important to U.S. national and economic security yet the national security space infrastructure has not kept pace. Organizationally, the first battle, in the form of efforts such as the Atlas project and the Navy's development of the technologically ambitious Sea Launched Ballistic Missile, went on to change the complexion of both the Cold War and the aerospace industry as the Atlas project alone eventually involved "over 18,000 scientists, engineers, and technical experts in universities and industry...and 500 military officers with technical backgrounds."

During the second battle, the U.S. military actively expanded its space capabilities concurrent with pursuit of a U.S. grand strategy of strategic engagement and a national doctrine of space control. Ronald Reagan's Strategic Defense Initiative, a concept based on a strong space-based component including satellite sensors, space-borne missile defense, and anti-satellite weapons, fostered the idea that a legitimate theater of conflict in space needed a command to lead such an effort. The 1980s saw a flurry of organizational space activity as Air Force Space Command was established in the fall of 1982 followed a year later by Naval Space Command and ultimately by the formation of a joint space headquarters, United States Space Command, in 1984. The Army followed with its own space command in

1988. United States Space Command was the first organization to truly tackle the tough issues associated with space doctrine and necessary military means in a major capstone document published in April 1998. The *U.S. Space Command Long Range Plan* held that three compelling circumstances had come together to set the stage for a bold new vision. First, the U.S. had entered a strategic pause in which it would face no global military peer within the next two decades; second, the nation had become vitally dependent on space capabilities; and third, space had true potential to lead to a "Revolution in Military Affairs."

U.S. Space Command left no doubt it was engaged when it claimed "*USSPACECOM Has The Lead:* As the single focal point for military space, the responsibility falls to USSPACECOM to ensure access to and protection of US interests and investments in space." This was the first in a series of bold moves to put military space organizations in the forefront of the debate over space capabilities and its role in the national agenda.

Within the joint structure, Air Force Space Command was the largest component under U.S. Space Command and represented the largest percentage of DoD space capability providing 90 percent of the space personnel and 85 percent of the space budget by the 1990s. Ultimately, a myriad of developments such as a dedicated Space Technology Center, the stand-up of a Consolidated Space Operations Center in Colorado to control DoD spacecraft, and the advent of the Space Warfare Center (SWC) to "support warfighters with space solutions…through innovation, testing, tactics development and training" embodied organizational space growth. Meanwhile, the Naval Space Command developed a rigorous capability to exploit national reconnaissance capabilities to benefit the fleet and took responsibility for training Navy and Marine Corps personnel concerning the potential contributions of satellite systems to their missions. In addition, they continue to maintain space expertise in the Center for Naval Analysis, Navy TENCAP, the Naval Post Graduate School, and the NRO.

During this same period, the Army took action to begin a space demonstration program and stand up its own Space Command tasked with the mission of operational space planning and support to the Army. The Chief of Staff of the Army, General Gordon Sullivan, summed up the Army Space Policy when he stated the Army would exploit space systems to ensure "space applications will be embedded in Army doctrine, training scenarios, wargames, exercises, and plans."

The organizational awakening to space as a contributor to warfighting was personified in the Technical Exploitation of National Capabilities (TENCAP) programs adopted by each service space component. A parallel push was made to teach space—the Air Force Institute of Technology and the Naval Post Graduate School each added masters degree level courses in space and the service's mid-level professional staff colleges began to include blocks of space instruction.

Ultimately, the build-up of a solid cadre of space experts defined one of the key elements that led to the U.S. winning the first two battles. It was not enough to simply have a threat that drove a grand strategy toward space—it took an organizational push from inside the military and industry to see the necessary technology and doctrine come to fruition. Entering the third battle, U.S. space organizations show signs of atrophy and must overcome significant challenges if they are to meet the goal of achieving space supremacy. Major issues to be addressed include consolidation in the space divisions of the military and industry, a brain drain of space expertise, and a changing operations environment. In addition, there have been numerous problems with acquiring systems to replace aging legacy space capability which raises tough questions about the ability of today's space organizations to develop tomorrow's space control systems.

Industry Consolidation Is Affecting the Third Battle

Organizational uncertainty has kept the U.S. national security space community from advancing a cogent naional strategy in space. In October 2002, the nation's single unified military command chartered with operational leadership of U.S. space forces, the United States Space Command, was disbanded and that mission was folded into the portfolio of United States Strategic Command (USSTRATCOM). Long charged with the command and control of the US nuclear deterrent force, USSTRATCOM is in its infancy as it relates to space power and the contributions of space to U.S. national security. In an article covering the merger, William Scott noted in Aviation Week that the new command is faced with "leveraging legacy orbital platforms while sorting out what warfighters absolutely must have in a new military and intelligence space architecture." While on the surface this appears straight forward, USSTRATCOM is burdened with an unwieldy mission set of which space is one small piece. Consider the command's five distinct missions:

- Global Strike: STRATCOM is responsible for the conduct of precision strikes anywhere in the world using bombers, ICBMs, or computer network attack tools
- Missile Defense: STRATCOM is responsible for planning and integrating global missile defense operations
- Intelligence, Surveillance, and Reconnaissance (ISR) Management: STRATCOM is responsible for coordinating ISR to apply the right asset at the right time in support of military and intelligence missions
- Information Operations: STRATCOM is responsible for DoD's emerging cyberwarfare capabilities to include computer network defense
- Space: STRATCOM is responsible for aggregating combatant commander's space requirements and performing key trade decisions over what systems to pursue

Some, such as retired General Thomas Moorman see the establishment of US Strategic Command with its expanded missions as "one of the most significant events in military organization since the National Security Act of 1947 established the Department of Defense and the CIA."

However, in terms of space, the unintended consequence was to deemphasize the space mission within the joint military arena. Much of this is due to the sheer size of the new mission USSTRATCOM inherited. No matter the dedication of the people involved, a single joint headquarters will most certainly have a hard time balancing priorities across such a wide mission set. As a result, the emphasis on the space mission can hardly help but suffer.

Perhaps a bigger issue is the loss of military officers with shared experiences in space that often drive doctrinal evolution. Stephen Peter Rosen, in his book *Winning the Next War*, argues that doctrine is often about distributing power and resources within an organization. If this is the case, space is receiving short shrift in the larger joint warfighting construct of the U.S. military. If space can't even reign supreme in its own unified command, it will be extremely difficult to gain priority in the military writ large. The de-emphasis of space in the primary warfighting organization that owns the mission does not bode well for continued organizational advancement.

While consolidation has impacted the military's ability to tackle the tough issues associated with space, the nation's aerospace industry has an even larger consolidation problem. The combination of major space producing aerospace contractors has significantly cut the number of viable space system developers the U.S government can turn to for complex space systems.

Over the course of less than ten years, the number of top tier Aerospace and Defense firms has dropped from 107 to just five in 2004. Although for the most part, a small stable of strong prime contractors can likely respond to U.S. defense needs, the consolidation has severely impacted second- and third-tier subcontractors who make many of the critical components necessary to build advanced space systems.

Much of the contraction in space was driven by the failure of a viable commercial space market to transpire. The vast potential once promised by commercial space business in the mid 1990's has all but dried up. In 1998, expectations were that the US and the world's other space faring nations, would pump $500 billion into space, launching at least 1,000, and possibly 1,500, new satellites." That same year 150 commercial satellites were launched around the world. Yet only three years later, in 2001, that total had dropped to 75 satellites—the lowest number launched in the past 10 years. The U.S. launch industry saw a decline of nearly 50 percent from an average of over 30 civil and military launches per year (from 1995-2000) to only 17 in 2002. 15 Worldwide, technical issues with launch vehicles and payloads kept the number of launch attempts to 54 in 2004, the lowest since 1961.

Evidence of the ramifications of these impacts can be seen in the fact that the U.S. defense department has been forced to support two launch vehicle manufacturers in order to maintain a viable industrial base. Critics note that consolidation following the Cold War was inevitable, but see the growing lack of indigenous U.S. space transportation manufacturing as a "national disgrace."

The Space Brain Drain

Failures in our national space agenda have affected the U.S. military's space work force. U.S. military space is a unique blend of military operators and acquisition managers working closely with the U.S. defense industry and government civilians to build, operate, and maintain complex space systems. To develop future space weapons, taskable sensors, and dynamic fire control systems will require a space cadre with extensive technical skills and firm grounding in space systems.

Knowledge loss is often an unintended consequence of downsizing and has been a significant problem in the aerospace industry. Rollbacks and consolidations following the Cold War as well as the 'dot.com' boom of the late 90's led to a significant reduction in aerospace technicians and engineers in industry. The ensuing brain drain was coupled with an aging workforce that has been increasingly difficult to replace.

This loss of technical skills in the space arena was not constrained to industry. The Deputy Assistant Secretary of

Defense for civilian personnel policy noted that downsizing and increasingly complex missions have left the DoD facing real challenges in retaining adequate technical skills in the civilian workforce. The Air Force predicts 45 percent of the civilian science and engineering workforce is eligible to retire in the next five years.

On the military side, accession and retention of skilled engineers and space operators has suffered as well. Air Force officers make up the largest majority of the military's space professionals in both the DoD and the NRO. A year-long review of the Air Force science and engineering community showed that the science and engineering career field in 2000 was "the most stressed career field in the Air Force. Among military engineers with seven to 13 years of experience, under manning is a particularly serious problem. At the critical mid-level officer level, Air Force Captains in the scientist and engineer career fields are manned at 40% and 50% respectively.

Technical expertise has also become a major issue in the Air Force's "Space Operations" career field, which contains nearly the entire military space operations workforce. In the early days of military space, satellites were flown by engineers in the Air Force's Systems Command which had the mission of acquiring and operating space systems.

The introduction of an operational Space Command ultimately led to the merger of space operations with the traditional missile operations career field. Officers educated as engineers and scientists (who had traditionally operated the complex one-ofa- kind satellites in the inventory) slowly began to be replaced by a new breed of space operators.

This new space and missile operations specialty did not require science or engineering degrees and drew much of its numbers from the ICBM crew force. Over time, the service began to operationalize many military space systems, eliminating the need for specialty engineers to solve rare on-orbit anomalies.

In parallel, there was a move to convert many space jobs to enlisted positions. Ultimately this led to a severe reduction in the number of officers, particularly those with science and engineering backgrounds, in the space and missile career field. As of 2005, only 9.% of the 3,400 officers in the career field carried college degrees in hard science or engineering disciplines. Overall, the brain drain in industry, civil service, and military space leaves one to wonder who will be left to develop the complex operations concepts and systems for the coming third battle.

Satellite Operations Are Changing—Is The Military Keeping Up?

The dilution of the technical base is not the only issue effecting organizational transformation in national security space. The Space Commission noted that the Air Force and the National Reconnaissance Office dominate satellite acquisition and operations in national security space. Due to basic differences in the force enhancement missions performed by the Air Force (i.e. navigation and satellite communications), and intelligence missions performed by the NRO (imagery and signals collection) these organizations run their organizations differently.

On the Air Force side, operators typically monitor health and status of spacecraft and only intervene in the case of an anomaly. In contrast, NRO operators are faced with a dynamic collection environment which requires rapid reconfiguration of spacecraft to meet evolving collection requirements. The advent of future taskable DoD systems such as the Space-Based Infrared System and the Space-Based Radar or any type of space- based weapons or tracking function will require an operational philosophy that is much closer to that of the NRO.

At issue here is whether the Air Force is grooming space expertise to tackle the challenges associated with much more complex and dynamic space systems or the command and control capabilities required to fly them. As discussed earlier, technical space skills in the Air Force are at a premium. Air Force Space Command's *Strategic Master Plan for 2006 and Beyond* calls for having "the world's experts in all assigned systems and in the application of space power during peacetime, crisis and war." Despite recent efforts to establish a "space cadre," the command is lagging in meeting this goal. Not only does the nation's lead space service lack officers formally schooled in science and engineering, but it is not growing a space cadre that will be suited to respond to the major issues associated with taking space to the next level.

In 1998, then Senator Bob Smith gave a speech he called "The Challenge of Space Power." In that speech, Smith noted that "Air Force Space Command includes 11 general officers. None are career space officers...a further breakout shows that five of the 11 are command pilots, five are command missileers, and one has a command and control background. To put this in context, consider how many general officers at Air Combat Command are not command pilots." Peter Grier, in an article titled *The Space Cadre*, notes that pilots, nuclear submariners, and others in specialized military fields typically spend about 90 percent of their careers within their specified field. In 2001, however, less than 20 percent of all of the flag officers serving in key operational space leadership positions had come from career space backgrounds. Since then the situation has improved, but there are indications at the lower levels in Space Command that the root of the issue has not been solved. In order to grow future space generals, we must start with space Lieutenants and Captains.

In response to the demands of the Space Commission, Air Force Space Command has tried to develop a cadre of "space professionals" who have the requisite education and experience to develop U.S. space power and apply it to combat, intelligence, and other national security missions. As of 1 Dec, 2004, Air Force Space Command it had 7,449 "credentialed" space professionals—5,982 officers and 1,467 enlisted members with "cadre" level experience.

What fails to show up in the statistics is the level of experience in particular weapon systems. The military services would never expect an F-16 pilot to be an expert in B-2 stealth strategic bombing or a Naval surface warfare officer to understand the nuances of submarine operations. In space, the "space professional" is expected to be able to coherently speak on all space-related topics from navigation satellites to missile warning to ICBM targeting.

This paradigm has kept the space services, primarily the Air Force, from growing true space weapon systems experts. That F-16 pilot can be expected to fly the same aircraft for 12 out of his first 15 years, becoming an expert in its employment. Conversely, a typical path for a young space officer starts with an assignment as an ICBM crew member, followed three years later by a job as a satellite officer doing command and control of the Global Positioning System, followed by a broadening tour teaching ROTC at a university.

While this type of rotation develops a certain amount of depth, it fails to develop weapons systems experts. The ramifications of this manifest themselves at the tactical and operational levels.

As an example, the 2nd Space Operations Squadron is charged with commanding the 28-satellite GPS constellation. In 2002, the average experience of an officer line crew member (typically a Lieutenant or Captain) was 3. months in the GPS weapon system, much less than necessary to be an expert in a system as complex as GPS. A large reason behind the low levels of experience was the cultural impetus in the space career field to continually move space operators to new and varied jobs (often away from line space operations) in order to keep them eligible for promotion.

In addition to the struggle to develop young space operators, it is also difficult to train older military leaders in the employment, capabilities, and limitations of space systems. It is very difficult to run military exercises that show the full impact of losing space capabilities—after all, you cannot shut off GPS to the world for a week to see how U.S. forces would be impacted. Thus, military commanders (who have limited space expertise in the first place) have had relatively little experience in learning to "cope with the loss or temporary interruption of key space capabilities, such as GPS, satellite communications, remote sensing or missile warning information."

United States Struggling To Upgrade Legacy Systems

A major issue that must be faced by the U.S. national security space system is how to modernize and replace nearly its entire space infrastructure due to "block obsolescence of many on-orbit systems now in service." U.S. legacy space systems are aging and in need of replenishment while the ability to develop new and innovative space systems withers on the vine. Satellites are typically designed with an expected life of 6-8 years.

The average age of U.S. military satellites on orbit is nearly 10 years and the satellite control network used to fly them is over 40 years old. The durability of US satellites is a boom and bust problem—because they are lasting so long, we are failing to replace them with new technology and new capabilities to solve long standing shortfalls. General Richard Meyers, current Chairman of the Joint Chiefs noted in 2000 "this is bad news because we have capabilities on orbit designed for a previous era and not responsive to our current needs."

In framing the debate on where the U.S. should focus its national security space investments, a review of military space systems in operation today tells the story. The U.S. continues to perform the missile warning mission using the Defense Support Program first launched in 1970 as an incremental improvement of the MIDAS system orbited in 1963. The satellite communications backbone remains the Defense Satellite Communications System designed in the 1960s with a first launch in 1971. The military weather satellite flying today, the Defense Meteorological Satellite Program or DMSP, was first launched in 1962. The superstar of the US space portfolio, the Global Positioning System (GPS), is in essence flying the same design as the spacecraft first launched in 1978 and has an average satellite age of 9. years—nearly two years longer than the satellite's design life of 7. years. The oldest GPS satellite in use today has been on orbit for over 15 years.

It is true that a number of systems are currently in development that aim to upgrade existing satellite constellations and ground control architectures. However, these space systems are all competing for a share of the DoD budget as the nation's military looks to modernize and recapitalize systems ranging from fighter aircraft to armored vehicles. Secretary of the Air Force Roche rightly recognizes that we cannot afford to backslide in terms of space support capabilities for they have become "like oxygen...if you have it you take it for granted, if you don't have it, it's the only thing you want."3 The 2001 Quadrennial Defense Review described six foundational operational goals, each relying in some respect on space capabilities. The space acquisition results since then cannot give space leaders confidence that the U.S. will be able to fully meet those operational goals. At issue here is whether the space acquisition system can support the DoD's transformation goals or even today's modest goal of maintaining existing capability in space.

As a gauge of how severe the problem is, the SBIRS and AEHF programs are a combined $8 billion over budget. 35 The NRO's new satellite imagery system (FIA) has been delayed by more than a year, scaled back the capabilities it planned to deliver, and its cost has increased from $6 billion to $10 billion. In 2003 alone, the Defense Science Board, Air Force Scientific Advisory Board, and the Government Accountability Office (GAO) published reports critical of the space acquisition process. Of the major space systems currently in development including missile warning (SBIRS), military satellite communications (AEHF) and Transformational Satellite Communications or TSAT) and the intelligence systems (Future Imagery Architecture (FIA) and Integrated Overhead Signals Architecture), all are over budget and behind their original deployment schedule. According to the Government Accountability Office, in a report published in March 2004, the procurement costs associated with the Space-Based Infrared System increased 143 percent between 1998 and 2003. The same report noted that the cost of the Transformational Communications Satellite system had seen program costs increase 148 percent in just two years since program inception.

Another issue with modernizing the U.S. space arsenal is how the burden should be shared amongst the services. According to the Government Accountability Office (GAO), the total programmed space budget for fiscal years 2002 through 2007 is about $165 billion. Of this, the Air Force is expected to spend 86 percent while the Navy spends 8 percent and the Army 3 percent (the remaining 3 percent is spent by other DoD agencies). While space is widely considered a "joint enabler," the lion's share of the burden for funding expensive space systems continues to fall on the Air Force. This debate is raging at the same time Air Force is facing tough modernization decisions on major weapon systems including the tanker fleet which averages over 40 yrs old and the fighter force which is flying F-15s developed in the 1970s. Until this problem is remedied, the challenge (for the Air Force anyway) will continue to be prioritizing space against other important Air Force missions and systems.

The bottom line is that U.S. national security space organizations are not equipped to handle the challenges of the third battle. Consolidation in military space and the supporting aerospace industry along with a brain drain of hard core space science and technology skills has impacted the ability to deliver new operations concepts and systems. The nature of space operations is changing with no evidence that space operators are keeping pace. Finally, the space acquisition system is not delivering the necessary systems. An organizational renaissance similar to those that powered the first and second battles in space is necessary.

THE SPACE TECHNOLOGY PARADOX IN THIRD BATTLE

During the past decade, technology has grown exponentially in key areas that would seem custom suited to the design of more capable space systems. One example is computing power, commonly measured by "Moore's Law", which has seen the number of transistors on an integrated circuit rise from 2,250 in 1971 to 410,000,000 in 2004 while processor performance has improved by six orders of magnitude in the same period. Another example is miniaturization. In building space systems, the limiting factor is almost always weight due to the excessive costs of lifting a spacecraft to orbit. Technologies such as micro electro mechanical systems (MEMS) and nanotechnology offer great promise for reducing weight on spacecraft.

Launch costs continue to be the largest drag on space systems. The U.S. launch business has seen not only a reduced launch demand, but the drive toward economic launch costs has been largely unproductive. According to Benjamin Lambeth in his article *Footing the Bill for Military Space*, the constant-dollar price of getting a satellite to orbit has not changed much over the past two decades. Putting a satellite in low earth orbit continues to cost between $3,600 and $4,900 per pound, while getting to geostationary Earth orbit runs $9,200 to $11,200 per pound. Through micro-technology advances in industry, materials have become lighter. Power, a definite limiting factor in space, has become more efficient with smaller more capable devices requiring less electrical power.

However, trends in military satellite development have not kept up with those in industry. Mass and power on defense spacecraft have leveled out. The average weight of a commercial geostationary communications satellite over the past 10 years has slowly come down, stabilizing at about 3750 pounds. Military communication satellites on the other hand have tended to be heavier with Milstar weighing in at 10,000 pounds and the new Wideband Gapfiller Satellite at 6,615 pounds. This weight differential is partly due to military unique components required to assure survivability or add jam resistance. Despite significant breakthroughs in electronics and miniaturization, we have yet to see corresponding improvements in our national security space systems. Like the advent of stealth technology and precision weapons transformed airpower, the U.S. must seize on the chance to develop leap-ahead technologies in space.

A large reason behind the lag in DoD space technology is driven by the way it does space acquisition. Because space systems are typically complex in nature, acquisition leaders commit to technology decisions early in a program in order to stabilize the future production cost and schedule. This creates what Douglas Lee calls a "technology paradox" in that any technical advantage a program gains is lost before launch of the first satellite. In the end, long development cycles and risk averse practices couple to make technology obsolescent before it reaches orbit.

Combined with typically long satellite development and production schedules (often 10 years from start to first launch), this paradox makes it especially difficult to respond with agility to a changing threat. Art Cebrowski, Director of the Office of Force Transformation pushes for tactically responsive space systems, claiming "What we want...are space capabilities in weeks and months and not decades." To date, the space acquisition system has not adjusted to this new timeline. Revolutionary transformation will require revolutionary new acquisition processes—and a solution to the technology paradox. Based on recent space system acquisition results, the U.S. space acquisition system is not moving in that direction. Failures in developing replacements for legacy systems raise serious questions about whether the U.S. national security space system can support more complex acquisition programs such as space tracking and targeting systems and space weapons.

Weapons in Space

Peter Hays spells out in his treatise *Current and Future Military Uses of Space*, that virtually all issues of space strategy are shaped by the broad spectrum of views on weapons in space. For 40 years since the U.S. put a man in space, the world's space powers refrained from putting weapons in space.

Even during the height of the Cold War, the two superpowers refrained from actively deploying weapons capable of shooting down satellites and signed the 1972 Anti-Ballistic Missile (ABM) treaty forbidding either side from tampering with satellites including "prohibiting a state-party from interfering with another state-party's national technical means of verification" or spy satellites.

The Space Commission report of 2001 documented how important space has become to our national well being. It also defined the role of space in the civil, defense, and intelligence sectors while assessing vulnerabilities and threats. Normally, this type of report would have fostered an intense debate on the future role of space in support of national grand strategy. Unfortunately, the events following the January 2001 release of the Space Commission report including September 11, the invasion of Afghanistan, and the ensuing war in Iraq have tempered the debate. The limited discourse has focused on two opposing positions: the need to maintain space as a sanctuary versus the need for space weapons.

The majority of world space interests have striven to keep space free of weapons, partly because the cost of fighting in space is beyond their means, but also because of deep rooted beliefs that space is indeed a sanctuary that should be free of conflict. Some argue that space warfare would be devastating to global commerce, especially those commercial transactions and telecommunications services (think pagers, cell phones, cable TV) that use satellites. Military leadership on the other hand is thoroughly convinced the US must move away from the sanctuary doctrine. Advocates of an aggressive military space policy argue that the US is more reliant than any other nation on space assets and is vulnerable to an asymmetric attack in space.

The Space Commission Report lays out three objectives for space: 1) promote peaceful use; 2) use the nation's potential in space to support US domestic, economic, diplomatic and national security; and 3) develop means to deter and defend against hostile acts directed at US space assets. The report then proceeds to spend only six of the remaining 92 pages on anything associated with peaceful use, economics, or diplomacy. It clearly advocates protection of U.S. space assets as its primary conclusion. In testimony before a Senate sub-committee in March of 2000, General Ralph Eberhardt, then the Commander of U.S. Space Command, captured the importance of space control when he said:

"Some may consider space a peaceful medium or even an international sanctuary for generating revenue. However, the dependence of our national security on orbiting satellites makes space a tempting target for terrorism and adversarial military operations. As these threats continue to evolve, the mission area of space control becomes even more important." From a US national security space point of view, the rhetoric points toward the dawn of a national space strategy focused on dominance in space. The Air Force Space Command vision focuses on "space warfighting forces ...that operate and employ space power in, from, and through space."

A RAND analysis performed in 2002 pointed out that prospective opponents will understand when space capabilities represent an easier target than other critical nodes and will interfere with them. The natural consequence of space integration into military activity is a more hostile environment for space." Evidence of a more hostile environment is documented in Air Force Space Command's *Almanac 2004-2005* which describes the command's future as transforming to provide "full spectrum kinetic and non-kinetic combat capabilities...and increase our focus on producing warfighting effects with space superiority and strike capabilities." All of this points toward weapons in space.

Before moving full speed to weaponize space, the U.S. must consider the broadest possible set of consequences. Economics play a part in the discussion. Between 1996 and 2002, world revenue for space systems totaled $517 Billion with a growth rate of about 15% per year during that time. In *Emerging Options for National Power*, the authors point out that force application missions have the least relation to U.S. economic interests. They do not generate revenue and in turn may discourage free market forces from moving to space. On the political side of the debate, the U.S. must tread lightly as it ponders a move toward weapons in space. Because space weapons are expensive and technically demanding, they are unlikely to be built for a low level conflict. This implies space weapons are only good for peer or superpower wars. If, as argued earlier, the U.S. maintains command of the commons and is facing no peer in space, to what end would we be the first to develop space weapons? If the U.S. does press down this road, it should develop only a "silver bullet" capability aimed at providing flexibility should a peer threat unexpectedly break out in the future.

In sum, politics have played a major role in shaping U.S. readiness for the third battle in space. The current grand strategy of primacy has led to an aggressive space control doctrine that may be overriding the need to upgrade existing force enhancement capabilities in space. Competition for space funding is further limiting the viable options in space while a technology paradox often makes systems obsolete before they are launched. Finally, the undercurrent of space Weaponization is ever present in the debate over how to proceed in the third battle.

FUTURE USE OF THE SPACE POWER

Pressure is building for greater military use of space, but no action should be taken without a broad public discussion.

The concept of space power has been receiving increased attention recently. For example, the Center for National Security Policy, a conservative advocacy group, has suggested that there is a need for "fresh thinking on the part of the new Bush-Cheney administration about the need for space power" and "an urgent, reorganized, disciplined, and far more energetic effort to obtain and exercise it." According to a recent report from the Center for Strategic and Budgetary Assessments, a mainstream defense policy think tank, "the shift of near-Earth space into an area of overt military competition or actual conflict is both conceivable and possible."

Some definitions may be useful here. The most general concept—space power—can be defined as using the space medium and assets located in space to enhance and project U.S. military power. Space militarization describes a situation in which the military makes use of space in carrying out its missions. There is no question that space has been militarized;

U.S. armed forces would have great difficulty carrying out a military mission today if denied access to its guidance, reconnaissance, and communications satellites. But to date, military systems in space are used exclusively as "force enhancers," making air, sea, and land force projection more effective. The issue now is whether to go beyond these military uses of space to space weaponization: the stationing in space of systems that can attack a target located on Earth, in the air, or in space itself. Arguably, space is already partially weaponized. The use of signals from Global Positioning System (GPS) satellites to guide precision weapons to their targets is akin to the role played by a rifle's gunsight. But there are not yet space equivalents of bullets to actually destroy or damage a target.

What is in question now and in coming years is the wisdom of making space, like the land, sea, and air before it, a theater for the full range of military activities, including the presence there of weapons. The 1967 Outer Space Treaty forbids the stationing of weapons of mass destruction in space, and the 1972 Anti-Ballistic Missile treaty prohibits the testing in space of elements of a ballistic missile defense system. To date, countries active in space have informally agreed not to deploy antisatellite weapons, whether ground-, air-, or space-based, and the United States and Russia have agreed not to interfere with one another's reconnaissance satellites. But there is no blanket international proscription on placing weapons in space or on conducting space-based force application operations, as long as they do not involve the use of nuclear weapons or other weapons of mass destruction.

For the new Bush administration, U.S. national security strategy will be based on two pillars: information dominance as key to global power projection, and protection of the U.S. homeland and troops overseas through defense against ballistic missile attack. Space capabilities are essential to achieving success in the first of these undertakings. Intelligence, surveillance, and communication satellites and satellites for navigation, positioning, and timing are key to information dominance. Space-based early warning sensors are also essential to an effective ballistic missile defense system that includes the capability to intercept missiles during their vulnerable boost phase; such a system appears to be under consideration. Using space systems in these ways would not involve space weaponization. However, under some missile defense scenarios, kinetic energy weapons could be based in space; they could thus become the first space weapons and open the door to stationing additional types of weapons in space in coming decades.

Worth particular attention as a likely indication of the administration's stance on space power issues is a report released on January 11, 2001, on how best to ensure that U.S. space capabilities can be used in support of national security objectives. The report was prepared by the congressionally chartered Commission to Assess United States National Security Space Management and Organization, which was chaired by Donald Rumsfeld, now the secretary of defense. It was created at the behest of Senator Robert Smith (R-N.H.), a strong supporter of military space power who has suggested in the past the need for a U.S. Space Force as a fourth military service. The conclusions and recommendations of the report deserve careful scrutiny and discussion; they sketch an image of the future role of space systems that implies a significant upgrading of their contributions to U.S. national security, including the eventual development of space weapons.

There is a common theme running through this and other recent space policy studies. In the words of the commission report, "the security and economic well being of the United States and its allies and friends depends on the nation's ability to operate successfully in space." This is clearly a valid conclusion, but one that has seemingly not yet made much of an impression on the public's consciousness.

The availability of the many services dependent on space systems appears to be taken for granted by the public. However, if space capabilities were denied to the U.S. military, it would be impossible to carry out a modern military operation, particularly one distant from the United States.

The civilian sector is equally dependent on space. Communication satellites carry voice, video, and data to all corners of Earth and are integral to the functioning of the global economy. The commission noted that failure of a single satellite in May 1998 disabled 80 percent of the pagers in the United States, as well as video feeds for cable and broadcast transmission, credit card authorization networks, and corporate communication systems.

If the U.S. GPS system were to experience a major failure, it would disrupt fire, ambulance, and police operations around the world; cripple the global financial and banking system; interrupt electric power distribution; and in the future could threaten air traffic control.

2

Creation of a Defence Space Agency and India's Space Security

Outer space exploration has turned into a key part of a modern society's functionality with several services including weather, communication, Internet, banking and navigation, supported by satellites orbiting the Earth. India being one of the major actors in outer space has in many ways led the usage of satellites for the benefit of the society. With the space infrastructure of India powering the economy, is there a case for exploring the defence of these vital systems? Moreover, given that the geopolitics and security scenarios are changing with respect to the utilisation of outer space, should India explore its capabilities and capacities built in the country for the past 50 years for dedicated space defence operations? The present work provides insights on the key question as to are we or are we not at a tipping point where the government needs to draw a vision in securing national interests via creation of a Defence Space Agency as an interim arrangement until a full-fledged Aerospace Command is in place. If so, what are its technological, organisational and policy facets?

The case for India's utilisation of outer space has traditionally been to "harness space technology for national development, while pursuing space science research and planetary exploration". Today, the global space economy is a key part of modern society infrastructure, providing connectivity, insights of the Earth from space and navigational support. In terms of financials, the space economy grew by 9 percent in 2014, reaching a total of $330 billion worldwide, with commercial space activities making up 76 percent of the global space economy with a growth of 9.7 percent (2014).

India, very much a part of the global space economy, has matured to be one of the key actors in outer space; and is one of those that reap benefits of infrastructure in space with the Indian Space Research Organisation (ISRO) operating one of the biggest fleets of satellites (remote sensing, satellite communications and navigation) in the world. Today, India's space programme is valued at more than $2.3 billion in assets already in orbit; this figure rises to around $37 billion ground-based infrastructure and value-added services are included. These satellites have facilitated governance, harnessing the advantages of space for its citizens.

However, given the changes in the international and regional security and geopolitics of outer space over the past two decades, one might argue that India needs to consider utilising its space capacities for securing its regional and territorial interests and the safety of its space infrastructure. Some steps in this regard have already been taken in an incremental style.

The first such concrete step was taken in 2010 with the creation of an Integrated Space Cell (ISC) under the Integrated Defence Services (IDS) Headquarters of the Ministry of Defence. The ISC has had a coordinating role between armed forces as well as with the Department of Space and Ministry of Defence for greater integration of space technology and assets into military operations. Following such developments, for the first time, ISRO built and launched dedicated military communications satellites, GSAT-7 (2013) for the Navy and GSAT-6 (2015) for armed forces. Further, the Technology Perspective and Capability Roadmap (TPCR) of the IDS details several space-based capabilities envisioned for India's expanding space-based security needs. With this dedicated infrastructure in outer space, experts within space security have signalled the threat to these assets due to our reliance on them. From technological, organisational and political perspectives, India needs to take a stand in active utilisation of outer space for meeting its security interests and affirming its position among the global space community in providing a transparent regime to utilise outer space for national security. Therefore, given the evident movement in utilisation of space systems for space-based security interests, formation of a dedicated defence space establishment in India seems a logical step in taking charge of these advances.

FACETS OF A DEFENCE SPACE ESTABLISHMENT

Following recent turn of events, there has been a movement towards opening up India's space security by a possible creation of a Defence Space Agency (DSA) as an interim arrangement until a full-fledged dedicated Aerospace Command is in place. This seems a case for the expansion of ISC for a more active role in utilisation of outer space within the armed forces. The case for a defence space establishment is not just of adding a final frontier edge to warfare or adding theatre capability via space assets to the armed forces. It is about developing a multi-dimensional approach to using outer space for strategic purposes.

Establish minimum technology umbrella: While creation of a DARPA-like agency in India may be thought off as a moon-shot, there is tremendous scope to establish certain minimum technology capacity umbrella that is at par with that of advanced militaries and spacefaring nations. This minimum technology umbrella will not only feed into the current requirements but also act as a catalyst to spin-off advanced requirement concepts for the future.

Space security doctrine: Declaring a space security doctrine that encompasses the military space utilities as well as spelling out the conditions under which India will consider the offensive and defensive use of space should be a priority. The doctrine should also factor in India's internal security challenges, including surveillance of the vast coastlines, porous border areas and other insurgency-related issues.

Capacity building in the industry: With the recent opening up of markets with a much more conducive environment via foreign direct investment, there are institutional challenges within the system that need to be addressed. While the private sector is now trying to move ahead with investments, there are still a lot of challenges in building up capacity in the private sector for it to deliver turnkey-level solutions for large/complex systems. One of the big challenges, however, is to strike a balance between the public and the private sector so that they co-exist without any conflict of interest.

Long-term roadmap & foundation for next generation systems: While the TPCR provides some sense of what space-based capabilities are of interest in the realm of defence and security, there is a need to develop a dedicated long-term roadmap for space security in India. One can draw inspiration from ISRO in developing such decade-long roadmaps and meeting technical challenges systematically in an effort to meet long-term goals. There is a need to develop mechanisms for the promotion of home-grown innovation in defence space systems (both in public and private sector) that will enable India to leapfrog in technologyand to build next generation systemsthat provide an edge in Command, Control, Communications, Computers, Intelligence, Information, Surveillance, and Reconnaissance (C4I2SR).

TECHNOLOGICAL CAPACITY INTERESTS

With the seed sown for space exploration right from the first satellite flown in 1957—being driven via defence interests—time and again, space capabilities have proven to bring an additional dimension to traditional defence capabilities that can support C4ISR.

Space Weather

With growing number of space assets, one of the major fields of growing importance to monitor the health and safety of all systems in space and their allied equipment on the ground is tracking space weather. This has emerged as a part and parcel of Space Situational Awareness (SSA), with a broad scope of monitoring and predicting near-Earth space environment that can degrade and disrupt the performance of technological systems due to adverse conditions caused by activities such as solar storm.

Space weather has gained such prominence that several spacefaring nations have developed preparedness strategies for space weather exigencies. For example, the Unither Kingdom has a National Space Security Policy (NSSP) whose objectives include resilience to the risk of disruption to space services and capabilities; and has developed a Space Weather Preparedness Strategy.

There are several mapped impacts of space weather situational awareness on the ability to use space assets for missions which include communication and navigation, among others.

From a space command and control perspective, these include decreased operational payload utility, decreased ability to control satellites, and loss of satellite tracking. From an ISR perspective, it would mean inaccurate position data or loss/degradation of intelligence due to radio frequency interference, range uncertainty, loss of target discrimination, spectral distortions, degraded system performance, reduction in resolution of SAR images due to solar flares, and ionospheric storms.

From a SatCom and long-range communications perspective, these would be inability to exercise C2, inability to send evacuation with life of small teams at risk. From a positioning, navigation and timing perspective, these include loss of navigation and manoeuvring accuracy for precision-guided munition, and decreased ability to synchronise ops with precision timing. Given these risks at large from space weather, there is a need to expand the scope of understanding the scientific phenomenon of space weather to turn around the knowledge of these effects (spacecraft charging and ground effects) to design inputs and operational strategies for critical systems, especially communications and positioning.

EO Small Satellites & Responsive Launch Vehicle

One of the major areas of low Earth orbit (LEO) exploitation in the recent times is in building low-cost small satellite (

Moreover, these networks of small satellites can also be launched on demand with retrofitting on Agni-5 with mobile launching capabilities. This has the potential to be developed as a responsive launch capability programme where a network of six to eight satellites can be launched on one rocket through a single plane to provide excellent coverage in swath. As far as coverage is concerned, a CARTOSAT provides coverage of about 10 km swath in a single satellite. However, having a network of these satellites on a single plane with an adjusted phase angle difference can provide a combined swath of 60-80 km, which has immense potential for exploitation in image intelligence. One has to also note the possible exploration of such a constellation in two or multiple orbits (one in polar sun synchronous and other in a slightly inclined orbit) to exploit security interests around the borders.

ASAT Capabilities

Following the Chinese ASAT missile test destroying an unused weather satellite in January 2007, there has been a debate on India's ability to develop and demonstrate ASAT capabilities, which can act as a deterrent against such adversaries in the final frontier. India recognises such tests as a threat to all space assets as well as being against the spirit of non-weaponisation & peaceful usage of outer space.

While most of the ASAT tests have been performed in LEO, there is speculation of China performing long-range ASAT tests that could threaten Medium Earth Orbit (MEO) and Geostationary Earth Orbit (GEO) satellites. From a 21st century strategic perspective one can argue that in advanced threat scenarios, assets in LEO—which typically are into Earth Observation (EO) and remote sensing missions—are more dispensable against assets providing navigational and communications capabilities from MEO and GEO. Removing the navigation and communications capability from space can have a crippling effect for large-scale military operations. From an Indian perspective, it is quite clear from several official statements at UN forums, such as the Conference on Disarmament in Geneva, that it is against weaponisation of outer space. However, India's stand on conducting ASAT tests is unclear. There are concerns that if it does not demonstrate such a capability, it will be left behind facing a repeat of what happened in the nuclear domain.

While India does have the fundamental building blocks for a kinetic-kill full-fledged ASAT weapon based on Agni and the ballistic missile interceptor, showcasing this capability has to be done in a responsible manner without creating huge amount of long-lasting debris that could damage existing satellites. A possible template to showcase technological capabilities may lie in following a strategic engagement of a low-flying asset that may not sustain any in-orbit debris but will completely be destroyed in entry and upper atmosphere. US performed such a mission as recently as 2008, launching a single Standard Missile-3 (SM-3) and destroying a 5,000-pound satellite with nearly 100 percent of the debris safely burned-up during re-entry within 48 hours and the remainder safely re-entering within the next few days. One has to note that India does not have any space asset at such a low altitude; and if such a capability has to be demonstrated, one of the dying satellites will have to be lowered to perform such a test.

While the policymakers may choose to make concrete decisions on such matters reactively, technologically the focus should be on having long-range tracking capabilities, on-ground development of technological building blocks to increasing reach to MEO & GEO, and systems of denial of service. Long-term technology focus can definitely pursue the potential of exploiting non-kinetic kill options by exploring cyber or focussed high-energy techniques.

Signal Intelligence

The need for satellite-based signal intelligence due to limitations of ground-based equipment (owing to radio horizon as well as such an equipment being compromised in advanced threat scenarios due to attack) is real. The field of satellite-based Signal Intelligence (SIGINT) encompasses Communications Intelligence (COMINT) with a focus on interception and decryption of military and strategic communications, Electronic Intelligence (ELINT) with a focus on developing technology for radio signals interception and decryption. The scope of SIGINT has also expanded towards capturing of telemetry signals with a special focus on missiles.

At present, India has extremely limited space-based COMINT capabilities with two GEO satellites supporting strategic communications with the multi-band communication satellite GSAT-7and GSAT-6.

However, China not only has full-fledged secure satellite communications networks, but also has expanded its satellite capabilities and may very well be equipped to use its network of LEO and GEO satellites to accurately track and target naval assets in near-real-time as part of its satellite-aided Anti-Ship Ballistic Missile (ASBM).

Similarly, from an air-defence perspective, ELINT capabilities may be used to precisely locate air defence systems, making such systems vulnerable. The Yoagan constellation launched by the Chinese is said to have capabilities of providing 16 targeting opportunities with less than 10-km location uncertainty for ballistic missile launch.

Given the modernisation of armed forces and the increased air and maritime interests, India should at least establish a minimum ISR capabilities starting with three dedicated satellites and expanding to six with wide band receivers to be able to monitor activities in the Indian Ocean and South China Sea. Use of an array of space-based sensors, along with other sensors using common standards and communication protocols for transmitting information automatically through machine-to-machine interfaces, are important. These become useful in the context of missile targeting as well as establishing data links in a multiple platform/command & control scenario.

GIS Cross Platform Integration

Geographic Information System (GIS) is a powerful tool to combine various spatial, spectral and other sources of data to generate key insights for security stakeholders. With the ever-increasing computational power alongside the increase in the number of sensors available, utilisation and integration of GIS into specific scenarios and actual traditional battlefield systems (such as UAVs, tanks, submarines, aircraft, etc.) will provide an edge over adversaries.

Post 9/11, US floated a dedicated National Geospatial-Intelligence Agency (NGA) in 2003 to provide geospatial intelligence putting policymakers, military, intelligence professionals and first responders at a decisive advantage. This dedicated agency claims to have helped track down al Qaeda leader Osama bin Ladin and shared insights with the special operations team that successfully stormed his compound in Abbottabad, Pakistan.

Tracking and visualisation of insurgent attacks based on their use of the geography, terrain, population density, and infrastructure with different mathematical models can be used to combat guerrilla warfare. This has tremendous scope for exploration from an internal security perspective for India.

Dedicated tools in GIS have been explored for coastal security by combining several data sources such as high-resolution images, Lidar, conduct of fleet/vehicle mobility analysis, continuous sea–land Digital Elevation Model (DEM) and geo-visualisation of changing shorelines with tidal levels in an effort to build a Littoral Warfare Database that enables commanders to take feasible and realistic decisions.

With the exponential dispersion of sensors (both in space, on ground and below) and emergence of technologies such as IoT/M2M, fusing all such data alongside GIS information will hold the key to taking intelligent decisions. There is no doubt that cross-platform integration of GIS technology as well as on-ground decision intelligence support system are the very basic needs of an effective network-centric warfare strategy.

Navigational Capabilities

India has completed the Indian Regional Navigation Satellite System (IRNSS) constellation for providing accurate position information to users in India as well as the region extending up to 1500 km from its boundary. This constellation can be used to aid in navigation for missions on land, in sea and in air; and can very well serve as an invaluable component of network-centric warfare.

While India is undertaking modernisation of its defence equipment, the integration of indigenous navigation systems at the user segment of these equipment will definitely be an important step towards self-reliance in defence technology. Typical examples of such uses shall be in the ballistic missile programmes such as Agni, and cruise missile programme such as BrahMos. The indigenous navigational capabilities have a wide array of other uses also, of course, outside of strategic areas—from most mundane such as location devices for infantry to smart bombs, covert surveillance and armoured warfare.

Space Situational Awareness

Satellites form an important part of network-centric warfare and therefore are prone to a broad range of natural disasters and intentional attacks, including cyber-attacks, space weather, space debris, collisions with other satellites and ASAT attacks. Therefore, it is necessary to have a military space situational awareness capabilities to not only track objects in space but also map the capabilities of various space systems and their implications for national security.

India right now has limited capabilities in the field of space situational awareness, with major asset for tracking objects such as space debris being carried out by ISRO's Multi-Object Tracking Radar (MOTR). While tracking is a major portion of space situational awareness, ground-based radar tracking may provide real-time collision analysis, given the cataloguing of the location and orbital information about all space objects. However, from a military dimension, there is a need to develop space-based systems that can help determine the capabilities of various space systems in-orbit and the intentions of its owner. Internationally,there have been recommendations made to develop radar-independent tracking methods such as lasers, coherent infrared sensors as well as developing space systems with a sole purpose of tracking the functional capabilities of suspected satellites that may serve the military functions.

A dedicated space situational awareness initiative within the defence space agency can serve for gathering space-based network-centric intelligence capabilities of adversaries and shall help map out evolving ground-based counter-capabilities. .

Communications Capabilities

The current satellite communications platforms for defence operations are served by GSAT-7 for Navy and GSAT-6 for the armed forces.

One of the significant areas to explore COMINT from a defence space perspective is its ability to exploit GEO platforms for data relay services for UAVs or other airborne platforms. Such airborne platforms can send their observation to a data relay satellite in GEO via an optical link. Subsequently, the satellite-based data relay services via high-speed laser communication can be used to replace expensive network of ground stations needed to constantly receive LEO satellite data.Moreover, there is also scope to explore inter-satellite links between GEO satellites that can be used to share resources and/or route traffic around a satellite network. In order to effectively exploit space, India also needs to focus on having orbital slots available in GEO, which shall be critical to have the necessary authorisation by International Telecommunications Union (ITU) to place satellites over the Indian-subcontinent.

Logic for A Space Security Doctrine

India's space programme has grown enormously over the past decade but without a broad strategic plan because India has lacked an overall strategic doctrine that lays out its long-term goals and objectives. As India's power and influence rises, there has to be greater clarity on what it wants to achieve as a nation in its overall security as well as within each of the important security domains such as nuclear and outer space.

India has many external security challenges, from cross-border terrorism and internal insurgencies to unresolved border and territorial issues, all of which call for a huge defence-space requirement. Repeated terrorist attacks in India, including on sensitive military installations, point to the need to better integration of space technology for military functions such as reconnaissance, and safe and secure communication channels, which put a premium on India's space capabilities. While space utilisation has picked up in the backdrop of these challenges, these are still being done in a haphazard manner.

India must also outline its red lines in space, that is, under what circumstances offensive use of space will be sanctioned. These must be laid down in clear terms to bring about clarity within the Indian establishment but also clarity in the minds of the adversary as to what is considered permissible behaviour and what might provoke a military response (intentional jamming and blinding, destruction, interference). This should include, for instance, a code of conduct and standard operating procedures for any threat to Indian space assets to avoid ambiguities.

The doctrine must also spell out how space assets will be put to use to deal with the internal security of India. The internal security challenges are very vast and these include surveillance of the cross-border areas, monitoring of the vast coastlines and water spaces, and monitoring naxal-affected areas. The cyber-outer space interface is another set of challenges that need to be factored within the doctrine. The growing linkages between cyber and outer space domains present India with new challenges, and India should develop a set of considered options that would protect against its vulnerabilities in space.

Space Security Strategies and Policy

Having established itself as a major space power, what India lacks is an overarching strategy that guides its space programme. In the absence of such a strategy, India's space programme and ISRO's attempts to cater to the wide-ranging demands have represented more of a piecemeal approach. India has to factor in the growing requirements of the space assets in social, economic and security arenas. A space security strategy will synchronise these growing requirements, taking into account India's total capacity, including political and economic capital. National space security strategy should also include the command and control structures to implement and respond to situations identified in the doctrine such as offensive uses of space and maintaining space deterrence.

Audit of Technology Integration and Performance

Even as ISRO has done a splendid job with India's space programme, there has to be better accounting and auditing of the technological developments and, more importantly, technology integration and performance. Providing constant insights on the performance of the programmes, the direction of the organisation, insights from an international technology and geopolitical perspective through a parliamentary oversight group or government-funded defence think tanks—such as the Institute for Defence and Strategic Analyses (IDSA), Centre for Air Power Studies (CAPS)—can be done via a dedicated Task Force created within the DSA for this purpose.

Conclusion

While there are significant opportunities to integrate satellite-based technologies into the defence realm, there is a need to carefully plan this technology integration. Given that DRDO does not focus its efforts on development of satellite platforms, there is tremendous opportunity for Indian industry to invest into such platforms.

Moreover, the defence space agency can act as an observer and regulator, which will constantly assess the needs of the armed forces and executes those needs via the industry. This provides a win-win situation for both the armed services and the local industry. This also ensures that there is scope for long-term capacity building in the country that can foster export of turnkey solutions for satellite-based products and services from India. Further, this will serve as a method of fruition of the tremendous efforts put forth by ISRO to develop a local industry ecosystem over the past 40 years.

Additionally, wherever there are gaps in state-of-the-art technologies, there is tremendous scope to explore closing such gaps with models such as international JVs under initiatives such as 'Make in India'.

From an organisational coordination perspective, there is a need to setup a clear protocol for coordination of defence space use between already established institutions—such as Defence Image Processing and Analysis Centre (DIPAC), Aviation Research Centre (ARC), National Technical Research Organisation (NTRO), Defence Intelligence Agency (DIA), Defence Satellite Control Centre (DSSC), and Research and Analysis Wing (R&AW). The critical aspect of the utilisation of the space dimension for intelligence gathering by these institutions can further elevate the quality of inputs to both investigative bodies as well as policymakers for internal and external security.

INDIAN MILITARY'S SPACE PROGRAM: IMPLICATIONS FOR PAKISTAN-ANALYSIS

The military role of space satellites has increased incessantly in last three decades. In the early 1960s, the first reconnaissance and surveillance satellites were launched by the United States, and the Soviet Union followed within a few years. In addition, military communications, navigation, meteorology and other satellites were developed during this period. By the 1980s, systems such as the Navstar Global Positioning System (GPS), as well as reconnaissance satellites were of major importance in the military affairs.

Military space satellites are used both for peacetime collection of intelligence of the enemy, as well as the location of targets, troops deployment and to support combat operations in modern warfare. Therefore India is heading towards development of space capabilities; such capabilities would revamp their overall surveillance and reconnaissance capabilities which is an essential element in the modern Warfare.

Indian military have used satellite imagery from Indian Space Research Organisation (ISRO) civil satellites since the early 1990s. Most civil satellites can also be used for military purposes. Most militaries in the world use commercially available imagery from satellites. Space satellites are vital for the C4I systems. India has acquired an Israeli RISAT-2 satellite in 2009 that has day and night viewing capability. This satellite will keep a 24/7 watch over Pakistan even when the landmass is covered by a thick cloud cover. This capability puts the satellite in the class of what are often called spy satellites. The launch of RISAT-2 satellite will give India the capability to closely track down military activities in Pakistan.

Indian Space Research Organisation (ISRO) is also developing its very own RadarSat at the cost of almost 400 million Indian rupees. Indian Defense and Research Development Organization's Chief Saraswat has announced "We are looking at launching one or two satellites every year to fulfill the requirements of all three military formations.................." Once these satellites are operational, we will be able to see troop movements along the borders,".......... "The key is high-resolution images with precision ....".........."Data and commands can be sent through these satellites to cruise missiles." These satellites in place would give India an edge in any future conflict or war against Pakistan.

These satellites will be developed and launched by ISRO based on requirements projected by the armed forces. Another important factor which needs an attention is the flow of high tech technology to India after the Indo-US deal 2008. Such a discriminatory policy of the international community would create strategic imbalance in south Asia, Pakistan's security will be in frenzy if India acquired such capabilities. In addition to that India is also developing Communication-Centric Intelligence Satellite (CCI-Sat). This satellite is being developed by the Defense Electronics Research Laboratory (DLRL) under the Defense Research and Development Organization (DRDO). This satellite will help Indian intelligence agencies to considerably improve their surveillance and reconnaissance capabilities vis-à-vis Pakistan and other neighboring countries.

Director (DLRL) G. Bhoopathy revealed this project on February 2010 and said, that "We are in the process of designing and developing a spacecraft fitted with an intelligent sensor that will pick up conversations and communications across the borders,". The satellite will be operational by 2014 and will also serve as a test bed for anti-satellite weapon development.

India is also developing a dedicated satellite to facilitate Indian Naval communication and network centric warfare will be launched into geostationary orbit by ISRO in 2010. This satellite will facilitate networking of Indian Naval warships, submarines and aircraft among themselves as well as with operational centres ashore through high-speed data-links, allowing Maritime threats to be detected and shared in real-time to ensure swift reaction. Indian military is developing a first dedicated Indian Air Force satellite which is scheduled for launch in 2011-12. According to IAF Chief Fali H. Major, the satellite will serve as the Air Force's eye in the skies. It will link up the six AWACS that the IAF is acquiring with each other as well as other ground and airbased radars.

Indian Military is regularly improving its surveillance and reconnaissance capabilities. From 2004-2011 it has carried out 12 major war games and in these exercises it has practiced its surveillance, reconnaissance and space imaging capabilities. In 2004 Indian army introduced Long-Range Reconnaissance and Observation System (LORROS) in this Exercise Divya Astra, which it has bought from Israel. LORROS is a high quality, remotely controlled ground based observation system designed for medium and long range surveillance. This kind of a system is good for intelligence gathering and reconnaissance purposes. In 2005 Indian military carried out Exercise Vajra Shakti. In this exercise Indian military practiced its satellite imaging facilities. First time, a Force Multiplication Command Post

(FMCP) was set up to integrate real-time flow of information as a principal tool for decision making and NCW capabilities in the Indian Army.

Most significant war game as far as satellite imagery is concerned was Exercise Hind Shakti in 2009. In this particular exercise Indian military practiced satellite imagery, helicopter borne surveillance systems, UAVs and ground-based surveillance resources such as LORROS, Battlefield Surveillance Radars (BFSRs) and Weapon Locating Radars (WLRs). In this exercise, India practiced latest weapons and equipments with the help of NCW and EW systems. Satellite imagery, modern surveillance and reconnaissance equipment will enhance Indian military's effectiveness to carry out synergized, limited, quick and swift operations.

In 2011 Indian military practiced Exercise Pine Prahar. In this Exercise Indian military rehearsed the capabilities to employ real time intelligence from unarmed aerial vehicles, geostationary satellites, ground-based sensors and human intelligence. These capabilities will enable the Indian military to fight a war in Network Centric environment and assist the field commanders in battlefield precision, fast decision-making and rapid execution of operations. It is a possibility that in next five to ten years Indian military will be able to fully employ satellite capabilities in its armed forces which could be a significant threat to Pakistan's military, nuclear and other sensitive installations.

Indian Military satellites would have wide range of implications for Pakistan and for the entire region. These satellites will improve Indian military's surveillance and reconnaissance capabilities; that would provide Indian military with round the clock coverage of Pakistan's military installations, deployment of Pakistan army close to the border with India. After acquiring such capabilities Indian military would be confident to launch a preemptive conventional strike against Pakistan's nuclear weapon delivery systems at their bases. Therefore Pakistan's missile forces and launching site will also be vulnerable of detection, monitoring and target by Indian military. Furthermore India's accesses to high tech international market after the Indo-US deal will impact negatively on strategic stability of south Asia. Therefore it is imperative for Pakistan Military's decision makers to closely monitor Indian military's space program and come up with adequate response to counter any future challenges and threats to Pakistan's security.

INDIA RACES CHINA IN SPACE FOR ASIAN PRESTIGE, MILITARY SECURITY

A surging space race between India and China is underway amidst nearly a dozen other Asian nations, like India, trying to avoid a loss of prestige or military security to China's aggressive space program. "There is definitely a space race between India and China for top regional prestige and influence," says James Clay Moltz, a professor in the U. S. Naval Postgraduate School's Dept. of National Security Affairs, Monterey, Calif.

"Evidence shows the two countries' are watching each other's activities in space very carefully and keeping score as to who is gaining and losing influence," Moltz told Space Quarterly.

China with seemingly no limits on its space budget or engineering talent is sailing a steady course. It is advancing across all space disciplines with no outward regard to India's space program, except for one important factor—"that India may develop retaliatory capabilities in response to China's 2007 ASAT test," said Bharath Gopalaswamy, associate director of Arms Control, Disarmament and International Security at the University of Illinois at Champaign-Urbana. He is a noted PhD analyst on India's nuclear and military space directions.

Even before China's ASAT test, the highly successful use of U. S. military space assets during the first Persian Gulf War "aroused some curiosity" within India's military services toward Indian development of its own military satellites, Gopalaswamy told Space Quarterly.

"With India what we have seen is a very significant change from a program that until recently was almost exclusively focused on space applications," said Moltz. "India has moved from mainly serving its population with remote sensing, telemedicine and transponders on fishing vessels, to one that has now adopted high prestige lunar and planetary science missions in addition to a fairly active military space program," he said.

There are also broader global power implications with the situation as India is more open to space cooperation with the U. S. and Russia to counter China.

Another perspective is that space rivalries are also growing across traditional Asian political lines, especially between Japan and China, South Korea and Japan and North Korea vs. South Korea.

Unlike the U.S. - Soviet race to the Moon, Asia's space rivalries are "more a long-duration cross-country race with many runners and different objectives," says Moltz in his recent book Asia's Space Race.

"China's rise in space also has had the influence of pushing very unlikely partners and former adversaries like Japan and Vietnam together into new strategic alliances,' Moltz said in an interview.

"One of the most fascinating examples is that Japan is providing Vietnam with more than $US 1 billion in space development assistance for the Vietnamese to build a National Space Center to develop and operate two radar imaging satellites," says Moltz. "These Vietnamese spacecraft will not only overfly Vietnam, but also China, gathering information that Vietnam will likely share with Japan."

While India and fellow west leaning nations seek to counter China's space power, China is using space to bring as many developing countries as it can under its sphere of influence. To do that it formed the Asia Pacific Space Cooperation Organization (APSCO). So far Bangladesh, Indonesia, Iran, Pakistan, Mongolia, Peru and Thailand are part of the group.

There is currently, however, virtually no chance for space cooperation between India and China.

China's growing military space prowess and India's perceived loss of prestige to China explains why India has suddenly decided to "very significantly expand its space budget and the range of its space activities," says Moltz. The key tipping points that sparked major changes in India's space program are China's aggressive military space development and growing ties with Pakistan, development of a human space flight program, its successful 2007 test of an ASAT weapon, China's successful 2007-2010 Chang'e-1 and 2 lunar orbit missions and development of a 2013 lunar rover.

All of these factors have resulted in India making pivotal changes to its space program including:

Major budget increase: In the last year India has increased it annual space budget by 38% for both civilian and military programs "in an all out effort to catch up with China," said Moltz. "This is a very large increase and indicates that India realizes that it has to step up its game if it is to remain at all competitive with China," he said.

Human space flight: In response to China manned space initiative, India is developing an Indian manned flight program with the launch of Indian astronauts planned by 2016-2018 using manned spacecraft and launch vehicles developed in India.

Russian Cooperation: After the U.S. declined an Indian request for manned space technology because of technology transfer issues, India sought similar technology help from Russia, which has agreed to provide some manned spacecraft technology. India is also seeking and likely to get some help from Russia with imaging reconnaissance satellite ground system technology, said Gopalaswamy.

Dueling lunar rovers: An Indian lunar rover mission is under development with Russian help for launch to the Moon in 2014. India's about 200 lb. lunar rover will use a Russian built lander similar to, but smaller than, the twin ramp landers that carried the 1 ton Soviet Lunokhod 1 and 2 rovers to the Moon in the 1970s.

If successful, the Indian launched mission will help counter Asian space leadership issues that will arise with China's lunar rover mission set for launch in 2013, if successful.

In 2008 India launched its Chandrayaan-1 lunar orbiter mission with U.S. and European instruments to counter the prestige gained by China with its Chang'e 1 and 2 lunar orbiters. But India's prestige related ham-handed secrecy may have fouled the water with NASA and ESA for future missions. India kept secret a serious thermal problem then nearly doubled the spacecraft's lunar altitude without telling its partners, confusing data reduction.

Mars exploration: India is developing a Mars orbiter for launch by 2018-2020 to focus on methane detection and to counter an expected Chinese Mars mission challenge.

Military Space: India's Ministry of Defense has formed a small Integrated Space Cell staffed with a few Army, Navy and Air Force officers to help plan near term space priorities with ISRO and also plan "what the Indian military services hope will become a much larger Indian Military Space Command in coming years," Gopalaswamy told Space Quarterly.

ISRO's military role: The Indian government has assigned the civilian Indian Space Research Organization (ISRO) to use its launch vehicles, personnel and facilities to provide capabilities for use by the Indian military, including an initial military spacecraft capability for each of the services. ISRO sought to remain in control of new Indian military spacecraft, but the government ruled they will instead fall under control of the military's Integrated Space Cell.

Israeli Collaboration: In order to obtain a 1 meter day/night all weather imaging capability to watch over China and Pakistan, the Indians collaborated with Israel for an Israeli TecSar imaging radar satellite that India designated Risat-2 and launched in 2009. Israel provided the satellite in exchange for Indian launch of an identical Israeli Air Force TecSar that Israel could not launch into a suitable orbit with its own smaller launch vehicle. The arrangement is likely to continue.

Indian Navigation System: In early 2013 India will begin the launch of its own seven navigation spacecraft under the Indian Regional Navigational Satellite System (IRNSS). The program will obviate the need for Indian forces to use the American GPS system.

Anti-Satellite Weapons: The Indian government asserts that it is prepared to fire an ASAT test of its own, using existing Indian antiballistic missile systems to convince China that India will defend its own space assets in the face of China's 2007 test of its own medium altitude ASAT capability.

Details emerging from China include evidence that top People's Liberation Army officers are writing in military circles about Chinese space security and other concerns should India decide to test its own ASAT.

Also in a mid October, noted defense writer Bill Gertz reported in Washington Free Beacon.com, that intelligence reports say China is ready to test a new "Dong Ning (DN-2)" ASAT missile designed to attack U.S. GPS spacecraft in 12,000 mi. (19,312 km) orbits and a wide array of International military spacecraft in geosynchronous orbit more than 22,000 (35,405 km) mi. high.

"The Indian response [to the 2007 test] has so far been measured and exploratory as far space security is concerned," said Gopalaswamy. But this report [of a higher altitude ASAT] and eventual test "will once again, reinforce and highlight Indian concerns and threat perceptions in space," he said.

"India already feels the necessity to develop retaliatory capabilities, but not necessarily test them. So this [high altitude ASAT] might not necessarily hasten or slow any Indian response, but rather serve as a validating point in India's course of fashioning technological and policy responses to China," Gopalaswamy told Space Quarterly.

There remains an active debate in India about whether India should hurry with an ASAT test to counter China's and also demonstrate capability before any ASAT test ban. India wants to win its space race with China and has made it clear that it is not going to take a secondary role to China in military space capability. But India is also just beginning to feel the high budget costs and the policy, engineering and organizational challenges it must overcome to achieve that goal.

INDIA'S MILITARY SPACE PROGRAM

The use of satellites for military purpose began in 1958 when the United States launched the communications satellite SCORE which simply transmitted a pre-recorded message from space. Since 1958, more than 2000 military satellites,.initially experimental and later operational, have been launched by the USA and USSR alone, so as to have a secure world-wide satellite communications network free from all interferences including jamming and deception.

Space now includes and will include for many years to come the military EW functions such as surveillance, reconnaissance, warning, survivable C3I, detection, targeting, weapon control, weapon delivery and target damage assessment.

The India-China military space relationship has been driven by the security dilemma in international relations. China pursues military space capabilities in part to counter perceived national security threats posed by the US quest for space dominance and missile defense. military doctrines and strategies change at a bewildering pace in the modern era and that technologies have to respond imaginatively to these changes.

Military space systems can gather information about distant battle-fields, transmit it in real time to command centres and inflict damage to targets through remotely controlled weaponry, without putting personnel at risk. Indian military and defense strategies have to respond to such realities.

The Defence Minister Shri AK Antony announced 10 June 2008 the formation of an Integrated Space Cell under the aegis of the Integrated Defence Services Head Quarters to counter 'the growing threat to our space assets'.

Addressing the Unified Commanders' Conference here, he said, although we want to utilize space for peaceful purposes and remain committed to our policy of non-weaponisation of space, 'offensive counter space systems like anti-satellite weaponry, new classes of heavy-lift and small boosters and an improved array of Military Space Systems have emerged in our neighbourhood'.

Shri Antony said the new Cell will act as a single window for integration among the Armed Forces, the Department of Space and the Indian Space Research Organisation (ISRO).

India began its unmanned RISAT-2 spacecraft based radar imaging program with the April 20, 2009 launch of a copy of the all-weather Israeli radar imaging surveillance program satellite TecSAR they had purchased for $200 million. This is to be utilized to address defense border security issues for India.

This RISAT-2 and the new in development dedicated Military Naval Satellite as well as in development RECSAT for India hearld a new era for India

Pushed by Indian immediate national security concerns that it not fall behind in intelligence surveillance advantage operational issues has sparked the Indian governments actions and its military with its security requirements responsibility on these programs.

Literally wartime like emergency requirements was applied to get this program moving on the path to launch as quickly as possible.

This is in addition to their new higher resolution daylight imaging spacecraft launched in 2008 and the existing low and medium resolution remote sensing satellites already being utilized by Indian Intelligence organization for the State and military.

The knowledge of terrain forms the essence of military operations. Geospatial tools for navigation, situational awareness, command and control, operations, or even training and maintenance, forms the core of any military's functioning. ISR is an area that has been revolutionised by geospatial technology towards improving situational awareness. Space-based surveillance and live data streamed from UAVs can drastically shorten sensor-to-shooter loop. Fusion of information from multiple sensors provides unprecedented battlespace transparency, enabling cooperative engagement over extended ranges. Jointness is the mantra for modern warfare. Therefore, common geospatial reference has enabled integration of situational data from different services for achieving operational synergy.

Space-based navigation is one of the major achievements of this technology with the GPS and GLONASS systems having existed for nearly two decades. However, concerns of data ownership, besides the needs for autonomy and redundancy, have driven the development of alternatives such as the EU's Galileo, China's Beidou and India's own IRNSS. Having an indigenous satellite navigation system will boost military capabilities across the spectrum, from basic navigation to high precision ordnance delivery. The armed forces are committed to self-reliance and would support all efforts of the industry in this direction.

The Integrated Space Cell (ISC, initiated in 2008) may want to put a long line of defense application oriented satellites into orbit. Already an "eye-in-the-sky" system for the Air Force is being considered. The Integrated Space Cell was operated jointly by the three service arms, the DRDO, and the ISRO, making it more of a central information network system than an offensive one. The CARTOSAT-2A, a dedicated satellite of the Indian Armed Forces, will also fall under the jurisdiction of this nodal agency. Although a fledgling agency, the ISC may be the stepping stone to a fully fledged Indian Military Space Command.

India, with a strong conviction on the vast potential of the use of outer space for peaceful uses, has been demonstrating it through various space based applications and services for national and societal purposes. India has been actively participating in the formulation of various international treaties on space law in Committees of United Nations. India has been using the space systems for national security purposes, as most other nations are also doing, since such uses are per se not prevented by the UN treaties on space law.

However, India strongly oppose to any attempt to place weapons in space or conducting any unconventional weapons tests in space, as it would pose a perennial threat to all space systems regardless of their use for civilian or military purposes. India is carefully watching the international developments and the attempts of few countries to formulate some legal instruments to prevent any arms race in outer space. Suitable steps would be considered / taken at appropriate time, without causing any prejudice to Indian national interests.

3

Information Warfare

The history of the Second World War offers great examples of the military and civilian leadership manipulating information, even in a very crude fashion, to achieve rather spectacular results. In those days, as we thought about dominating the information spectrum, we turned to the cryptographers who were on the leading edge of these efforts, the so-called "code breakers." These specialized folks focused intently upon breaking the Japanese and German codes. In Europe, the ULTRA project -- "ULTRA" for the "ULTRA secret" -- produced spectacular results. Our code breakers literally worked miracles.

After the Normandy invasion, the German 7th Army attempted a counterattack to drive the Allied forces from the rather tenuous beachhead that they held. But with the help of ULTRA's ability to read the German mail and message traffic, we knew precisely what they were doing as they began to gather their forces to make this attack. We were able to put the British Second Tactical Air Force and the United States Ninth Tactical Air Force immediately upon these armor formations just as they massed. ULTRA gave us the critical information that allowed us to defeat the German forces before they ever came in contact with our ground forces.

By comparison, if you think to December of 1944 and the Battle of the Bulge, we see an example of where the Germans were able to catch us by surprise. They used an alternative communications network, and the Allies did not realize that the Germans had made this switch. It was our lack of information that really fueled the initial German success in the Battle of the Bulge. We had come to rely on ULTRA and had developed a little bit of self-delusion -- and the Germans took advantage of it very effectively.

Our ability to monitor the enemy's communications and use that information as an integral part of our operations is really nothing new. There is another example we should not forget. That's how we control the information that we allow the enemy to receive. Again, I am going back to the Second World War and talking about disinformation, particularly the disinformation campaign that centered on General Patton before and during the D-Day landings. At that time, the Allies understood the other guy's ability to intercept our open signals, so we devised a rather elaborate plan that played to this emerging capability on the part of the Germans. The Allies set up a fake Army headquarters and generated false communications transmissions in England. As a result, the Nazis ended up with a significant number of troops placed in the wrong positions.

Even as they started to pick up indications that there was this great Allied armada that was going to invade Normandy, the Germans refused to believe that there could actually be an Allied invasion of Europe led by anyone but Patton. We played on that expectation in a way that kept Patton associated with his fake headquarters. Even as the Germans began to get higher and higher fidelity intelligence that indicated a real attack at Normandy, their leaders were frozen in indecision and, as a result, tied down considerable forces in France across from the shortest invasion route from England.

For instance, the aircraft we will fly over this time frame are fundamentally the same kinds of aircraft we are flying today. Some will have more advanced avionics, more advanced stealth characteristics or other features; but in the main, aircraft will remain fundamentally aircraft as we know them today. Ships will remain fundamentally ships as we know them today. The same holds true for tanks and armored personnel carriers.

Information warfare is not the exclusive domain of the Air Force, or any other service. I think information warfare has different meanings to a soldier, sailor, Marine, or airman. For instance, the soldier's focus may be on what happens at the corps level and below. The sailor's and Marine's focus is on the maritime and littoral regions. At the same time, an airman's focus is theatre-wide, from the front lines to the adversary's capital. You begin to see how IW covers the entire battlefield. But, because of these divergent views and unique needs, I think it's critical that all services come to grips with and develop capabilities for their respective mediums of operations -- that is land, sea, and air. Then, it falls to the joint force commander, or the regional commander-in-chief, to integrate these capabilities to accomplish the mission.

The Air Force has put considerable effort into developing our concepts. In fact, over the past four months, we have had a team travel to every commander-in-chief (CINC) of a U.S. unified command and brief them on our efforts to incorporate IW into our doctrine and to integrate these concepts into our force employment. Most importantly, we want to be sure that what we are doing and how we approach the subject as an institution will be consistent with the way the CINCs intend to fight. And we want to make sure that what we are doing will meet their needs.

As a practitioner of the profession of arms, I view information technology advances with a single-minded interest. I am motivated by the fact that throughout history, soldiers, sailors, Marines, and airmen have learned one extremely valuable lesson relative to engagement with an opposing force. That is, if you can analyze, act, and assess faster than your opponent, you will win.

The information explosion discussed here today is going to make dramatic changes in how this nation fights wars in the future. Such technology will allow a commander's vision and view of the battlefield to be shared at the lowest level -- to the flight for the airman, to the company on the ground, and to the ship's bridge. Simultaneously, soldiers, Marines, sailors, and airmen on the front lines will be able to see and exploit opportunities as they occur.

What this means is our joint forces may enjoy what some are calling "dominant battlefield awareness." We have some of this kind of capability today. We've made significant enhancements to our ability to leverage our forces with faster command and control and intelligence networks. Among other capabilities, these networks are dramatically reducing the time required to detect and destroy a target.

This process starts with how we gather data. Our intelligence, surveillance, and reconnaissance efforts have been significantly and dramatically improved since Desert Storm. If you are familiar with our TALON programs, you will appreciate what we are doing to reduce the sensor-to-shooter loop -- that is injecting what is detected by our space-based assets directly into the cockpit or a flight deck. We are making similar advances with the systems that operate within the earth's atmosphere. For example, our AWACS early warning aircraft have been greatly improved. Their current radar upgrade allows us to detect cruise missiles at twice the range that we could previously. The AWACS is being fitted with the Joint Tactical Information Distribution Systems, or JTIDS. We will start the initial JTIDS operational test this August. Expect that we will reach full operational capability before the end of the decade. JTIDS alone will give us some pretty significant capabilities. It is not restricted just to AWACS. It also gives our warfighters a secure and jam-resistant data link between Air Force, Navy, Army, and Marine units and future coalition partners -- on land, at sea, and in the air. What that really means is all the players will have a real-time picture and awareness of both what is happening on the ground and what is going on in the air above those forces. JTIDS will give us a tremendous capability to know, at a much higher fidelity, the location of both the enemy and our own forces.

We are also making similar improvements in how we plan and control air operations. Today, we are fielding CTAPS -- the Contingency Theatre Automated Planning System. CTAPS will connect our command and control from the joint forces air component commander (JFACC) to the air wings and the base-level planning cells. It will allow us to generate, disseminate, and monitor the progress of the daily air tasking order much faster than we ever have been able to do before. CTAPS also will tie in with the Combat Intelligence System which will provide us the enemy's order of battle through imagery and integrated threat data.

What does this really mean to us? During Desert Storm, it took us about 48 hours to plan and disseminate the ATO. That doesn't mean that it took 48 hours to execute a request from the field. But, it means that the deliberative process that planners went through to service targets was a 36- to 48-hour process. And you had to have someone manually intervene with an immediate air request to get inside those planning cycles. What the CTAPS system will do for us is take this 48-hour cycle and compress it to 12 hours. This really isn't some pie-in-the-sky system that we're dreaming about or visualizing. This is something that is in full use in exercises today and will be operational across the force next year. We have a similar planning tool that has been operational with our global air mobility forces for about three years.

These are a couple of examples of the kinds of tools we are putting in place. They are going to do more than replace the grease pencil and butcher block paper that (retired Air Force General) Chuck Horner and his staff had to use to run the air war during Desert Storm. These systems are going to help us dominate the information spectrum. I am convinced that this capability will be critical the next time our forces are employed in combat.

If you recall, I described information warfare in terms of how we deny, corrupt, or destroy our adversary's information base while we protect our own. Much of this activity has a very offensive element to it. I think we have been doing this for some time, but perhaps we didn't use that term. For example, during Desert Storm, we targeted many of the Iraqi communications nodes and physically destroyed Saddam Hussein's ability to talk to his troops through normal channels. We forced him into sub-optimum modes of communicating.

In the future, we will approach this objective by viewing our adversary's information activities as a system, and we will engage that system in a variety of ways. In fact, rather than put a precision guided munition into the central telephone exchange in Baghdad and destroy it next time, we may elect to leave it standing so we can better exploit it through our advances in information warfare. So, there will be trade-offs between lethal and non-lethal dimensions in the IW arena.

In the same manner, we have been doing some things along the way that we could properly classify as offensive information operations. There are ways that we corrupt information available to the enemy to deceive him. They include using psychological operations and our electronic warfare assets, like the Compass Call aircraft. I think that these kinds of measures that are designed to corrupt information the enemy has are really critical tools that we provide to the CINCs today. They open the envelope for the potential of further operations tomorrow. Again, if you think back to what we did on D-Day with disinformation, and you consider the tremendous advances in technology since 1944, you begin to appreciate the tremendous potential that exists in this area.

If we recognize an adversary's information network as a lucrative target, an adversary will view our data banks and weapon systems the same way. Information security -- the classic OPSEC, COMSEC, and the more recently stressed computer security -- takes on a whole new level of urgency. As a result, the Air Force is taking some rather significant measures to safeguard our assets. This year, we are spending more than $80 million on defensive measures alone, including establishing a base network control center to protect access to computers and communications. This same center will permit us to see if someone has tried to gain access to our system and, hopefully, will allow us to track down who tried to intrude on the system. These initiatives are important because we run a tremendous risk if we look at information warfare as something that is unique to America. It is not, and by the same token, the U.S. military is not alone in this vulnerability.

Our commercial sector, other elements of the government, and our industrial sectors rely on information systems just as much, if not more, than the military. If you've read Tom Clancy's recent thriller, Debt of Honor, you're familiar with what may be plausible. In this fictional tale, Clancy describes the problems caused when someone infects the stock exchange's computers with a virus, literally bringing the stock market to a standstill. To me, Clancy's work reinforces how the information threat is more than just a unique military concern.

As I look at information warfare and how it relates to the services, I'm reminded of a story about a football team. It seems that during one of the games, the local team had to put in a back-up quarterback late in the fourth quarter. They were ahead, and they were just trying to hang on. So, they put this relatively untested young man into the game, and all he had to do was avoid making a mistake and the team would win. So, the coach grabbed the guy as he was about to go on the field and said, "OK, here's what I want you to do. Run the ball three times, and then punt." So, the kid understood that and goes out onto the field.

His first run gains 20 yards -- great. On the second play, he gains 30 yards. Now, this is going a lot better than he ever expected. On the third play, he gains 30 more yards.

Now they are down on the 10-yard line, the fans are going crazy, and it appears they're going to wrap this thing up. All he has to do is score, and he'll seal the victory for sure. So, the center snaps the ball to him and he punts. Everyone is stunned by this. His coach pulls him over to the sidelines and asks him what he was thinking. And the quarterback replied, "I was thinking that since you didn't change that play, I must have the dumbest coach around."

It is not enough to make a game plan and go with it. You must act and react to what is happening around you. What we're doing today with information warfare is a little bit like that football game -- IW gives us the ability to plan faster with better information so that we can call the optimum play. It may allow us to know what defensive stunt the other team is going to use. It may allow us to give our opponent false information on what play we're about to use. And, most importantly, it may allow us to call an audible and adjust to a fluid situation.

But unlike the game that I just described, when America sends her military forces into action, we don't want a close, exciting game, and we don't want an inexperienced quarterback. This nation has come to expect in our military operations nothing but blow-outs -- 100 to nothing is a good score. And, I believe that exploiting this new and emerging information technology is going to be the key to making this happen. As we approach tomorrow, we need to do more as a service and with the other services. Let me touch just briefly on what we are doing in terms of changing the way we organize, train, and equip our forces.

First, in terms of organizing, in September 1993, the United States Air Force stood up the Air Force Information Warfare Center in San Antonio. This center has more than 1,000 men and women chartered to support IW planning, intelligence gathering, weapon system analysis, and related activities. This group will be a source of IW support teams to go out and assist the CINCs and JFACCs during crises or exercises. They will help build information warfare into the air campaign planning and execution. The Air Force is not alone in this. The Army has an Information Warfare Center at Fort Belvoir, Virginia, and the Navy has created a center at Fort Meade, Maryland.

Additionally, the Air Force is adjusting our training and education programs to include IW concepts. We have had a course for our major air command and numbered air force staffs to give them basic understanding of the issues. We are incorporating IW into our doctrine, so that airmen everywhere will share a common foundation and a common terminology. We're adjusting our mid- and senior-level professional military education schools at Maxwell Air Force Base, Alabama. You see part of this effort here today. We have four Air Force officers attending the inaugural class of the National Defense University's School for Information Warfare.

Finally, and most significantly, we are beginning to procure weapon systems with a mindset that places high priority on maximizing their performance as an information warfare platform. One example of that is the United States' new air superiority fighter, the F-22. This aircraft is the first platform to be built around information technologies. This was an established objective when we started the program, not something added after the fact. A lot of people have heard about the F-22's stealth. You've heard about its supercruise capability -- that is the ability to cruise faster than the speed of sound in military power. And possibly you've heard about the fact that it has tremendous agility in the air-to-air arena. But, you cannot begin to appreciate its potential until you sit in the concept demonstrator and see how the F-22's integrated avionics work. The quality of the composite picture that's compiled from a variety of sources will literally water your eyes, particularly if you're an old-time fighter pilot. For the first time, you'll be able to sit with those flat glass displays and have tremendous situational awareness readily available to you. That is something we've needed for years, and we're finally in the process of getting it. It will allow our pilots to act and assess faster even when outnumbered. And I tell you it isn't just a concept -- it's being put into production today! The F-22 is just one of many Air Force programs that we're continuing to push forward. You see the same thought processes in the space-based infrared system, in our Joint STARS, and in our precision munitions program. As we move forward, we are establishing an additional requirement for our weapon systems -- that is security against the information threat -- that's being written into the requirements documents.

This new mindset is found throughout our acquisition strategy. We are changing how we view our modernization needs. We're taking another look at IW capabilities, like those associated with command and control, and we're treating them more like force structure than support structure. It's part of how we must change the way we do business to incorporate the fundamentals of information warfare.

This broad approach means that we must get the lawyers involved. When I first heard about bringing in the lawyers, I thought we had really slipped off the deep end one more time. I apologize if I offend any lawyers out there -- I always have held lawyers in fairly high esteem. The more I thought about bringing the lawyers into the equation, the more I realized we need their expertise. Because exploiting the information spectrum will readily cross international borders, we must be cognizant of what the law allows and will not allow.

When do you begin information warfare in the spin up to a conflict? When do you begin to go out there and intrude in somebody's banking system? When do you begin to get into somebody's telecommunications system? These are all very difficult questions. Clearly, information warfare is not something that is focused solely on the confines of a constrained battle area. While we will fight in a theatre, information warfare will force us to be engaged worldwide. Thus, we must have some good advice as we pursue this capability.

I appreciate this opportunity to share with you what the Air Force is doing to try and keep up with the information technology explosion. The American way of war has very strong roots in understanding the value of exploiting information to deny information to our adversary, to corrupt what data he has, and to exploit what we know.

World War II was filled with many examples of information warfare. Perhaps Winston Churchill offered the best summary of its importance. At the Tehran conference, when discussing the Allied plans to manipulate information before D-Day, many of these same ethical questions came up. When do we do it? How do we do it? Who are the innocent victims of this thing? And Churchill, addressing the other Allied leaders said, "In wartime, truth is so precious that she should always be attended by a bodyguard of lies" (Anthony Cave Brown, Bodyguard of Lies (New York: Harper and Row, 1975), p. 10). Something to think about. Later, there was a book written with that title by

Anthony Brown. If you read his thick volume, it is rather chilling to see what was possible in that era, and then think about how much more is possible today with the technology that's available. Today and in the future, information warfare is, in fact, going to be this nation's bodyguard. It is essential for the success of our joint forces. To succeed, we are going to need help from a lot of people, including all the very interested people in this room. You understand the far-reaching implications of systems like LANDSAT or SATCOM which are readily available and widely employed at relatively low cost. You appreciate the potential for information technology to allow an adversary to build small, capable, autonomous, operating systems that can threaten U.S. forces on land, sea, or in the air. Such devices might operate relatively unseen and unobserved until they unleash their destructive power.

DEFINITION OF INFORMATION WARFARE

Information Warfare (IW) was formally launched in December 1992 with the dissemination of DOD Directive 3600.1. From the outset, widespread discussion and understanding of IW were hampered by its Top Secret classification. In September 1995 the Assistant Secretary of Defense for Command, Control, Communications and Intelligence) published the formal DOD unclassified definition of IW:

Actions taken to achieve information superiority by affecting adversary information, information-based processes, and information systems, while defending one' s own information, information-based processes, and information systems.

This description clearly underscores both the defensive, as well as offensive aspects of IW. In the summer of 1994, the Defense Science Board (DSB), drawing heavily from expertise within DOD, published the most comprehensive and authoritative discussion of IW to date. The report highlighted the distinction between information in warfare and information warfare. Information in warfare pertains to "getting [information] it where it is needed in a timely and reliable manner."It encompasses the collection, processing, and dissemination of information and is synonymous with the "C4I for the Warrior" vision released by the Joint Staff in 1992.

C4I for the Warrior addresses the concept of a global Command, Control, Communications, Computer, and Intelligence system directly linking military units around the globe in an interoperable, fully integrated fashion spanning the range of military operations from peace to war. Information in warfare capitalizes on the national information infrastructure (NII). Characterized as an "information highway,6 the NII is the growing worldwide information infrastructure which transcends industry, media, and the military and includes government and non-government entities.

Most activities now rely on the information infrastructure including the banking' transportation, manufacturing, and electrical power industries. The Defense Information Infrastructure (DII) is an integral part of the NII with over 95 percent of DOD' s worldwide telecommunications needs satisfied by commercial telecommunications carriers. Military activities relying on the DII include transportation, logistics, financial, manpower, and personnel and training.

While C4I for the Warrior focuses on harnessing ever-increasing computer storage and exchange capabilities, IW targets these information systems. The distinction between C4I for the Warrior and IW is extremely important.

IW employs offensive techniques such as deception, electronic jammers, munitions and advanced technologies to deceive, deny, exploit, damage, or destroy adversary information systems, while at the same time protecting friendly information systems from disruption, exploitation and damage by an adversary. The target of IW may range from influencing national level decisionmakers to corrupting the automated control of transportation systems. Defensive IW protects friendly information systems from disruption, exploitation and damage by an adversary. or example, the Army's ongoing digitization of the battlefield is an application of information in warfare at the operational and tactical levels. Defensive IW, on the other hand, focuses on identifying and protecting vulnerabilities which arise from this increased reliance on technology.

Organizational Imperative

IW, as this definitional discussion highlights, is a complex issue. Organizations are essential in actually implementing this new concept and achieving a viable IW architecture. IW will only become institutionalized if activities actually take responsibility for planning and executing IW. Today IW offices have been stood up throughout DOD focusing on offensive and defensive IW capabilities, but for the most part the budgets and staffs of these elements are very limited. They represent an important start in what will likely be a long and slow process.

IWExecutive Board: The Deputy Secretary of Defense chairs an IW Executive Board established in May 1995 which comprises senior officials within the department including the Vice Chairman Joint Chief of Staff (VCJCS). Supporting the IW Executive Board is an IW Council chaired by the Assistant Secretary of Defense for Command, Control, Communications and Intelligence (ASD(C3I)).

The Executive Board is chartered to address IW roles and responsibilities and serve as the DOD focal point for IW discussion at the national level. The Board is a welcome addition as it demonstrates an awareness by senior DOD officials of the need to coordinate IW, not only within the department, but in the interagency arena. However, senior officials are too busy to spend a great deal of time on any one issue, particularly one that has not reached crisis proportions. This is the point Robert McNamara makes in his book In Retrospect when discussing the evolution of U.S. policy in Vietnam during the Kennedy and Johnson administrations and the same is true today. You need to have the pull from the top, but it is important that lower levels are fully energized.

ASD C31: The ASD(C3I), as the senior IW advisor to the Secretary of Defense, has organized a small IW Directorate comprising less than ten personnel to help him execute his responsibilities. It was the forerunner to this office which drafted the original IW directive in 1992. The IW Directorate conducts centralized planning, coordination, and oversight for IW and conducts program reviews of selected Service and defense agency IW efforts. In May 1995 the IW Directorate sponsored an IW wargame for senior government officials designed to raise the profile of the threat to the U.S. information infrastructure.

The IW Directorate has also focused on initiating a DOD "Red Team" effort. This was one of the IW recommendations from the 1994 Defense Science Board report to "jump start Defensive IW." Under this concept personnel knowledgeable in adversaries' offensive IW form a team to "attack" the DOD information infrastructure. Given the magnitude of the vulnerabilities, the objective would be to have this capability distributed throughout DOD and carried out at various levels and locations. This concept dovetails with the Computer Emergency Response Team (CERT) which reacts to real world intrusions into computer systems. The Defense Information Systems Agency (DISA) has stood up small offices which accomplish both these tasks, but a more comprehensive program is necessary. In the twelve months prior to July 1994 DISA detected roughly 3,600 attacks on military networks, but officials estimate they detected only two percent of all the attacks, raising the estimated number to 182,000.

The "Red Team" program is designed to increase awareness throughout DOD of the vulnerabilities of automated systems and improve the overall security posture. A comprehensive "Red Team" effort can significantly reduce vulnerabilities in the near term as many existing problems are attributed to inadequate training of operators and system administrators. As the head of a CERT team stated, "the problem...is a lack of understanding and awareness and a lack of training and technical competence on the part of the user community." The "Red Team" is a laudable objective, but ASD(C3I) presently only coordinates and does not direct action. The Joint Staff has designated the Joint Command and Control Warfare Center (JC2WC) at San Antonio, Texas as executive agent to support the OSD IW Red Team effort. However, implementation of the

"Red Team" concept is evolving slowly given budget constraints and manpower reductions in the Services and defense agencies.

USD(P): In 1995 the Under Secretary of Defense (Policy) (USD(P)) created an Infrastructure Policy Directorate. This office focuses on emergency preparedness and shaping the role of DOD in the protection of infrastructures, including coordination between DOD and nonDOD government, and civilian/corporate owned infrastructures. These are important responsibilities which clearly fall under the heading of defensive IW. As this office matures, it will be incumbent upon the IW Council and Executive Board to insure IW activities within ASD(C3I) and USD(P) are delineated and deconflicted, if necessary.

Joint Staff: In the Joint arena, IW organizations have also emerged. On the Joint Staff, proponency for IW is now shared between the Directorate for Operations, J3, and the J6, Directorate for Command, Control, Communications, Computers, and Intelligence (C4I) under a Memorandum of Understanding signed in October 1994. While conceptually this may have merits with each directorate bringing a unique dimension of IW, in reality as Lt Gen Clapper, former Director, DIA, has recommended, the Operations Officer should be the overall staff coordinator as he is for all other operations issues.

The current arrangement on the Joint Staff presents some unique challenges as no one is actually in charge. The J3 and J6 principals are too busy to dedicate the constant attention this area requires and day-to-day responsibility for IW on the Joint Staff is delegated. A need exists for direct flag officer sponsorship to orchestrate joint IW policy and doctrine development, conduct operational planning, and establish requirements. A dedicated flag officer sponsor would greatly facilitate coordination with Services, OSD, the Intelligence Community and as IW matures, the interagency and civilian sectors. It would also send a strong message that IW is an important joint warfighting issue requiring immediate highlevel attention. Within the Joint Staff J3, responsibility for offensive IW now resides within the Information Warfare /Special

Technical Operations Division (IW/STOD). This division is responsible for coordinating compartmented planning between the Services, Combatant Commands, and DOD agencies. Bob Woodward writes in The Commanders, the Special Technical Operations Center (STOC) is "a command and communications center for operations involving the sensitive "black" programs known only to those cleared to the special-access compartments." The IW/STOD also has responsibility for coordinating all facets of C2W for the Joint Staff including policy, doctrine, and operational issues. It is this office which authored MOP 30, led the preparation of Joint Pub 3-13 and will draft IW doctrine. This arrangement underscores the important linkage between C2W and IW. As the military proceeds to operationalize IW, the IW/STOD represents the linchpin for ensuring the integration of all dimensions of joint IW.

It has been suggested that, just as we continue to use a Single Integrated Operational Plan (SIOP) for strategic nuclear warfare, DOD might consider the use of an "IW SIOP" which addresses offensive and defensive deconfliction and intelligence equity issues. If this were implemented, the task would be assigned to the IW/STOD to coordinate the task. Today the IW/ STOD focuses principally on support to the Combatant Commands, but as IW matures with both its non- lethal and deterrence potentials, greater interagency participation and coordination will undoubtedly occur.

JC2WC: The activation of the Joint Command and Control Warfare Center (JC2WC) at San Antonio, Texas in October 1994 provided a valuable resource for the Commanders of the Combatant Commands (CINCs). (Note 26 As a field-operating agency of the Joint Chiefs of Staff and headed by a flag officer,the JC2WC is fully engaged in the warfighting application of IW. With 163 assigned personnel, the JC2WC dispatches tailored teams to augment CINC and Joint Task Force staffs and provide C2W expertise in all joint exercises and contingency operations. Personnel from the JC2WC have participated in U.S. efforts in Bosnia and contingency operations in both Kuwait and Haiti. Given the high turnover of personnel on CINC staffs, the JC2WC is very much in demand for its C2W expertise. The JC2WC is in the unique position of being able to cross fertilize and share C2W lessons learned between the Combatant Commands. Accordingly, the organization has played a major role in developing joint C2W doctrine and will contribute significantly to the preparation of a follow-on C2W Joint Tactics, Techniques, and Procedures (JTTP) publication. At the present time, the JC2WC is fully engaged accomplishing its assigned tasks with respect to C2W. It is only now beginning to analyze its newly assigned responsibilities as executive agent in support of the OSD IW Red Team effort. As IW evolves and DOD' s role in the larger IW arena is clarified, a natural progression will be for this organization to serve as the nucleus for a Joint IW center.

Joint COMSEC Monitoring Activity. The JCMA is another field operating agency of the Joint Chiefs of Staff having IW applications. It was created in 1993 by a Memorandum of Agreement between the Service Operations Deputies and Directors of the Joint Staff and NSA. The JCMA is charged with conducting "COMSEC monitoring (collection, analysis, and reporting) of DOD telecommunications and automated information systems (AIS) and monitoring of related noncommunications signals."Its purpose is to identify vulnerabilities exploitable by potential adversaries and recommend countermeasures and corrective actions. The JCMA focuses on unencrypted DOD systems and "does not perform traditional telephone monitoring," as this function remains a Service responsibility.The Joint Staff Director for Operations has been assigned primary responsibility for JCMA affairs. This facilitates coordination between the JC2WC and the JCMA. The JCMA supports both real-world operations, as well as joint exercises and DOD systems monitoring. The JCMA, more so than the JC2WC, already has the expertise to perform the Red Team mission. Rather than further diluting the already stretched resources and expertise of the JC2WC, it would make better sense to designate the JCMA as executive agent to support the OSD Red Team IW initiative.

Joint Spectrum Center. The DOD Joint Spectrum Center (JSC) was activated in September 1994 under the direction of the Joint Staff J6. The JSC assumed all the mission and responsibilities previously performed by the Electromagnetic Compatibility Center, as well as additional functions. The JSC deploys teams in support of the CINCs and serves as the DOD focal point for supporting spectrum supremacy aspects of IW. Notably the JSC assists warfighters in developing and managing the Joint Restricted Frequency List (JRFL) and assisting in the resolution of operational interference and jamming incidents. While informal coordination occurs on IW related issues between the Joint Spectrum Center, the Joint COMSEC Monitoring Activity, and the Joint C2W Center, each organization interfaces separately with the CINC staffs. No formal mechanism is yet in place to ensure the warfighters obtain a coordinated IW support package.

Combatant Commands: The focus of warfighters at the Combatant Commands remains planning and executing C2W. All of the geographic CINCs now have C2W staff officers assigned in their Operations Directorates, but organizing the diverse elements which comprise C2W is a challenge for CINC staffs. U.S. Central Command (CENTCOM) has actually physically consolidated the staff officers responsible for orchestrating electronic warfare, operational security, military deception and psychological operations into a single branch.

This organization can serve as the nucleus as new IW capabilities emerge and are apportioned to the CINCs. Defensive IW poses a more significant challenge. While the CINCs can take incremental measures to unilaterally reduce vulnerabilities of their information systems, given their ultimate dependence on the national information infrastructure, defensive IW must be undertaken as part of a larger DOD sponsored initiative.

Services: Each of the Services have created or are participating in Information Warfare Centers or Activities. The Air Force leads the Services and in September 1995, the Chief of Staff and Secretary of the Air Force published the 17 page, Cornerstones of Information Warfare which describes how "Air

Force doctrine should evolve to accommodate information warfare."The Air Force was also the first to establish their Information Warfare Center (AFIWC) at San Antonio, Texas in October 1993. This was accomplished by consolidating the Air Force cryptologic support center and the electronic warfare center. The AFIWC serves as the Air Force command and control warfare executive agent with approximately 1000 military and civilian personnel assigned. The Center is subordinate to the Air Intelligence Agency closely aligning it with the Intelligence Community. The Center applies the teaming concept integrating the intelligence component with operators, engineers, communications and computer specialists, both offensive and defensive.The AFIWC also has an ongoing "Red Team" and CERT effort designed to improve network security in the Air Force. The Center is collocated with the JC2WC and both organizations work closely together. Personnel from the AFIWC regularly team with the JC2WC on major deployments.

On 1 October 1995, the Air Force created its first Information Warfare Squadron at Shaw Air Force Base, South Carolina. The squadron's primary purpose will be to protect Air Force computers and communications, as well as assisting in "infiltrating an enemy's computer and communications systems."The squadron will support the 9th Air Force commander who is assigned the Central Command area of operations. Eventually, the Air Force will set up more squadrons to assist air commanders responsible for other geographic areas. While the IW Squadron at Shaw AFB presently only has two officers assigned, there will be as many as 40 by August 1996, when the squadron is slated to be operational. Eventually, the squadron might grow to 85 people.The Air Force recognizes it is pushing the envelope, but as General Joseph Ralston, chief of Air Combat Command, stated:

You can sit around for another 10 years and debate about what some of the problems might be [with setting up an information warfare squadron]...but you will never know until you actually get into them and try to make it work operationally.

The Navy established the Navy Information Warfare Activity (NIWA) in August 1994 to serve as their focal point for IW activities.Directly subordinate to the Naval Security Group, the NIWA is located at Fort Meade, Maryland and is closely linked to the National Security Agency.

Given the rapid pace of advancing technology the Navy has given the NIWA special authority to generate requirements and procure systems. Traditionally there has been a sharp separation in the Navy between organizations responsible for setting requirements and those charged with overseeing their acquisition. However, with new generations of computers and information systems unveiled on average about every 18 months, the Navy has adopted a more streamlined approach. As John Davis, technology adviser to the Navy's Space and Electronic Warfare Directorate, indicated, "If we fall more than one cycle behind. we could find industry putting information warfare systems into potentially hostile nations at the same time that US force receive the same equipment."

The Navy also has established the Fleet Information Warfare Center (FIWC) at Little Creek, Virginia from existing Fleet Deception/C2W Group assets.The FIWC serves as the link between the NIWA and the Atlantic and Pacific Fleets. With personnel deployed on carrier battle groups throughout the world, the FIWC fulfills a similar mission for the Navy that the JC2WC does for the joint warfighter. The IW organizational structure created by the Navy enables the FIWC to focus on near term operational requirements, while the NIWA assumes a more long-term perspective keeping abreast of IW advances and developing and acquiring systems.

Rather than create a separate IW organization, the Marines intend to assign liaison officers to the respective Service IW centers to benefit from their efforts. The Navy and Marines have also teamed up to develop policy guidance for Navy and Marine IW/C2W operations. In February 1995, the Marine Corps Commandant and Chief of Naval Operations approved a plan which states, "Navy and Marine Corps must have a fully integrated IW/C2W capability...team must organize, train, and equip its forward deployed forces to conduct IW/C2W." The Army is the latest Service to establish an IW activity. Officially activated in May 1995, the Land Information Warfare Center (LIWA) is subordinate to the Army Intelligence and Security Command (INSCOM) but is under the operational control of the Headquarters Department of the Army, Deputy Chief of Staff for Operations (DCSOPS).

As with the Air Force and Navy, the Army has closely aligned its IW effort with the Intelligence Community. The LIWA is a totally new organization in contrast to the Air Force and Navy efforts which reorganized existing activities. It is also the smallest of the three Service IW activities with a projected end strength of 50-75 personnel.

The primary focus of the LIWA is to provide operational support at the Army Corps and higher levels. The Army is also coordinating closely with the Marines to assign personnel to the LIWA. Given its small size, the LIWA draws upon existing capabilities in the Army including psychological operations, electronic warfare, and operational security. The Army is in the process of institutionalizing a "Red Team" effort from existing INSCOM assets, and there is close coordination and collaboration with NSA on mutual IW efforts.

The Services' efforts during a period of serious budget constraints underscore a recognition of the importance of IW. Except for the general responsibilities delineated in the original DOD IW directive, Services have received no additional policy guidance on how to implement IW. In reviewing Service responses to IW, they have established organizations which best suit their near term needs. Manpower and funding for Service IW initiatives have been reallocated internally with the Air Force taking the most aggressive approach.

Over time Service organizations can be expected to evolve as IW matures. Today much of their focus is on implementing C2W, the military application of IW. Services have also implemented "Red Teams" to train personnel and improve security awareness of the vulnerabilities associated with information systems. Additionally, while the linkages of Service

IW organizations with the Intelligence Community is valuable, it is important IW does not become an intelligence activity. IW needs to be controlled and fully managed by the warfighters as an integral part of an overall strategy. In that regard, the recent activation of the IW Squadron by the Air Force, separate and distinct from the AFIWC, is a positive step.

Intelligence Community: Within the Intelligence Community there exists an acute appreciation of the enormous impact IW has on their efforts. Each organization, DIA, CIA and NSA has established an office to orchestrate IW related activities and satisfy the needs of their consumers. NSA, in addition to it its intelligence mission, has a unique responsibility for developing "standards, techniques, systems, and equipment" for classified information.NSA has demonstrated success at protecting classified systems, but has achieved less success in the increasingly vulnerable area of unclassified computer networks where it plays a supporting role.

Under the 1987 Computer Security Act, the National Institute for Standards and Technology (NIST) was assigned responsibility for developing government wide standards and guidelines for "unclassified, sensitive information."The law also directed NIST to draw upon technical computer security guidelines developed by NSA.To clarify the relationship between NIST and NSA, a Memorandum of Agreement (MOW) was formalized in 1989 establishing mechanisms for implementing the Computer Security Act of 1987. The MOU has been controversial because of concerns in Congress and elsewhere that it cedes NSA much more authority than was intended under the act.The act envisioned NIST requesting NSA expertise as needed, but instead the MOU has involved NSA in all NIST activities related to information security.

Protecting unclassified, sensitive information is essential in developing an effective IW architecture. Given the growing threat to our information system, NSA officials are lobbying for increased efforts to protect unclassified networks.While NSA certainly has tremendous expertise and is the national authority on cryptographic protection, there are reservations about having it assume a greater role. Some perceive a conflict of interest between NSA's information protection role and its principal intelligence mission. Additionally, leadership in cryptography does not imply leadership in other areas of defensive IW. DOD has assigned the responsibility of protecting its own information infrastructure to the Defense Information Systems Agency.As national defensive IW policy is formulated, the security of unclassified, sensitive information must be addressed.

Non DOD Organizations: Although defensive IW has not been officially embraced outside of DOD, several standing organizations focus on this issue. The National Communication System (NCS) was established in 1963 to coordinate the planning of national security and emergency preparedness communications for the federal government under all circumstances, including crisis or emergency, attack, recovery, and reconstitution. The NCS receives policy direction directly from the National Security Council (NSC) but is managed through the Department of Defense.The NCS's National Coordinating Center for Telecommunications is staffed full time by both government and telecommunications industry representatives whose mission is to respond to both military and civil emergencies: ea., Desert Storm, Hurricane Andrew and, more recently, the bombing of the Federal building in Oklahoma city.

The National Security Telecommunications Advisory Council (NSTAC) was established during the Reagan Administration to advise the President on national security and emergency preparedness issues. This senior body is composed of presidents and CEOs of major telecommunications and defense information systems companies. NSTAC works closely with NCS.

The Federal Communications Commission (FCC) also plays a strong role in reliability and privacy issues regarding the public switched telephone network. The Network Reliability Council (NRC) was created in 1992 by the FCC to investigate the reliability of the public switched network following a series of service outages in 1991. The efforts culminated in a one-thousand page document, "Network Reliability." The FCC expanded the membership of the NRC in July 1994 and gave it a new charter. Today the NRC is composed of CEOs from telephone companies, equipment suppliers, state agencies, and federal, corporate, and consumer users.

Each of these organizations, as well as NIST, are involved in aspects of defensive IW. What is lacking, however, is an overarching framework linking these disparate efforts into a coordinated effort. Within the government someone needs to be in charge. The NCS may serve as a blueprint for this effort. Not only does it have in place representatives and links to all major government agencies, including the Intelligence Community, but it is a model for governmentindustry cooperation. To be successful, defensive IW must have the support of private industry. Not only must awareness of vulnerabilities be increased, but coordinated steps taken to reduce the risk. That is the exactly the success which NCS has achieved in the telecommunications sector. As national policy is developed for IW, strong consideration should be given to creating an organization like the NCS to serve as the focal point for this effort and having it possibly work directly for the Vice President. DOD should play a role in the organization but as an active participant, not the leader.

IMPACTS OF INFORMATION AGE TECHNOLOGIES

To understand the future one needs to develop at least a broad conceptual understanding of the nature of the impacts that these technologies are likely to have. The impacts that these technologies are projected to have can be grouped into the following six areas. First, the speed at which information can be transmitted, managed, manipulated, and interpreted will increase significantly. Information flows within and between organizations and among organizations and international actors will also accelerate, although at differing rates depending upon a host of factors. Increased speed will matter more for some uses than for others, and some international actors will benefit more from more rapid information flows than will others. But in general, the increased speed of information flow will increase the tempo of interactions within and between international actors. Second, the capacity to transmit information will also increase significantly. Again, increased capacity will become available at different rates to different international actors. As with increased speed, greater information and communication capacity will benefit some organizations and international actors more than others. Here, however, the point to stress is that for many international actors, the ability to transmit and interpret greater amounts of information will mean that decision makers could have a greatly enhanced picture of the world, themselves, and others upon which to base their decisions.

Third, Information Age technologies will enhance the flexibility of information flows. Those needing information will be able to reach out and get it from more sources. Those needing to communicate with someone will find it ever more easy to do so quickly and directly. Put differently, these technologies will decrease the location-dependence of information and communication transactions. This greater flexibility will be available to some more quickly than to others, will matter more for some than for others, and will be embraced more quickly by some than by others.

Fourth, these technologies will provide more and more individuals greater access to more and more people, organizations, and information than ever before. This, some observers have argued, will lead to the democratization of information and communication flows throughout the world, that is, a decreased ability of a few (e.g. governments, businesses, and the other "haves") to dominate information and communication channels. This will free information from the hierarchy, or in the case of the military, from the chain of command. Although this may be true, improved access will not occur—or in some cases, be permitted—at the organizations, societies, and international actors.

None of these anticipated impacts means that time, distance, or location no longer matter—they still do. Indeed, as pointed out several times above, Information Age technologies will be absorbed, diffused, and operationalized by different international actors in different ways and at different speeds. This will lead to different types and rates of change in different international actors. Factors that will influence the way and rate in which advanced technologies will be absorbed, diffused, and operationalized include but are not limited to:

1. purchase and upkeep cost;
2. age and utility of in-place technology;
3. an actor's social and cultural receptivity to new technology;
4. degree of insularity within an actor;
5. level and reliability of an actor's human, technical, and economic support infrastructures;
6. level and strength of traditional values and outlooks within an actor;
7. levels of concern over sovereignty on the part of states, and over control of decision-making processes on the part of the actors; and
8. many political, social, and economic factors idiosyncratic to each actor and therefore impossible to detail.

Despite these constraints on adoption, Information Age technologies are indeed lessening the role that time, distance, and location play in human interactions. It is also noteworthy—and fraught with implications for national security—that this process is uneven and will create new "gaps" and a new power relationship among players on the world stage.

Information Age

The Information Age (also known as the Computer Age, Digital Age, or New Media Age) is a period in human history characterized by the shift from traditional industry that theIndustrial Revolution brought through industrialization, to an economy based on information computerization. The onset of the Information Age is associated with the Digital Revolution, just as the Industrial Revolution marked the onset of the Industrial Age.

During the information age, the phenomenon is that the digital industry creates a knowledge-based society surrounded by a high-tech global economy that spans over its influence on how the manufacturing throughput and the service sector operate in an efficient and convenient way.

In a commercialized society, the information industry is able to allow individuals to explore their personalized needs, therefore simplifying the procedure of making decisions for transactions and significantly lowering costs for both the producers and buyers.

This is accepted overwhelmingly by participants throughout the entire economic activities for efficacypurposes, and new economic incentives would then be indigenously encouraged, such as theknowledge economy.

The Information Age formed by capitalizing on computer microminiaturization advances.This evolution of technology in daily life and social organization has led to the fact that the modernization of information and communication processes has become the driving force of social evolution.

Internet

The Internet was conceived as a fail-proof network that could connect computers together and be resistant to any single point of failure.

It is said that the Internet cannot be totally destroyed in one event, and if large areas are disabled, the information is easily rerouted.

It was created mainly by DARPA on work carried out by British scientists like Donald Davies; its initial software applications were e-mail and computer file transfer. Though the Internet itself has existed since 1969, it was with the invention of the World Wide Web in 1989 by British scientist Tim Berners-Lee and its introduction in 1991 that the Internet became an easily accessible network. The Internet is now a global platform for accelerating the flow of information and is pushing many, if not most, older forms of media into obsolescence.

Progression

Library Expansion

Library expansion was calculated in 1945 by Fremont Rider to double in capacity every 16 years, if sufficient space were made available.He advocated replacing bulky, decaying printed works with miniaturized microform analog photographs, which could be duplicated on-demand for library patrons or other institutions. He did not foresee the digital technology that would follow decades later to replace analog microform with digital imaging, storage, and transmission mediums. Automated, potentially lossless digital technologies allowed vast increases in the rapidity of information growth. Moore's law, which was formulated around 1965, calculated that the number of transistors in a dense integrated circuit doubles approximately every two years.

The proliferation of the smaller and less expensive personal computers and improvements in computing power by the early 1980s resulted in a sudden access to and ability to share and store information for increasing numbers of workers. Connectivity between computers within companies led to the ability of workers at different levels to access greater amounts of information.

Information Storage

The world's technological capacity to store information grew from 2.6 (optimally compressed) exabytes in 1986 to 15.8 in 1993, over 54.5 in 2000, and to 295 (optimally compressed) exabytes in 2007. This is the informational equivalent to less than one 730-MB CD-ROM per person in 1986 (539 MB per person), roughly 4 CD-ROM per person of 1993, 12 CD-ROM per person in the year 2000, and almost 61 CD-ROM per person in 2007.

Information Transmission

The world's technological capacity to receive information through one-way broadcast networks was 432 exabytes of (optimally compressed) information in 1986, 715 (optimally compressed) exabytes in 1993, 1.2 (optimally compressed) zettabytes in 2000, and 1.9 zettabytes in 2007 (this is the information equivalent of 174 newspapers per person per day). The world's effective capacity to exchange information through two-way telecommunication networks was 281 petabytes of (optimally compressed) information in 1986, 471 petabytes in 1993, 2.2 (optimally compressed) exabytes in 2000, and 65 (optimally compressed) exabytes in 2007 (this is the information equivalent of 6 newspapers per person per day). In the 1990s, the spread of the Internet caused a sudden leap in access to and ability to share information in businesses and homes globally. Technology was developing so quickly that a computer costing $3000 in 1997 would cost $2000 two years later and $1000 the following year.

Computation

The world's technological capacity to compute information with humanly guided general-purpose computers grew from 3.0×10^8 MIPS in 1986, to 4.4×10^9 MIPS in 1993, 2.9×10^{11} MIPS in 2000 to 6.4×10^{12} MIPS in 2007.

Relation to Economics

Eventually, Information and Communication Technology—computers, computerized machinery, fiber optics, communication satellites, Internet, and other ICT tools—became a significant part of the economy. Microcomputers were developed and many businesses and industries were greatly changed by ICT. Nicholas Negroponte captured the essence of these changes in his 1995 book, *Being Digital*. His book discusses similarities and differences between products made of atoms and products made of bits. In essence, a copy of a product made of bits can be made cheaply and quickly, and shipped across the country or internationally quickly and at very low cost.

Impact on Jobs and Income Distribution

The Information Age has affected the workforce in several ways. It has created a situation in which workers who perform tasks which are easily automated are being forced to find work which involves tasks that are not easily automated. Workers are also being forced to compete in a global job market. Lastly, workers are being replaced by computers that can do their jobs faster and more effectively. This poses problems for workers in industrial societies, which are still to be solved. However, solutions that involve lowering the working time are usually highly resisted. Jobs traditionally associated with the middle class (assembly line workers, data processors, foremen and supervisors) are beginning to disappear, either through outsourcing or automation. Individuals who lose their jobs must either move up, joining a group of "mind workers" (engineers, doctors, attorneys, teachers, scientists, professors, executives, journalists, consultants), or settle for low-skill, low-wage service jobs.

The "mind workers" are able to compete successfully in the world market and receive high wages. Conversely, production workers and service workers in industrialized nations are unable to compete with workers in developing countries and either lose their jobs through outsourcing or are forced to accept wage cuts. In addition, the internet makes it possible for workers in developing countries to provide in-person services and compete directly with their counterparts in other nations.

This has had several major consequences, including increased opportunity in developing countries and the globalization of the workforce.Workers in developing countries have a competitive advantage which translates into increased opportunities and higher wages. The full impact on the workforce in developing countries is complex and has downsides.

In the past, the economic fate of workers was tied to the fate of national economies. For example, workers in the United States were once well paid in comparison to the workers in other countries. With the advent of the Information Age and improvements in communication, this is no longer the case. Because workers are forced to compete in a global job market, wages are less dependent on the success or failure of individual economies.

Automation, Productivity, and Job Loss

The Information Age has affected the workforce in that automation and computerization have resulted in higher productivity coupled with net job loss. In the United States for example, from January 1972 to August 2010, the number of people employed in manufacturing jobs fell from 17,500,000 to 11,500,000 while manufacturing value rose 270%. Although it initially appeared that job loss in the industrial sector might be partially offset by the rapid growth of jobs in the IT sector, the recession of March 2001 foreshadowed a sharp drop in the number of jobs in the IT sector. This pattern of decrease in jobs continued until 2003. Data has shown that overall, technology creates more jobs than it destroys even in the short run.

Rise of Information-intensive Industry

Industry is becoming more information-intensive and less labor and capital-intensive. This trend has important implications for the workforce; workers are becoming increasingly productive as the value of their labor decreases. However, there are also important implications for capitalism itself; not only is the value of labor decreased, the value of capital is also diminished. In the classical model, investments in human capital and financial capital are important predictors of the performance of a new venture. However, as demonstrated by Mark Zuckerberg and Facebook, it now seems possible for a group of relatively inexperienced people with limited capital to succeed on a large scale.

Innovations

The Information Age was enabled by technology developed in the Digital Revolution, which was itself enabled by building on the developments in the Technological Revolution.

Computers

Before the advent of electronics, mechanical computers, like the Analytical Engine in 1837, were designed to provide routine mathematical calculation and simple decision-making capabilities. Military needs during World War II drove development of the first electronic computers, based on vacuum tubes, including the Z3, the Atanasoff–Berry Computer, Colossus computer, and ENIAC.

The invention of the transistor in 1947 enabled the era of mainframe computers (1950s – 1970s), typified by the IBM 360. These large room-sized computers provided data calculation and manipulation that was much faster than humanly possible, but were expensive to buy and maintain, so were initially limited to a few scientific institutions, large corporations and government agencies. As transistor technologyrapidly improved, the ratio of computing power to size increased dramatically, giving direct access to computers to ever smaller groups of people. Along with electronic arcade machines and home video game consoles in the 1980s, the development of the personal computers like theCommodore PET and Apple II (both in 1977) gave individuals access to the computer. But data sharing between individual computers was either non-existent or largely manual, at first using punched cards and magnetic tape, and later floppy disks.

Data

The first developments for storing data were initially based on photographs, starting with microphotography in 1851 and then microform in the 1920s, with the ability to store documents on film, making them much more compact. In the 1970s, electronic paper allowed digital information appear as paper documents.

Early information theory and Hamming codes were developed about 1950, but awaited technical innovations in data transmission and storage to be put to full use. While cables transmitting digital data connected computer terminals and peripherals to mainframes were common, and special message-sharing systems leading to email were first developed in the 1960s, independent computer-to-computer networking began with ARPANET in 1969. This expanded to become the Internet (coined in 1974), and then the World Wide Web in

1989. Public digital data transmission first utilized existing phone lines using dial-up, starting in the 1950s, and this was the mainstay of the Internet until broadband in the 2000s. The introduction of wireless networking in the 1990s combined with the proliferation ofcommunications satellites in the 2000s allowed for public digital transmission without the need for cables. This technology led to digital television, GPS, and satellite radio through the 1990s and 2000s.

Computers continued to become smaller and more powerful, to the point where they could be carried. In the 1980s and 1990s, laptops first allowed computers to become portable, and PDAs allowed use while standing or walking. Pagers existing since the 1950s, were largely replaced by mobile phones beginning in the 1980s, giving mobile networking ability to a few at first. These have now become commonplace, and include digital cameras. Starting in the 1990s, tablets and then smartphones combined and extended these abilities of computing, mobility, and information sharing.

Information Age Strategic Environment

The Information Age, like the agricultural and industrial ages which preceded it, is a global phenomenon. Global communications are virtually instantaneous, computers and other Information Age technologies are found in even the most underdeveloped states, and almost every country has least one system connected to the Internet.

However, again like the preceding agricultural and industrial ages, changes being introduced by the Information Age are not equally pervasive everywhere. Change induced by Information Age technologies is taking place in different countries at different rates of speed, with different impacts, different organizational characteristics, and with different strategic implications. As pointed out earlier, different societies absorb, diffuse, and operationalize Information Age technologies at different rates because of cost and cultural considerations. These factors include the age and utility of in-place technology; a society's social and cultural receptivity to new technology; the degree of insularity of a society; the level and reliability of a society's human, technical, and economic support infrastructures; the level and strength of a society's traditional values and outlooks; the level of education within a society; the degree of technical sophistication of users and potential users of Information Age technology within a society; the level of concern over sovereignty on the part of states, and over control of decision-making processes on the part of a society's leadership elites; and many other political, social, and economic factors idiosyncratic to each society and therefore impossible to detail.

What, then, will the emerging strategic environment look like? Here, we will begin with the view of Alvin and Heidi Toffler as a point of departure. This view is criticized by some as being too simplistic and by others as overlooking important historical facts. However, it is a widely recognized view that provides a common reference point, one whose assumptions can be "tested" in a systematic way.

To the Tofflers, the world is moving toward a global socio-economic revolution that will lead to the development of a global "trisected power structure." This new strategic environment will entail a trisected global power structure that will supersede the Industrial Age's bisected structure in which states that developed industrial "smokestack" based economies enjoyed economic, social, and military superiority over more primitive agriculturally based societies.

In the Information Age, the Tofflers argue, those states that use and benefit most from Information Age technologies will be at the apex of a new three-tiered global power structure dominated by knowledge and knowledge-related "intangibles." They will be superior in capabilities to those states that remain dependent on either an industrial or agricultural economy.30 In an effort to gain the advantages afforded by Information Age technological capabilities, some states may even attempt to bypass the industrial stage of development, moving directly from an agricultural economy to an information economy. But all three types of societies, with many countries not fitting clearly into one or another of the three dominant types, will coexist even as they coexist in today's bisected power structure. Countries at the apex of this trisected global power structure will be more dependent on the technologies of the Information Age than will those states that remain with an industrial or agricultural economy. Because of this greater dependency, they as societies will be more vulnerable than industrial or agricultural societies to any alteration, disruption, or destruction of the technologies upon which they rely (e.g., information or critical infrastructure warfare), much the same way as industrial societies are more vulnerable to the disruption or destruction of energy and fuel supplies than are agricultural societies. Despite the enhanced economic and military capabilities that flow from the technologies of the Information Age, the security equation for post-industrial states will be complicated because of this vulnerability.

At the same time, as the trisected global power structure emerges, the capabilities provided by the technologies of the Information Age are likely to further blur the boundaries between domestic and international affairs. In the emerging strategic environment, the combination of increased speed, capacity, and flexibility of information flow combined with greater access to, more types of, and heightened demand for information will make it increasingly difficult for states to control inward and outward information flows. Some states will try to control access to freely available information, as China has with access to Internet sites. However, few will succeed unless they are willing to impose truly draconian social or technological solutions to their perceived problem. Such solutions might include capital punishment or long-term imprisonment for accessing information sites deemed unacceptable, restricting Internet access via licenses to only a few loyal subjects, or otherwise restricting access to advanced information and communication technologies. States that apply such solutions, while perhaps maintaining control of information flows, will suffer other social and economic losses, including limiting their ability to move from agricultural or industrial level to an information based level of economic development.

Because of the capabilities that they provide, the technologies of the Information Age are also likely to increase the role that non-state actors play in the international system. Multinational corporations have long been major actors in the international scene, but they are likely to grow even more influential as businesses becomes increasingly regionalized and globalized.

Already, taking advantage of opportunities afforded by advanced information and communication technologies to increase the speed, capacity, and flexibility of information flows, many businesses have made geography and national borders less relevant as they have created an international marketplace and increased profitability by moving their labor intensive back room operations to countries where labor costs are low. Similarly, nongovernmental organizations (NGOs) have proliferated, increasing in number from perhaps four thousand such organizations in the late 1970s to perhaps as many as thirty thousand in the late 1990s. A significant but uncertain percentage of this growth is undoubtedly due to the ability that like- minded or like-interested people now have on a global base to share information and to collaborate. Thus, the emerging strategic environment will be more complex than the one that exists today.

If this analysis is substantially correct, more fissures of change and potential conflict will divide the global community than in the past. Inevitably, the technologies of the Information Age will continue to be absorbed, diffused, and operationalized at different speeds and with different results in different countries. Without denying that states will, for the foreseeable future, remain the dominant type of international actor, more types of actors, and more actors of each type, will gain importance on different issues. Given the potential provided by Information Age technologies for collections of individuals to articulate and perhaps act on their viewpoints, the strategic environment of the Information Age may well be far more complex than that which preceded it. This view is contrary to those who argue that the Information Age will drive us to global homogeneity.

There are at least four views about the speed with the Information Age will usher in changes to the strategic environment, and about how extensive those changes may be. A few voices urge caution about leaping to conclusions that the Information Age is truly upon us. These analysts do not deny that change is taking place nor that advanced technologies provide humankind with capabilities far beyond those previously available, but they are skeptical that, in the final analysis, much other than capabilities will change. This perspective is not widely shared, but it can not be overlooked.

One such skeptic is Frank Webster, who has observed that there are immense difficulties in measuring what is meant by an Information Age. He also warns that information by itself means nothing, and that humankind must take into consideration the meaning and quality of information, not just its quantity. Even with the proliferation of information-related technologies, Webster wonders whether society has or will change profoundly enough to warrant calling the near term future an Information Age. While Webster and others with similar perspectives fully admit that information technologies provide humankind with capabilities that were unimaginable a few short years ago, their premise is that little in human interrelationships or organizations has changed fundamentally or is likely to change fundamentally as a result of advanced information and communication technologies.

What does this imply for national security affairs? If Webster's view is accurate, this means that new and emerging technologies will continue to enhance military capabilities, but that the strategic environment will change little. Military systems, weapons platforms, and kill mechanisms may grow more capable, more lethal, more accurate, and obtain greater reach, but national security planners and strategists will be able to proceed with their planning as if little else other than capabilities have changed.

A second perspective sees strategic change taking place in an evolutionary rather than revolutionary way. Without denying that the cumulative impact of new technologies will be revolutionary, this school nonetheless sees change occurring in a paced and evolutionary manner. Advocates of this school of thought accept that future human and organizational relationships will be fundamentally different from past relationships, but that these changes will unfold over time, permitting individuals and organizations to adjust slowly or coevolve.

INFORMATION WARFARE AND DETERRENCE

It is clear that the information age has spawned new relationships and greatly expanded the range of possible interactions. It is no longer possible to separate and isolate military, national, public, and private systems. Thus, concepts of national security, to include protecting information systems and deterring attacks, need to be expanded to consider the full range of likely interactions. This would help to determine where the boundary between DoD and the rest of the national information infrastructure should lie. It was in this context that the workshop primarily addressed the relationship between information warfare and deterrence.

At the abstract level, the interface between these two concepts is dependent on setting the context clearly. First, deterrence is always from an actor toward a target. The very nature of the actor and target, as well as the degree of asymmetry between them is important. A nation state has much greater power than an individual hacker and has broad powers of law enforcement that can be brought to bear if the individual is within its borders or the reach of accepted international laws. However, two nation states are, at least in legal terms, equal and must exercise the international system (diplomacy, warfare, etc.) to influence one another's behavior. Moreover, the nature of the relationship between the parties is important to the analysis. The use of deterrence is unlikely in cooperative arrangements, more likely in competitive ones, and most likely in conflictual patterns. Finally, substantive context may also make a difference. For example, deterrence is most likely in military arenas where the credibility of threats is greatest and easiest to assess. Hence, specification of the context (type of relationship, nature of the actors, substantive domain) is essential before any conclusion is possible about the effectiveness of deterrence.

The Steamroller and the Wrench

The most important insight arising from looking at the two concepts however, is the fact that they are only relevant to one another in highly selective contexts. The analogy that emerged was that of a steamroller and a wrench. Both are tools and depending on the situation, appropriate wrenches may be useful for, or even crucial to, the operation of the steamroller. However, most of the things the steamroller does are irrelevant to the wrench and most of the things the wrench can be used for do not involve a steamroller.

In many cases, therefore, the workshop found itself venturing away from a pure consideration of the two concepts and into meaningful discussions in areas related to one or the other of the two central topics. These discussions revolved around the concepts, but kept slipping tangentially to more familiar issues such as command and control warfare (C2W), or IW in some other context such as retaliation in kind for an IW attack. It eventually became apparent that the main reason for frustration was that the related concepts and issues are grossly mismatched. IW is just too big and encompasses so much (particularly in the context of information dominance), while deterrence is limited and almost always case specific.

In retrospect, the revelation should not have been surprising. While workshop participants noted that certain IW actions are as old as warfare (a bluff for example), the exploding vistas of information technology and cyberspace are only beginning to be understood. Several of the participants were comfortable discussing deterrence as it might be related to command and control warfare (C2W). In this application there are five clearly defined "Pillars" which include Operational Security (OPSEC), Electronic Warfare (EW), Psychological Operations (PSYOPS), Military Deception, and Physical Destruction.

The pillars are arrayed both offensively as "Counter-Command and Control" and defensively as "Command and Control Protection." Both arrays are dependent on and supported by intelligence. Any one of the pillars can have a deterrent effect. For example, in EW the presence of anti-radiation missiles may deter the use of air defense radar. Likewise, the adroit use of psychological operations might disrupt the enemy decision making process to the point where they are deterred from action, or at least their C2 process is greatly slowed.

While we believe that we understand C2W, the workshop brought into clear focus the fact that C2W is only a very small subset of IW, and it is that larger context that needs further exploration and analysis. Likewise, one size IW deterrence does not fit all. Equally important to the action itself is the intended recipient. Without getting into the adversary's mind and understanding his social, cultural, and religious values, as well as his education and past history, IW deterrence actions may be like the tree that falls in the forest and goes unheard. They may even be misunderstood and, therefore, have unintended consequences. The earlier discussion of deterrence stressed that creditable deterrence requires that the message be communicated clearly. Knowing how the adversary receives and understands messages is essential. It also became increasingly clear that IW deterrent actions must be part of an orchestrated and integrated effort. Seldom will an IW action in and of itself be a creditable deterrent. However, skillfully combined as part of an overall information dominance concept, some combination of IW and other actions may produce the desired deterrence.

4

Information Warfare: A Threat to International Space Security

Russia's interest in influencing the democratic processes of the West is a very hot issue in the international security debate. The threat of Russia's information warfare is prominently indicated in the National Security Strategy of the United States, released last December, where it is stated (pages 35) that "Russia uses information operations as part of its offensive cyber efforts to influence public opinion across the globe". Proofs of Russia's meddling in the last US presidential elections' public debate raised serious concerns across the Atlantic. The President of France, Emmanuel Macron, announced this January that he will soon propose a law to tackle the issue of fake news, especially during electoral campaigns, for instance by requiring a more transparent profile of the authors of online content.

Last October, Germany approved the law on the "Enforcement on Social Networks": it is one of toughest laws in the Western world, designed to ensure that social media platforms remove fake news and hate speech within set periods of receiving complaints, and foreseeing fines of up to 50 million Euros if they persistently fail to comply. Last November, at the traditional Lord Mayor's Banquet, Great Britain's Prime Minister, Theresa May, warned: "So I have a very simple message for Russia. We know what you are doing. And you will not succeed. Because you underestimate the resilience of our democracies, the enduring attraction of free and open societies, and the commitment of Western nations to the alliances that bind us".

The issue is also relevant to Italy in the wake of the general elections due in a few months. Former Italian Prime Minister, Matteo Renzi, recently warned about the risk of "weird connections" between some of his political opponents and media outlets allegedly involved in influencing the public opinion with manipulated information; its Democratic Party launched last December a monthly bulletin to "name and shame" fake news. Connections between some Italian political parties and Russia were, instead, given for certain in the last December's issue of Foreign Affairs by former US Vice President, Joe Biden, and former US Deputy Secretary of Defence, Michael Carpenter, who overtly accused Russia of attempting to stir the discussion around the December 2016 Italian referendum on institutional reforms. The Italian intelligence community promptly denied that any such interference occurred in the past, but remains vigilant.

CHANGING TRENDS IN SPACE SECURITY

The changing trends in space security are outgrowing the existing international governance framework for outer space. It is no longer accurate to claim that there is progressive development of international space law. Two key developments in international law and policy illustrate what is not taking place. First, the Conference on Disarmament (CD) has been stalled on a programme of work since 1998, preventing formal discussion and negotiation of an agreement to prevent an arms race in space. Second, efforts to extend the mandate of COPUOS to include issues related to the militarization of space have also been waylaid. Diplomacy is failing to keep pace with innovations in who uses outer space, how it is used and for what purposes.

In a shift of strategy, however, the international community is beginning to respond to growing governance challenges in outer space by adopting more flexible and less formal approaches to space security. Recent proposals tabled at the CD have sought to broaden the space security debate from a narrow focus on weapons to include issues such as transparency- and confidence-building measures. States are also expressing more support for a code of conduct for space or voluntary "rules of the road" for space operations. Initial progress in this new approach is evident with the adoption of the voluntary guidelines on space debris mitigation at COPUOS, which will be referred to the UN General Assembly in the fall of 2007. There is potential for COPUOS to apply this same technical approach to space traffic management. The ability of this approach to maintain the security of outer space will depend on its capacity to address some of the more controversial issues challenging space security, particularly those related to military and national security uses of space; this may be a function of political will rather than process.

Moving forward on Space Security

Outer space now effects almost every person around the globe in ways that were hardly imaginable 50 years ago. The duty to preserve outer space as a global commons for the benefit of all peoples has become more vital at the same time that the task of safeguarding the security of outer space has become more challenging. Moreover, some of the most pressing security issues are not being addressed in traditional forums. Additional steps must be taken to ensure that the security of outer space is sustained. The role of the SSI is to provide a tool to inform policy. The analysis of changing trends in space security captured by the SSI indicates critical issues that must be addressed by the international community in order to protect the security of outer space.

The specific process of the SSI, however, also sheds light on how these issues are best addressed. First, any efforts to preserve and enhance space security must include the relevant actors and stakeholders—governments, militaries, scientists, industry, consumers and civil society. Second, these efforts must not be too narrow—arms control issues cannot ignore concerns for space debris, peaceful exploration, commercial access, and so forth. Third, these efforts must prioritize the security of outer space as an environment, which means the safe and sustainable access to and use of outer space, and freedom from spacebased threats. This means taking issues and actors out of discrete contexts such as national security, scientific and technology advancement, revenue, convenience, and so forth, and examining them in the broader context of space security.

Above all, this process must begin with the OST. A famous adage states that "the more things change, the more they stay the same" and this is no less true in outer space. Many of the challenges to space security captured by the SSI are reminiscent of an earlier age in outer space, when it was threatened by competing interests. It is in this context that the OST was negotiated, to maintain security and stability in space. The OST is a guide, however, and not a panacea. The methods used to achieve the goals that it sets out must change to keep pace with the growing number of actors, stakeholders, uses, technologies and concepts that shape the security of outer space.

Precis: The Talk's Main Argument

A scrutiny of Silent Service contributions in war and peace proves that American submariners and submarines consistently display unique attributes of agile, stealthy, persistent access to denied areas for superbly completing anticipated mission taskings. Perhaps more importantly, they possess the adaptability and small footprint needed to complete inevitably unanticipated critical new undersea warfare mission taskings better than any other military platform.

Missions Matter Most

Why scrutinize mission types? They explain what subs and their crews are for. Missions describe what they do. Unlike arcane details of technology and tactics, crucial parts of which must remain classified, overview mission descriptions can speak to everyone. Unlike stirring tales of great battles and the heroes who fought them, which are embedded in the past, mission tasks emphasize benefits to come today and tomorrow.

Missions: Expected vs. Actual, First 50 Years

In the pre-World War One era, a leading role for submarines was harbor defense. Subs then were mainly coastal craft. Their ability to submerge gave stealth, which provided surpriseandsurvivability that surface warships lacked. Used in an outer ring of harbor defense vessels, subs expanded the zone of jeopardy, and warning time, against approaching hostile fleets.

That was not the only mission submarines were asked to perform early on. During the First World War they scored some great successes against capital ships farther out over the continental shelf. Nowadays we would call this a part of anti-surface warfare. ASuW was contemplated long before WWI, since the ASuW mission was carried out unsuccessfully (though survivably) by *Turtle* in the War of Independence, and successfully (though fatally) by *CSS Hunley* in the War Between the States. But few pundits had predicted that subs would be effective well outside harbors— yet they were.

Subs in the Great War also played a big role in commerce warfare, previously earmarked as a task mainly for surface raiders. Once Germany declared unrestricted submarine warfare, this "*guerre de course*" reached a level of lethality, and of sheer brutality, hardly imagined in the lead up to 1914. German U-boats in WWI sank more British merchant shipping tonnage than they did in WWII — the first vivid demonstration of the enduring value of subs as a maritime striking force that could assist materially in bringing a warfighting opponent toward his knees on the intercontinental and thus essentially nautical stage.

Looking back, we can say that subs in the WWI era quickly proved their value at stealthily penetrating denied areas, since warship formations and escorted convoys would do their violent utmost to deny marauding subs the least bit of access.

WWI subs and their crews were called on for other pressing missions that no one had thought much about before. One of these was aviator rescue, which arose as soon as the war ushered in combat aircraft. A particularly intriguing WWI chore sometimes assigned to submarines, because they showed they could do it surprisingly well, was anti-submarine warfare. In WWI, ASW targets were diesel subs surfaced over the continental shelf.

In the pre-World War II era, major powers resumed the competition for worldwide supremacy, which couldn't be won without fielding a first class navy. Submarines were viewed as the advanced guard for battleships, as fleet scouts that would locate the enemy formations, report on them, and soften them up before that long anticipated but ever ephemeral "decisive fleet action on the high seas."

U.S. submarine designs were given greater cruising endurance, speed, and payload capacity, so they could range ahead of the capital ships and pack a punch when they came upon the adversary. These enhanced capabilities soon proved of tremendous import — but mostly not for fleet scouting.

After direct U.S. involvement in World War II began with the shock of Pearl Harbor, the submarine force, especially in the early dark days in the Pacific, carried the fight to the enemy.

But subs were not after all best used for open ocean fleet scouting. American ASuW against warships and merchant shipping reached unsurpassed levels of intensity and effectiveness. Subs served potently as intelligence trip wires, ultra-smart minefields, and mobile covert coast watchers, in the constricted, disputed waters where so much of the naval combat actually took place. Once again, the best way for subs to accomplish war aims was to use their stealth to penetrate denied areas and strike with surprise and survivability. Little of this was articulated, or even much suspected, before December 7, 1941.

And once more, submariners and their subs were drawn into ASW. During WWII, the targets for ASW work were diesel subs running on the surface, occasionally in deep water. This was a heck of a stretch for both men and machines, but they did it, while deployed *out there* in the hostile front line environment — which again shows the adaptable nature of subs and their crews.

An additional unanticipated role for subs was also invented of necessity, on the spot: radar picket.

This was forced on the U.S. Navy as a desperate response to the lethality of another unexpected weapon, the kamikaze human guided cruise missile. Early warning of inbound massed kamikazes was needed for defense of island hopping landing forces and self-defense by their escorts. When lone destroyers sent far forward turned out to be overly vulnerable to kamikaze attack themselves, submarines were tapped for the radar picket role. The subs, again because of their stealth, could operate largely unimpeded, while unsupported, in otherwise denied areas.

Missions: Expected vs. Actual, Second 50 Years

By 1950, a Cold War was definitely on between East and West. Once more subs and their people were stretched to the very limit of capabilities and endurance.

This was in part due to the extreme secrecy of the Manhattan Project, which prevented senior Silent Service leadership and military contractors alike from envisioning submarine roles in a world possessing the atom bomb — until that world, via Hiroshima and Nagasaki, was suddenly and mercilessly thrust upon them. The men and machines of undersea warfare rose to the occasion, and then some. With nuclear weapons proliferating in a face off between two big opposed camps; a new mission emerged: *indications and warnings*.

When a thermonuclear holocaust might start with a surprise attack in which one bomb could wipe out a whole city, it was vital to know in advance if the enemy was beginning to think about any belligerent move. Electronic countermeasures became an ever more valuable way to spy, an indispensable part of intelligence, surveillance, and reconnaissance.

Given the way many emanations hug the surface of the earth as they dissipate with distance, subs were uniquely able to get close in shore, with stealth, in enemy home waters, for clandestine, prolonged, uninterrupted interception, with favorable signal to noise ratio, of naval and national information of great import. Stealth now served the purposes of survivable physical *and* electromagnetic access into otherwise denied areas — access which was dramatically extended by special operations divers accomplishing amazing feats of undersea espionage and salvage.

In the ominous Cold War context, remaining undetected in order to eavesdrop effectively became especially acute. And as events like the U-2 shootdown would demonstrate, submarine undetectability was key to avoiding the local act of access turning into a conspicuous, undeniable provocation of global scale. Not even the Space Age's constellations of spy satellites could satisfy equally well all these demanding mission parameters.

Everything on the undersea front changed profoundly with the advent of *practical nuclear propulsion.* The anti-submarine role for U.S. Navy submarines changed along with it; instead of being a mere supplement, they quickly became the platform of choice. With a few notable exceptions, the targets for ASW work were nuclear subs operating submerged in deep water.

The mating of hydrogen bomb warheads to long range delivery platforms ushered in an arms race in which it was paramount to assure a viable second strike option against a nuclear exchange ever breaking out. Bombers and land based missiles were augmented by what stands as the greatest defense system design-engineering-construction-deployment accomplishment of all time, nuclear subs carrying highly accurate submerged launch nuclear armed ballistic missiles. SSBNs with SLBMs form the most stealthy, survivable leg of America's thermonuclear triad.

For the first time but not the last, several different submarine missions comprised one big, complex, dynamic, integrated global mission. As a package, indications and warnings, anti-submarine warfare, and the survivable second strike option allowed the aggressive pursuit of proactive undersea strategic deterrence. The posture wasn't to just build more and more overkill weapons in a dreary and dangerous perpetual stalemate. Proactive strategic deterrence, by flexing submarine muscle and demonstrating undersea superiority, achieved war-winning soft power via the flaunting of barely restrained hard power. The Silent Service gained the ultimate access into denied areas, helping shape influential minds throughout Soviet society. No one could have possibly predicted that in 1950.

COUNTERING THREATS THROUGH CYBERSPACE

In the United States, surveillance has been at the heart of changes in traditional defence, as well as attempts to counter so-called "asymmetric" security threats. Guided by the principle that "what can be seen can be hit," battlefield surveillance was at the heart of the U.S., "revolution in military affairs" during the 1970s, 1980s, and 1990s. Two asymmetric threats in particular have caught the imaginations of those within the United States who have worked consistently to increase government surveillance capabilities: the threats of terrorism and cyber attack.

The idea that information-age conflict in general, and the fight against terrorism in particular, constitute a global "battle for hearts and minds" has been popular among U.S., defence and security professionals for at least a decade. Various observers have worried about terrorist use of the Internet as a tool for fundraising, organising, recruiting, and propaganda. It is in this spirit that Arquilla has urged the U.S., government to remove terrorist web sites from the Internet. Likewise, it is in this spirit that groups of self-organised, online volunteers engage in various types of online activities in support of the U.S., "war on terrorism," including intelligence gathering and counter-propaganda activities.

The work of Shannen Rossmiller and her group Phoenix Global Information Systems is the most notable example of intelligence-focused, volunteer cyber-counterterrorism. In response to the terrorist attacks of September 11, 2001,

Rossmiller, a municipal judge from a small town in Montana, began trolling jihadist web sites to learn more about those who had attacked the United States and what they might be planning next. In January 2003, Rossmiller joined forces with at least six other individuals whom she met in the online discussion forum. They created a web site and began calling themselves 7-Seas Global Intelligence.

Members of 7-Seas live in the United States, Canada, Australia, and Singapore and include an economist, a physicist, a computer systems engineer, a corporate security consultant, and a private investigator. Rossmiller and members of 7-Seas have used a number of techniques to gather intelligence about terrorists online. These have included creating multiple false personas complete with pictures and detailed life histories. To appear as convincing as possible to her targets, Rossmiller has learned Arabic, studied the Quran, and read Arabic literature. They also employ translation software, tools to map the IP addresses of the online jihadists with whom they interact, software to mask their own IP addresses and make it appear that they are located in the Middle East or South Asia, and even spyware that is remotely installed on the computers of some of those that they investigate.

While their initial goal was to predict future terrorist attacks, they soon shifted to gathering and analysing information from terrorist web sites, forums, and chat rooms, and then turning that information over to authorities. Rossmiller's efforts in particular have contributed to two high-profile arrests of would-be terrorists, including the 2004 case of Specialist Ryan Anderson, a Washington state National Guardsman who attempted to sell classified information about vulnerabilities of U.S., weapons systems to an al-Qa'ida member that he met online.

That al-Qa'ida member was actually Rossmiller. Anderson is now in prison serving five consecutive life sentences, the harshest penalty yet dealt to an American in the war on terrorism. In another case, and again posing online as a member of al- Qa'ida, Rossmiller uncovered a plot by Pennsylvania resident and al-Qa'ida sympathiser, Michael Reynolds, to blow up several gas pipelines and oil refineries in the United States. Reynolds was convicted and is now serving fifty seven years in prison. Rossmiller is reported to have provided information to U.S., law enforcement or intelligence in as many as 240 other cases, leading to the detention of dozens of suspects worldwide and even some arrests and deportations of terrorism suspects from the United States. For all the success that Rossmiller and 7-Seas has had, there remains a great deal of ambivalence, ambiguity, and tension in their relationship with authorities.

On the one hand, the volunteers are motivated in part by calls by authorities to be vigilant. They believe authorities' claims about the seriousness of the threat of terrorism and want to help. One the other hand, they are also motivated by feelings that the government is either unable or unwilling to counter extremists' use of the Internet.

Similarly, while Rossmiller has received a great deal of praise and assistance from authorities—the FBI has compensated her for her expenses, provided her with Arabic translation services, and provided her with security, a former Secretary of Commerce has said that she deserves a medal, she has been consulted by the Defence Intelligence Agency, and she has been an invited speaker at an FBI cyber security conference—these agencies have also sometimes expressed concern or doubt about her work and the work of others like her.

For her part, Rossmiller has at times complained that her work is being undervalued by authorities and has been clear to assert her independence from the state. But for all the tensions between authorities and volunteers, and for all that Rossmiller and 7-Seas have tried to distance themselves from the authorities, they nonetheless seek both approval and profit from the authorities. Both 7-Seas and later Phoenix Global Intelligence Systems have sought government contracts and intelligence and security consulting work for government clients.

In 2009, Rossmiller announced at an FBI-sponsored cyber security conference that she had formed a company and was seeking a partnership with a defence contractor to offer cyber-intelligence training and services to the government. She has been encouraged to do so by former CIA Director, James Woolsey. In the end, there are real reasons for tension and for concern. Both sides are right. The authorities likely cannot monitor and analyse that much Web content, making the work of the volunteers indispensable.

However, the volunteers do not have the ability to physically arrest suspects or materially disrupt terrorist planning or operations in any significant way, making the capabilities of the state indispensable in achieving their goals. Additionally, there are clear difficulties in making the relationship work. Sometimes authorities and volunteers can work at cross purposes. If authorities rely too much on volunteers, or if the role of volunteers becomes formally institutionalised, then their main value can be compromised. Finally, Michael Reynolds' defence strategy—i.e., claiming that he too was just trying to catch terrorists online like Rossmiller—also points to some of the potential difficulties in this new relationship between producers and consumers of security online.

RUSSIA'S APPROACH TO THE "INFORMATION SPACE"

Back in 1998 (while Operation "Moonlight Maze", one of the first and most devastating cyber campaign ever orchestrated by Russia's intelligence against US military targets, was well underway...) the Russian Federation presented to the UN General Assembly a proposal for a Resolution titled "Developments in the field of information and telecommunications in the context of international security". The Russians wanted to discuss both cyber security and the limitations to destabilizing online content (revealingly gathered together by Moscow under the label of "threats to the information space"). The West refused to have that discussion, on the ground, essentially, of its self-proclaimed moral superiority: if we want to safeguard an open Internet and freedom of expression, the West argued, it is not possible to negotiate about information's content. Ironically, almost twenty years later, the West is forced to discuss with Moscow about the threat of manipulated online content, which probably is, in itself, a score on the Russian side.

The approach highlighted in the Resolution of 1998 reflects Russia's strategic thinking: cyber-attacks and information warfare (we could also add electronic warfare, hybrid warfare,...) are, in Moscow's view, on an operational continuum. Cyberspace, in Russia's view, is one part of the broader "information space", which includes also ICT hardware and software, data and human information processing. This is confirmed in the Russia's Information Security Doctrine of 2000, which identifies two types of so-called "informational attacks": technical and psychological ones. If we assume that the ultimate strategic objective of Russia is that of undermining the cohesion and the stability of NATO and the European Union in order to renegotiate - from a better position - a new European security architecture, then, in order to obtain this overarching strategic goal, it does not really matter to Russia whether it is more suitable, in a given tactical context, to hack the opponent's networks or, so to say, "hack his mind" ("cognitive hacking"), or do both. Russia has an integrated and holistic approach to the "information space": while digital sabotages (CNOs) aim to infiltrate, disorganize, disrupt or destroy a State's functioning, psychological subversion (information warfare) aims at deceiving the opponent, discrediting its decision makers, and disorienting and demoralizing its public and armed forces. This is reflected in the current 2014 Russia's Military doctrine, the "New Generation War" doctrine (also known as "Gerasimov doctrine", from the name of the Russian pro tempore Chief of General Staff, Valeriy Gerasimov). The "New Generation War" doctrine enshrines a combination of hard and soft power (encompassing also economic warfare, energy blackmailing and pipeline diplomacy, support to political oppositions and agents of influence abroad, and other active measures) across different domains and through a skillful application of coordinated military, diplomatic and economic tools. In this context, "informational attacks" become the "system integrator" of both kinetic and non-kinetic military means as well as of government and non-government actors; they are waged during peacetime and wartime in domestic, the adversary's, and international media domains, and they are perceived as one of the most cost-effective tools of non-nuclear coercion, and an essential instrument to minimize kinetic engagements.

A textbook example of "informational attack" (or, in our lexicon, "cyber-enabled information warfare" - CEIW), that clearly combines both offensive cyber capabilities and information warfare, is Operation "Grizzly Steppe": the US Intelligence community assesses with "high confidence" (notwithstanding President Trump's skepticism) that Russia's intelligence (GRU) gained access to the Democratic National Committee (DNC) computer networks in July 2015, and maintained it until at least June 2016. By May, Russia's Intelligence had exfiltrated large volumes of data from the DNC. Someone under the name of "Guccifer 2.0" subsequently leaked to Wikileaks.com and DCLeaks.com the material stolen from the DNC. The scandal that followed was exploited by a massive PsyOps to discredit Hillary Clinton and, more importantly, to erode trust in US institutions.

Considering the relevance of the "information space" in Russia's security strategic thinking and the intrinsic ambiguity of cyberspace, "informational attacks" seems perfectly suited for the job of the intelligence community that is so relevant in Russia. Cyberspace provides both unprecedented access to compromising material (available online or "securely" stored in PCs...) and a safe, efficient, effective and global distribution platform for gaining maximum strategic effect from its use. In order for data to became weaponised information, it does not really matter whether the content is forged or non-attributable; it is instead crucial to "make the first impression", to create the "sense of doubt" in the public opinion, to trash the information space with multiple truths - ultimately, to hack the cognitive domain. Moreover, the State's control over the "information space" is critical also at the domestic level: everywhere in the world, autocratic governments view the Internet as a threat to their grip on power - an information platform that must be monitored, censored and manipulated. Social media servers located outside of the government's control are an intrinsic threat, as Moscow's strict control over the Internet in Russia shows. The relatively low impact among the Russian public opinion of the Panama Papers' leak - that uncovered the personal wealth hidden abroad by Russia's leadership - is probably the result of such a control.

What's At Stake?

If operations in the "information space" are so critical in Moscow's "New Generation Wars", what does the escalation in directness, level of activity and scope of effort of Russia's activism in cyberspace tell us from the point of view of international security? Truth is, we do not really know. But it is reasonable to assume that much of what is going on in cyberspace (military and intelligence cyber campaigns; reconnaissance of networks; signaling about cyber capabilities in order to establish deterrence; information warfare,...) is part of a much greater game. How does what happens on global ICT networks relate, for instance, with the signaling concerning the level of readiness of conventional and nuclear forces? Ironically, understanding the ongoing political-military confrontation in cyberspace would require decoding an ongoing heavily encrypted interaction taking place on multiple tables and at the global level, just like hackers do.

Our limited perception of the ongoing confrontation in cyberspace is worrisome, for two reasons. First, there is an actual risk of misperceptions and miscalculations involved in States' responses to CEIW campaigns, as the tensions following Moscow's meddling in the US presidential elections' debate show. Second, the use of cyberspace for projecting a State's power is endangering a free and open Internet, is fuelling the proliferation of aggressive capabilities through reverse-engineering of cyber weapons, is providing motivation and resources for hackers and organized crime engaged in identifying zero-days vulnerabilities and in developing cyber weapons, and is hijacking trust both among common Internet users and within public-private partnerships – which typically take years to develop. Our individual freedom and our societies' independence will be increasingly relying on a free, open and resilient Internet, and it would therefore be of key importance to safeguard it as a critical global common. We are unfortunately drifting toward a different scenario: sovereign States will inevitably aim at establishing information superiority over potential adversaries for the achievement of their own national security. Therefore the crucial question becomes: what can we do if we want to preserve our open democracies and one of the greatest accomplishments in human history against the risk of cyberspace becoming a warfighting domain? The general lack of awareness and consideration about the dangers and the responsibilities involved in this dilemma is a question of serious concern.

MOUNTING A MULTI-FACETED RESPONSE

What can we do to protect our democracies from the threat posed by fake news and cyber-enabled information warfare? The answer is multi-faceted, in as much as CEIW is an emerging asymmetric threat that forces us to innovate our security approach in many ways. Investments in technological innovation and cyber capabilities aside, there are probably at least five major endeavors.

If foreign influence is the virus that attacks democracies, the first aspirin (or, if you will, the most effective firewall) is awareness & education. Awareness about the threat, the game at play and the price at stake, both among the general public and at the top institutional level, is the first line of defence. Education in dealing with the cyber threat, in particular, is a powerful ally against CEIW, as reducing cyber vulnerabilities, enhancing the resiliency of our ICT infrastructure, and encouraging cyber hygiene in the general public would drastically reduce the potential damages of cyber attacks (for instance: the malware "Wanna Cry", that affected so many computers in 2017, used a well-known vulnerability, that was patchable long time before the campaign was launched). Cyber hygiene would also greatly contribute to the fight against cybercrime, which is the gym, the ATM, the fog of war of a far more dangerous game entailing state-actors' attacks for espionage, intelligence, surveillance and reconnaissance (ISR), deterrence, targeting, war fighting prepositioning. We are not saying that cyber hygiene and a greater awareness about the cyber threat will, per se, protect countries from cyber advanced persistent threats (APTs), hybrid scenarios or "New Generation Wars", but they are an easy and relatively inexpensive measure that could allow us to devote our scarce financial and technological resources to face even more serious threats and challenges. Explaining to the general public the dangers of manipulated information will also constitute an efficient cultural barrier against fake news, while our societies develop a healthy skepticism as they learn to manage, interpret and evaluate large volumes of non-intermediated information. Education, in other words, reduces the "eco-chamber effect" of social media, ultimately making us better citizens.

A second critical element for countering CEIW is our societies' coherence with their core values: information warfare represents an attack to an unavoidable vulnerability of open democracies, but this does not mean we shall question or negotiate our commitment in transparency, openness and the rule of law. While we must confront foreign information warfare head-on, and we must increase transparency in political funding in order to avoid foreign meddling in our democratic processes, we must also, at the same time, avoid a witch-hunt against whoever is ideological aligned with Moscow's stances: such a course of action would ultimately erode the legitimacy of our democratic institutions, with the effect of dissipating precisely what we wanted to preserve. Instead, open democracies should work on reinforcing their institutions and the public support they deserve. The best way to do this is proving how they are able to deliver innovative solutions to manage the complexity of today's world. In this context, one discussion that seems urgent is the one concerning the strategic relevance of public-owned ICT infrastructures and independent media. Revealing, in this sense, is the discussion underway at the global level (but not much in Italy...) about net neutrality. The new US administration's decision to abandon President Obama's choice on net neutrality reflects the idea that the Internet is primarily a commercial environment and that market forces are best suited for ensuring its growth. But the Internet is clearly much more than this: it is, primarily, an infrastructure that is essential for the functioning of modern societies. Not recognizing this role at the domestic level risks undermining our ongoing international efforts to ensure an open Internet at the global level. Coherence to our values means, also, that politicians should refrain from undermining public opinions' faith in the free press just because they are the objects of unflattering but genuine journalism, because disinformation works best precisely where there is a lack of trust.

Another important element in our response to Russia's CEIW is to refrain from launching, at least in peacetime, retaliatory strategic communication (Stratcom) on our own citizens or on citizens of allied countries, as this would ultimately undermine faith in the free press and trust in international relations. Likewise, retaliatory Stratcom would most likely reinforce (and, to a certain extent, even justify) Russia's perception that information campaigns have been and are implemented by the United States and the West in order to influence the course of a series of regime change over the last two decades ("Color Revolutions" and the "Arab Springs"). The danger, in other words, is that of fuelling an escalation in the conventional domain with relevant repercussions. Instead, a viable option, although a very challenging one, is to respond to information warfare not retaliating in kind, but countering its desired effects. ISPI, for instance, is one of the many think-tanks that launched a fact-checking initiative to expose fake news; likewise, many institutions are focusing not on developing a counter-narrative, but rather on exposing the mechanism behind fake news, such as the "EU-East StratCom Task Force" launched in 2015 to counter Russian propaganda in Eastern

Europe, the "EU myth-buster" and the US State Department's Global Engagement Center. The new US National Security Strategy seems to point to this direction, where it declares (p. 35): "We will craft and direct coherent communications campaigns to advance American influence and counter challenges from the ideological threats that emanate from radical Islamist groups and competitor nations. These campaigns will adhere to American values and expose adversary propaganda and disinformation."

A fourth initiative to counter CEIW is strengthening our governance and response-mechanisms at the institutional level. Michael V. Hayden, who served as CIA Director under President George W. Bush, described the Russian interference in the last US presidential elections as the political equivalent of the 9/11 attacks - an event that exposed a previously unimagined vulnerability and required a unified American response. The transformation underway at NATO, which is actively involved in developing doctrines, structures and mechanisms to counter hybrid threats, shows that new institutional and operational arrangements are needed. As suggested by Prof. Adriano Soi in his contribution to the second ISPI's Dossier on cybersecurity, maybe it is time to update even at the domestic level our decision-making processes and to develop an ad hoc strategy and specific structures and procedures for countering the emerging threat of CEIW.

Finally, the West should build on the idea that, in order to counter an asymmetric threat, the best possible strategy is partnering with those that are defending against the same menace. At the international level, this means strengthening both at the strategic and at the operational level our cultural, political and military alliances, and working actively to establish confidence building measures (CBMs) and norms of States' behavior in cyberspace. At the domestic level, CEIW compels us to actively engage in a coordinated effort all relevant public-private stakeholders, key ICT infrastructures' owners and operators and, also, media outlets, building within this communities as much trust as possible. Private companies should not be the arbiters of truth, but they do, however, have an interest in preserving a safe space for genuine content, and this interest could and should be leveraged. The success in engaging Internet providers and social media operators in countering online jihadist propaganda and radicalization, gained by the G7 Ministries of Interior last October at the meeting organized by Minister Marco Minniti in Ischia (Italy), is an excellent example of what can be done to develop a shared responsibility among key stakeholders, and could be fruitfully pursued also in the response to cyber-enabled information warfare.

PERSPECTIVES ON INFORMATION SECURITY

Efforts to achieve effective collaboration will need to overcome the understandably different perspectives that organizations bring to the table.

Commercial organizations traditionally treat events such as Everyday attacks as simply a cost of doing business not significantly different than pilferage euphemistically referred to as inventory "shrinkage." Countermeasures have a definite expected value and are employed when their costs are less than their expected value. Private sector organizations traditionally respond to relatively low probability events with potentially large costs by either purchasing insurance or providing self-insurance.

The perspective on information security taken by organizations entrusted with information and systems deemed vital to our national security is quite different. Unlike many information attacks on private sector systems, the cost of a breech in security of national security information can not easily be determined. Overshadowing the actual costs of a particular incident is the fact that the very protection of the integrity of national security information and the systems that handle it is considered to have intrinsic value in and of itself. Risk avoidance is the ingrained response in these situations.

Given the nature of the IW threat topology, national and private sector information security are now inexorably intertwined. Attacks on the national or global information infrastructure can seriously affect private sector organizations and attacks on key private sector organizations that provide vital services have definite national security implications. These situations are contained in the Potentially Strategic region of the threat topology. It is proposed that, in this region, rather than take a simple "dollars and cents" approach as in the Everyday region or a risk avoidance approach as taken in the Strategic region, we should take a collective risk management approach. This is clearly an area which requires defenses to be closely coordinated.

Managing the Solution

Given what we have seen about the nature of this problem as we have considered the different areas of the threat topology, it should be clear that any attempt to try to manage IW-D using a centralized approach is doomed to failure. If one has any doubt, they should be reminded of the weak threat to organizational mapping which prevents effective delegation of the problem with clean "chains of command" and the considerable limits on the ability of the Government or any single organization to control significant relevant variables.

Given the urgency and importance of this problem, a proactive stance is required. Therefore, it should be equally obvious that a laissez-faire approach is also doomed to failure. A form of collective orchestration is needed to develop the degree of awareness and understanding of the threat and to develop the necessary defenses. The Government needs to lead by establishing what I have called a "framework for progress." The specific roles and responsibilities of the private and public sectors will vary as a function of the threat as we have seen in our brief look at each of the three major regions of the threat topology. While this discussion has focused on the roles, responsibilities and need for collaboration among U.S. players, the problem of IW-D transcends national boundaries. Without appropriate international agreements and cooperation among nations and international organizations, our collective ability to handle threats will be severely hampered.

Framework for Progress

While we have come a considerable distance in our journey to better understand the nature of this problem, many of us have been frustrated by the lack of a supportive environment for progress.

Although we can continue to make progress, even on the rocky path we are currently forced to travel, progress in the six areas identified in the graphic will greatly smooth out our path and accelerate our progress.

First, one of the key prerequisites for progress is to create awareness of the problem and its complexities, as well as to foster a climate that will facilitate discussion and cooperation among the many groups and organizations that need to be a part of this effort. Given recent events surrounding some aspects of information security, we need to start by rebuilding bridges between some public and private sector groups and organizations.

Second, it is important that we work toward a well-defined vision that clearly lays out what we are trying to achieve and the appropriate role of the Government.

Third, the "rules of the game" need to be developed and promulgated. Many of our current laws and regulations have not caught up with the realities of the Information Age. A set of rules needs to address the establishment of information security standards, or a minimum level of defense to be associated with different kinds of data and information services. These would be similar to the recent development of privacy standards.

Fourth, self-interest, even enlightened self-interest and the desire of individuals and organizations to be good citizens, are not enough to ensure that appropriate actions and defenses will be developed and employed. Resources need to be provided for government organizations to help implement this framework for progress and to develop and implement the needed defenses. We also need to provide incentives that encourage public sector organizations to do what is collectively needed. In some specific cases, the Government will need to actually provide funds to private sector organizations to implement enhanced security.

Fifth, the solution to this problem depends on a great deal of cooperation among disparate groups and organizations. Mechanisms to facilitate and enhance cooperation (including the establishment of panels, groups, and clearinghouses) need to be developed.

Sixth, we need to fix responsibility for the many tasks involved in IW-D. We need to decide questions of jurisdiction. We need to make liabilities known and well defined. Finally, we need to clearly establish the responsibility of each organization. The nature of organizational responsibilities is discussed in more detail below.

None of these six aspects of the framework for progress is likely to be accomplished anytime soon. One only need review the legislative process and experiences with the translation of privacy concerns into a set of rules of the game to realize that it will be quite a while before each of these foundational pillars is in place. However, we must begin now to foster discussion of these issues and try to keep attention focused on this subject.

Allocation of Responsibilities

The responsibilities of public and private sector organizations differ as a function of the threat region. In all regions of the threat from everyday to strategic, however, each sector of society has some responsibility.

Responsibilities for Everyday Threats

The primary responsibility for the Everyday region of the threat topology falls upon the private sector. First and foremost, private sector organizations must assume responsibility for the protection of their own systems. When security laws and regulations are legislated and formulated, these organizations will, of course, also be responsible for adhering to these rules of the game.

Given the time it may take to develop and put in place a legal and regulatory framework to deal with the myriad of information security issues, it is proposed that on a voluntary basis, private sector organizations assume the responsibility for reporting incidents. It is hard to overstate the importance of the collection of information related to information attacks and their analysis. Without the development of a body of knowledge concerning these attacks, efforts at building defenses will be severely hampered.

The Government (including the federal, state, and local levels) must assume certain responsibility for this region of the threat topology as well.

Clearly, the Government bears the responsibility for protecting its own systems and for the enforcement of appropriate laws and regulations. Given the importance of gaining international cooperation on this problem that knows no state boundaries, the Government must take on the negotiation of the necessary treaties and agreements.

Clearly, the collection of incident data with respect to its own systems is also a Government responsibility. But given the importance of pooling information to gain a more accurate situation assessment, the Government must also put in place appropriate mechanisms for data sharing, analysis of data, and the dissemination of results. Issues related to classification and security of these data and the products of these analyses will need to be addressed. A way must be found to get the information that individuals and organizations need to defend themselves to those involved in the effort.

Responsibilities for Strategic Threats

The Federal Government has the responsibility for the defense of the Strategic region of the threat topology, albeit with some support in selected areas from the private sector and state and local governments. Given the dynamic and interactive nature of this situation, it is important that the current and emerging threat be as fully understood as possible. Therefore, utilizing information collected as well as information reported by others, the Federal Government has the responsibility to perform strategic threat analyses on an ongoing basis.

The Federal Government also needs to develop an appropriate deterrence strategy designed to dissuade potential attackers. Strategic systems must be monitored and surveillance operations must be mounted.

Obviously, the Federal Government has the responsibility for protecting strategic information and the systems that collect, store, process, and disseminate this information.

Finally, the Federal Government needs to develop plans for reconstitution of damaged or disrupted systems and lost, compromised, or damaged information and for implementation of these plans should an event occur.

The private sector also has a role to play in this region of the threat topology. First, many strategic systems depend to some extent on the availability and integrity of private sector or state and local government information and systems. Second, some private sector or state and local government information and systems may be so critical that they are, for all intents and purposes, strategic. In both these cases, organizations need to cooperate with the Federal Government to protect these systems and the information they handle. Developing an adequate understanding of the threat requires that all organizations report incidents and share data related to attacks, whether successful or not. Thus another responsibility that must be assumed by private sector organizations is the prompt reporting of incidents and related information.

5

Space Weapon and Warfare

Space weapons are weapons used in space warfare. They include weapons that can attack space systems in orbit (i.e. anti-satellite weapons), attack targets on the earth from space or disable missiles travelling through space. In the course of the militarisation of space, such weapons were developed mainly by the contesting superpowers during the Cold War, and some remain under development today. Space weapons are also a central theme in military science fiction and sci-fi video games.

SPACE-TO-SPACE WEAPONS

The Soviet Almaz secret military space station program was equipped with a fixed 23mm autocannon to prevent hostile interception or boarding by hostile forces. The Soviet unmanned Polyus weapons platform was designed to be equipped with a megawatt carbon-dioxide laser and a self-defense cannon.

Earth-to-space weapons

Anti-satellite weapons, which are primarily surface-to-space and air-to-space missiles, have been developed by the United States, the USSR/Russia, and the People's Republic of China. Some test firings have been successful in destroying orbiting satellites.

In general use of explosive and kinetic kill systems is limited to relatively low altitude due to space debris issues and so as to avoid triggering the Kessler syndrome.

Strategic Defense Initiative

On March 23, 1983, President Ronald Reagan proposed the Strategic Defense Initiative, a research program with a goal of developing a defensive system which would destroy enemy ICBMs. The defensive system was nicknamed Star Wars, after the movie, by its detractors. Some concepts of the system included Brilliant Pebbles, which were Kinetic Kill Vehicles, essentially small rockets launched from satellites toward their targets (a warhead, warhead bus, or even an upper stage of an ICBM). Other aspects includedsatellites in orbit carrying powerful lasers or particle beams. When a missile launch was detected, the satellite would fire at the missile (or warheads) and destroy it. Although no real hardware was ever manufactured for deployment, today the military is testing the use of lasers mounted on Boeing 747s to destroy missiles. The tests are taking place at Edwards Air Force Base.

WEAPONS OUTTA SPACE

Although U.S. citizens may not be familiar with the full sweep of the U.S. space military plans, because of a media lazy or worse, other nations are.

On November 20, 2000, because of the U.S. plans, a resolution on "Prevention of An Arms Race In Outer Space" was voted on before the UN General Assembly. The resolution sought to reaffirm the Outer Space Treaty and specifically, its provision that space be set aside for "peaceful purposes." Some 163 nations voted in favor. Abstaining were the U.S., Israel and Micronesia, a cluster of Pacific islands dependent on U.S. aid, Canada, certainly in no way a potential foe, has been highly active at the UN in seeking to strengthen the Outer Space Treaty with an agreement to ban all weapons in space.

In a UN presentation in October, 1999, Marc Vidricaire, counselor of the Permanent Mission of Canada, noted that "Canada first formally proposed... a legally binding instrument" for a "ban of the weaponization of space" in January 1997 and "renewed our proposal" earlier in 1999. He cited the U.S. Space

Command's Long Range Plan "including its recommendation to 'shape [the] international community to accept space-based weapons'" The Canadian diplomat said: "Our objective is to ensure that pursuing the concepts of space control and force application are not extended by any state to include actual deployment of weapons in outer space."

On October 19, 2000, Vidricaire was again sounding the alarm on behalf of Canada at the UN. "Outer space has not yet witnessed the introduction of space-based weapons. This could change if the international community does not first prevent this destabilizing development through the timely negotiation of measures banning the introduction of weapons into outer space," he said. "It has been suggested that our proposal is not relevant because the assessment on which it rests is either premature or alarmist. In our view, it is neither. One need only look at what is happening right now to realize that it is not premature..."

Vidricaire said: "There is no question that the technology can be developed to place weapons in outer space. There is also no question that no state can expect to maintain a monopoly on such knowledge-or such capabilities-for all time. If one state actively pursues the weaponization of space, we can be sure others will follow."

Russian President Vladimir Putin, in his first address at the UN, to the "Millennium Summit" on September 6, 2000, stated that "particularly alarming are the plans for the militarization of outer space." In Canada in December 2000, he and Canadian Prime Minister Jean Chretien issued a joint statement announcing that "Canada and the Russian Federation will continue close cooperation in preventing an arms race in outer space." Interestingly, it was the U.S. that was deeply involved in initiating the Outer Space Treaty, according to Craig Eisendrath, a former U.S. State Department officer who helped in its creation. The Soviet Union had launched its Sputnik satellite in 1957 and "we sought to de-weaponize space before it got weaponized."

A model the State Department used for its draft of the Outer Space Treaty, says Eisendrath, was the Antarctic Treaty, barring weapons from that continent. The Soviet Union and the United Kingdom joined the U.S. in presenting the treaty, adopted by the UN General Assembly in 1966. It entered into force in October 1967.

The intent of the Outer Space Treaty is "to keep war out of space," said Eisendrath, who went from the State Department to becoming an educator and is now a senior fellow at the Center for International Policy in Washington, `, D.C. He is a co-author of the forthcoming book, The Phantom Defense: America's Pursuit of the Star Wars Illusion.

Eisendrath views as "a violation" of the Outer Space Treaty the deployment in space of weapons such as the lasers that the U.S. military has been and is pursuing.

The final wording of the treaty provides for a ban on "nuclear weapons or other kinds of weapons of mass destruction." Endeavoring to clear up any confusion and specifically bar all weapons in space have been Canada and China. But the U.S. has successfully fought back those efforts-and this was before George W. Bush and Richard Cheney took office.

With the assumption of power by Bush and Cheney and a U.S. administration intimately linked to corporate and right-wing interests committed to expanding space military activities, Star Wars has received a huge boost. The corporate links include Cheney himself, a former member of the TRW board. His wife, Lynne Cheney, was until January a member of the board of Lockheed Martin. There is no subtlety. "I wrote the Republican Party's foreign policy platform," Bruce Jackson, vice president of corporate strategy and development of Lockheed Martin, proudly told me. Jackson was selected as chairman of the Foreign Policy Platform Committee at the Republican National Convention, at which he was a delegate.

Thus the Bush-Cheney administration is using a foreign policy platform written by a top executive of Lockheed Martin, the world's biggest weapons manufacturer and a kingpin in U.S. space warfare preparations.

Jackson said that during the campaign, advocacy on space military activities was done by Stephen J. Hadley, an assistant secretary of defense for international security policy and member of the National Security Council in the administration of Bush's father and partner in the law firm of Shea & Gardner-which represents Lockheed Martin in Washington.

"Space is going to be important. It has a great future in the military," Hadley, speaking as "an adviser" to Bush, told the Air Force Association in an address at its national convention September 11, 2000. He became deputy director of the National Security Council in the Bush II administration.

Jackson and Hadley worked closely on an entity called the Committee to Expand NATO. Jackson was president, based in the Washington office of the right-wing American Enterprise Institute; Hadley was secretary. Cheney, before becoming vice president of the U.S., was a Distinguished Fellow of the American Enterprise Institute.

In the Bush choice of Donald Rumsfeld as Secretary of Defense, the U.S. got a man whom the pro-Star Wars ultra right-wing Center for Security Policy describes as a "trusted adviser" and a financial supporter and who in 1998 was awarded its "Keeper of the Flame" award.

The Center's advisory board includes such Star Wars promoters as "the father of the H-bomb" Edward Teller and Lockheed Martin executives including Bruce Jackson.

Says Gagnon of the Bush-Cheney administration, "This so-called election is a major victory for those who intend to put weapons into space at an enormous cost to the U.S. taxpayer and to world stability."

MILITARY: MOVEMENT TOWARD SPACE WEAPONS

There is no question that outer space is already militarized. Indeed, from the dawn of the space age, the two Cold War superpowers were already focusing on developing space assets for military uses: from early warning to strategic communications to verification of arms control treaties and even to efforts to build anti-satellite (ASATs) weaponry. In recent decades, as the inevitable march of technology and the spread of information has quickened, it would be fair to say that the militarization of space has become more profound and embedded. While according to U.S. Air Force officials there are only eight to 10 countries routinely applying space capabilities to their military operations, there are another 40 or so nations with civil space capabilities that could eventually be applied to military uses. The trend line seems clear: the coming decades will see more and more nations able to harness the advantages of space-based assets to improve their military command, control and communications, strategic and battlefield surveillance, weapons targeting, and perhaps even missile defenses.

What remains unclear is if this increased militarization of space will inevitably lead toward the actual weaponization of space. The answer to that question, however, lies less in the progress of technological know-how and more in the realm of geo-political calculations outside the scope of this chapter. At the same time, there are ongoing technology and political developments that may lead some countries to seek this path – sooner rather than later.

This chapter will review major technology development efforts among today's space-faring powers that bear relevance to the possibility of elevating the battlefields of the future to the heavens. One caveat: it must be remembered that despite the ongoing research into weapons-related technology, there are no formal programs in any country to procure or deploy space weapons. This is in large part due to the fact that the technologies necessary to do so remain immature and costly to pursue.

The United States

There is no question that the United States is the world leader in military exploitation of space. According to the Stockholm International Peace Research Institute, the United States at the end of 2001 had nearly 110 operational military-related satellites, compared to 40 for Russian and 20 for the rest of the world combined. The United States outspends the rest of the world by vast amounts in the military space arena, accounting for almost 95 percent of global military space spending in 1999, according to the French space agency CNES. The U.S. military uses satellites – both dedicated military satellites and those owned by private firms – for weather prediction; strategic and tactical communications including ship-to-ship; Earth imaging; surveillance and reconnaissance (including optical, infrared and radio frequency systems); and tracking and monitoring objects in space, including potentially dangerous debris.

Since the early 1990s, the military has used the Global Positioning System (GPS) satellite navigation network to time and synchronize operations, as well as increasingly to target precision-guided munitions. Also since the Information Revolution of the 1990s, the U.S. military has exponentially increased its use of satellite communications, not only for voice but also for transmission of imagery to the battlefield and Internet communications. According to a senior Army official, some 380 megabits of bandwidth were used by the U.S. military during Operation Iraqi Freedom (as compared to 99 megabits in Operation Desert Storm) for both communications and imagery transmission, with about 80 percent of it supplied by commercial not military assets.

Suffice to say that space assets are now critical to the American way of war, providing rapid global power projection and ever- greater precision war- fighting. This fact has led to growing concerns within the U.S. military about protecting its own space assets, and about the ability to, in future warfare, keep opponents from using space assets in a similar manner to increase their military effectiveness and erode the U.S. military edge. It is also driving a renewed push toward the weaponization of space by the faction of the U.S. political/military spectrum who believe that space weapons are required to maintain U.S. military dominance into the next century. Currently, the United States is the country most capable, both technically and economically, to undertake a serious space weapons program, and the country most clearly starting to move in that direction – both from a technology development viewpoint and a policy perspective.

Besides ramping up programs to, for want of a better word, "passively" protect U.S. space assets – such as the planned improvements to the Global Positioning System to better protect it against jamming or degradation – current long-term planning and budget documents envision a number of programs to develop so-called "active" defenses as well as offensive capabilities against enemy space assets, some eventually to be based in space.

Offensive systems are are defined as "counterspace operations" in the Air Force Space Command's most recent long-term planning document, "Strategic Master Plan FY04 and Beyond" published in November 2002. As the chart below explains, "defensive counterspace" operations not only include attack detection and reporting, but in the roughly 2016-2028 timeframe, the deployment of "active on-orbit protection" – which one must assume includes "shooting back" in some fashion at a potential or ongoing attack from another space-based object, although the Master Plan is less than clear on what exactly is being considered.

According to the Master Plan, the desired capabilities in "offensive counterspace" are first concentrated on three ground-based systems: the mobile Counter-Coummunications system to jam uplinks and downlinks of enemy satellites; the Counter-ISR system to blind optical sensors; and the Counter-Navigation system to prevent adversaries from using space-based navigation signals.

However, in the 2016-2028 timeframe, the plan envisions the availability of "space-based counterspace" systems, which most of us would probably define more simply as anti-satellite weapons (ASATs). The plan elaborates intentions to field "full-spectrum, space-based OCS systems capable of preventing unauthorized use of friendly space services and negating adversarial space capabilities from LEO to GEO altitudes."

At least some of these counterspace programs already have made an appearance in the DoD fiscal year 2004 (FY 04) budget request. Overall, the Pentagon asked for $82. million for counterspace technologies (at the engineering, manufacturing and development level of so-called 6-4 funding) in FY 04, and a total of $325. million between FY 04 and FY 09. Included under that line are: the Counter Satellite Communications System at $9. million in FY 04 and a total of $42. million from FY 04-FY 09, and the Counter Surveillance Reconnaissance System (referred to in the Master Plan as the Counter-ISR system) funded at $66. million in FY 04 and a total of $152. million over the FYDP.

While Air Force Space Command officials have not said much about these programs, except for maintaining that the goal of both programs is develop temporary, reversible and/or non-destructive methods of accomplishing the counterspace mission. 6 While, as noted above, both these programs are being designed as ground-based systems, there is no reason to believe that there is not interest in miniaturizing laser and other jamming technologies – indeed, the Air Force has a number of ongoing efforts at miniaturization of such technologies, especially lasers.

The Air Force budget request also included another $138. million over the FYDP in Space Control Technologies, aimed at technology development, demonstration and prototyping. Somewhat confusingly, Space Control is defined by the Air Force as including Space Situational Awareness, Defensive Counterspace and Offensive Counterspace – but the budget breaks out counterspace technologies separately, with the exception of the Kinetic Energy Anti-Satellite (KE-ASAT) program, which is funded under Space Control Technologies. However, the small amount of money included in the Air Force budget for KE-ASAT was inserted by Congress; the Pentagon did not ask for it. This is in keeping with the KE-ASAT's long history – its development, began in 1989 as a technology demonstration, is primarily due to the championship of former Sen. Bob Smith of New Hampshire, who for many years pushed funds for the program on the Army, the program's original owner. While senior Air Force officials in the past have expressed concerns about the use of kinetic energy weapons in space due to the creation of space debris – and there has been a long-running argument about the debris-creating potential of KE-ASAT itself — there are currently rumors that the service is looking at asking for money in the FY 05 budget to flight test at least one of the three KE-ASAT prototypes.

Besides KE-ASAT, the other key U.S. Air Force programs that seem to be at least partially aimed at developing future space-based ASAT capabilities are clustered in a group of microsatellite technology projects. Microsats are usually described as those weighing less than 100 kg. The Air Force long has been interested in reducing the size of satellites due to potential benefits in reducing launch costs – still the major expense in any space program, hovering between $11,000 per kg and $22,000 per kg. In fact, microsats are not new at all, in that the first military communications satellites in the 1960s, the Defense Satellite Communications System, weighed about 45 kg. 8 Since that time there have been at least 20 U.S. militaryon-orbit microsat tests; however, there are only few examples of microsats actually performing operational missions.

In recent years, however, as technology has improved, there has been more interest from the U.S. military (as well as commercial satellite firms) in microsat technology. The latest U.S. Air Force Space Command study on microsats, "The 1999 Microsatellite Technology Requirements Study," concluded that microsat development should be pursued as rapidly as possible.

For the three major Air Force microsat activities – known as MightySat, TechSat21 and the XSS Experimental Satellite series – there is $68. million in the FY 04 budget request, and a total of $502 million over the FYDP. With regard to possible future weapon applications, the XSS program is the most interesting. The first of the series, XSS-10, was launched Jan. 29, 2003. Weighing 28 kg, the XSS-10 successfully maneuvered autonomously around another space object (a Delta II upperstage) and took images. A follow-on, XSS-11, is to be launched in late 2004 and is expected to remain on orbit for a year, with the experiment involving "navigating larger distances and performing more extreme maneuvers" with a more specific sensor payload. While the XSS experiments so far have involved only maneuvering and imaging, the Air Force has envisioned possible future ASAT uses and the technologies being demonstrated – particularly the capability to maneuver into a near-by orbit and move closely around another on-orbit object — have applicability to such missions. The 1999 Microsatellite Technology Requirements Study done for Air Force Space Command strongly called for "the deployment, as rapidly as possible, of XSS-10-based satellites to intercept, image, and if needed, take action against, a target satellite." There is apparently on-going discussion within the Air Force about melding KE-ASAT technology into the XSS program; there also has been discussion of equipping XSS-like satellites with a kind of ink-jet like system to blind a target satellite. However, exact plans for this program remain somewhat opaque, with Air Force officials downplaying their possible role as ASATs.

The United States could also acquire space weapons and/ or ASATs through the ongoing Missile Defense Program. There are three programs that if successfully deployed would be technically capable, provided slight modifications, of an ASAT mission. At the same time, the three programs are technically challenging and costly; thus there remains some question about their future viability.

Space-Based Boost-Phase Interceptors. The Missile Defense Agency (MDA) currently has tentative plans under its boost-phase interceptor development program to orbit a "test bed" of space-based boost-phase interceptors sometime in the 2007/08 timeframe. There is $14 million in the FY 04 budget for a concept study, and $119 million in 2005 for granting design contracts. Congressional cuts to the overall pot of money slated for boost-phase intercept programs have made the fate of the space-based interceptor effort somewhat unclear, however. MDA announced in August that due to immature technology and cost issues, its plans for the program were on hold.

Space-Based Laser. The Space-Based Laser program officially was canceled in 2002 due to technical and cost challenges, there remains in the MDA budget a line item for exploring laser technologies.

Airborne Laser. The ABL was budgeted at $345 million in FY 04. MDA has been planning to conduct its first lethality demonstration in 2004-05, but the development effort has been plagued by cost and weight issues and the program was heavily criticized by the General Accounting Office in a July 2002 report. Lastly, there has been some consideration in military and space circles in the United States about the possibility of basing kinetic energy weapons in space designed to destroy hardened and deeply buried targets, weapons sometimes referred to as "Rods From God." Indeed, such ground-strike weapon systems have been looked at for many years – but there remains a serious question about the technical and cost viability of such weapons, as the engineering required to overcome the physics challenges are large.

China

China is the only other nation whose political/military establishment seems to be having an ongoing debate on the potential value of space weapons, especially ASATs. This is despite the fact that official Chinese policy is in support of a space weapons ban, and the fact that China is less dependent on satellites than the United States. China's military does have communications satellites, remote sensing satellites, and weather satellites; in addition two Bei Dou navigation satellites out of a planned four have been launched. According to the latest Pentagon report on Chinese military capabilities, "China's leaders probably views ASATs – and offensive counterspace systems, in general – as well as space-based missile defenses as inevitabilities. In addition to passive counterspace measures – such as denial and deception – China is said to be acquiring a variety of foreign technologies which could be used to develop an active ASAT capability." Indeed, there are increasing signs that the United States and China are poised at the edge of a potentially destabilizing space arms race. Both countries are increasingly suspicious of each other's ambitions in space and perhaps convinced that they need to prepare for a future space war. Chinese media reports and official statements have also expressed concern about the U.S. use of space for global power projection. In a July 2000 article, Chinese defense analyst Wang Hucheng posited that: "For countries that can never win a war with the United States by using the method of tanks and planes, attacking the U.S. space system may be an irresistible and most tempting choice. Part of the reason is that the Pentagon is greatly dependent on space for its military action" From the U.S. side, China's excessive secrecy about its space program, especially its military projects, spurs concerns.

China just became the third nation to put a man in orbit. While it is inevitable that the manned program is having, and will have, technology spin-offs for military capabilities – indeed it is believed that the orbital module left behind by the Shenzou V launched Oct. 14 is carrying an imaging payload – it is not China's ambitious manned space effort that is of the most direct concern to U.S. military officials (although the program is managed by the PLA). Rather it is suspected Chinese efforts to develop a number of satellite jamming technologies and ASAT weapons. According to the Pentagon report, China may be developing Global Positioning System jammers and may already have the "capability to damage, under specific conditions, optical sensors on satellites that are very vulnerable to damage by lasers." The report goes on to assert that China may have acquired laser technology that "probably" could be used to develop ground-based laser ASATs. China has made laser research a high priority, and independent experts also believe that "ground-based laser technology is well within China's reach."

Hong Kong newspapers in January 2001 also claimed that China had developed a "parasitic" microsatellite (presumably a kinetic energy or explosive device that could attach itself to a target satellite) – a claim the Pentagon report says still "is being evaluated." China is actively pursuing microsat and nanosat technology and small launchers for then, ostensibly for communications, earth imaging and other civil uses.

Beijing (along with a number of other countries) has worked with the U.K. University of Surrey, a leading developer of microsatellites. For example, China's Tsinghua University participated in a Surrey Space Centre experiment in 2000 with a co-designed 50 kg microsatellite called Tsinghua-1. In addition, the university's majority owned company, Surrey Satellite Technology Ltd., intends to launch in 2005 a disaster monitoring satellite for China with a 4 meter resolution as part of a larger international constellation.

However, many independent experts have cast doubt on the idea that China has developed a microsat ASAT. There has been little in the scientific research to support the idea that actual work on such a system is ongoing, and no obvious on-orbit testing. In addition, several scientists have noted that development of such a weapon would require space capabilities (such as sophisticated orbital maneuvering) that even the United States has yet to demonstrate.

China also lacks some key capabilities that would make a space weapons program currently possible. These include limited tracking and launch capabilities. Another issue is costs, given China's extensive domestic development problems. And given China's vocal public support of a space weapons ban, it may be that China would be reluctant to be the first nation to pursue space weapons options – instead more likely to hedge its bets while hoping to avoid such an expensive undertaking.

India

India, too, has a sophisticated space program, building and launching its own satellites since 1980, now in both LEO and GEO orbits. Primarily, India is focused on using satellites for communications and remote sensing – but New Delhi also has said it is considering planetary exploration and possibly even a manned mission to the moon. 28 In addition, India hopes to sell its launch services to other nations. India is an active proponent of the rights of developing countries to use space, with keen interest in things like telemedicine. India is also officially a proponent of a space weapons ban and active in pushing for such negotiations at COPUOS in Geneva. However, India too may be researching options for disrupting or destroying enemy satellites in wartime. Just prior to arch-rival China's launch of an astronaut Oct. 15, the chief of the Indian Air Force, S. Krishnaswamy, told reporters that India was planning a new aerospace force command that would eventually develop space weapons. Krishnaswamy claimed that the Indian Air Force already has "started work on conceptualizing such weapon systems and its operational command system," arguing that this was necessary because "advanced countries are already moving toward laser weapon platforms in space and killer satellites."

India also has been working on laser technologies for military applications since the mid- 1990s. A recent story in *Bharatvarsha 1947* maintains that India's chiefs of staff have asked for a feasibility study of space-based lasers, and that the Indian defense research organization, DRDO, is already doing research on a system called Durga (directionally unrestricted ray-gun array) as well as on a "kinetic attack loitering interceptor" known as Kali. The credibility of this report may be somewhat doubtful, however, as the author seems to be mixed up on the differences between laser and kinetic energy weapons.

Considering India's current state of technology development, and official tendencies to "hype" military research and development progress, it is somewhat unlikely that India has made much real technical progress on this front. The political impetus to spend money and effort on space weapons, however, would be present if China were to develop and deploy such weaponry.

Other Nations

There is no body of evidence indicating that any other nation is seriously interested in space weapons. However, a number of countries have, or are developing, capabilities that could be applied to ASAT programs. In addition, progress in a number of key technology areas indicates that this trend could speed.

Russia

Since the launch of Sputnik, Russia has built and maintained a sophisticated civil and military space program, and, as noted, in the past has pursued ASAT capabilities. From 1968 to 1971, the then-Soviet Union successfully tested a radar-guided co-orbital ASAT system. Another set of tests took place between 1976 and 1982, when Moscow unilaterally suspended testing – despite the failure of negotiations with the United States on an ASAT ban.

Like the United States, Russia maintains a full spectrum of military-dedicated satellite systems for early warning, communications, navigation, optical reconnaissance and signals intelligence. Its Glonass navigation system is the only other in the world besides the U.S. GPS. The Russian space industry is large, well entrenched and technically capable.

Thus, Russia would certainly have the technical capability to pursue space weapons if it so chose. In particular, Russia is researching and development microsat technology and has also worked with Surrey, with many Surrey satellites launched on Russian rockets. Russia also has a long history of work on laser programs. However, the Russian military space program is currently suffering from disarray, both in its management and in the fact that it is being starved of funding. None of its military programs are functioning at full operational level – for example, Glonass is supposed to comprise a network of 24 satellites but at the moment only eight are operational. Several other programs are thought to be practically non- functional, and others are being phased out.

Officially, the Russians, like the Chinese, are strong backers of a space weapons ban – the two countries have jointly introduced draft treaty language to the UN Committee on Peaceful Uses of Outer Space. And the 2001-2002 *Jane's Space Directory* characterizes the Russian ASAT program as "inactive." That said, Russian military officials have expressed concerns similar to those of their Chinese counterparts regarding the intentions and directions of the U.S. military space program. Upon his appointment as commander of the new Russian Space Forces in April 2001, Col.-Gen. Anatoliy Perminov warned that the international community "should be on guard regarding the American policy of the military utilization of outer space" – citing in particular U.S. doctrine "reserving the right to employ force to conduct military operations in space, through space and from space." Thus it seems logical to assume that while Russia would not welcome a space arms race that would further tax their struggling space program, Moscow might feel the need to purse space weaponry if other nations did so – and given enough funding, such a Russian program would be technically feasible.

United Kingdom

While there is little or no evidence that Britain has interest in space weapons per se, as noted the University of Surrey is a leading producer of microsatellites and nanosatellites. According to a university press release, Surrey has launched 23 small satellite missions for international customers over the last 22 years. It also designed and launched one of the first advanced nanosatellites, the 6. kg SNAP-1, in June 2000. SNAP was able to take images of other on-orbit objects and to maneuver into a docking orbit with Tsinghua-1, and use GPS to determine its on-orbit position. 34 According to an annex to the U.S. Space Commission, Surrey has cooperated with Russia, China, Pakistan, Chile, Thailand, Portugal, Singapore and Malaysia on microsatellite research and development. Surrey also is building a 120 kg Earth observation satellite with a 2. meter resolution for the U.K. Ministry of Defense.

TERRESTRIAL-TYPE WEAPONS IN SPACE

Soviet, and later Russian, cosmonauts have regularly carried small arms (handguns) on spacecraft, as part of the special emergency kit included in landing capsules. The weapon was included to protect the cosmonauts from wild animals after reentry if the capsule landed in a wilderness area and could not be quickly retrieved. United States Astronauts are also provided a firearm for similar use.

The Russian space station Salyut 3 was fitted with a 23mm cannon, which was successfully test fired at target satellites, at ranges from 500 m to 3000 m.

Mass-media portrays numerous examples of the possibility of both conventional or nuclear missiles in space which could reach targets on the ground. While such a system is technically feasible, and would allow for their operator to reach practically anywhere on earth within minutes (instead of half an hour or longer compared to land-launched ballistic missiles) such a system would also be incredibly expensive for the operator both in development and in real terms as missiles are extremely heavy compared to most satellites. While space is an attractive prospect for a nuclear base, all but guaranteeing a second strike capability, such stations would also be fragile and open to any number of unforeseen problems. Conventional missiles would similarly present a problem, as such munitions are much more likely to used thus necessitating either resupply or continual replenishment of the satellites. When compared to missiles on ballistic missile submarines, and air-launched missiles from long-range tactical bombers, satellites' only advantage is the ability to strike quickly, before normal forces could redeploy.

Space Warfare

Space warfare is combat that takes place in outer space, i.e. outside the atmosphere. Technically, as a distinct classification , it refers to battles where the targets themselves are in space. Space warfare therefore includes *ground-to-space warfare,* such as attacking satellites from the Earth, as well as *space-to-space warfare,* such as satellites attacking satellites.

It does not include the use of satellites for espionage, surveillance, or military communications, however useful those activities might be. It does not technically include *space-to-ground warfare,* where orbital objects attack ground, sea or air targets directly, but the public and media frequently use the term to include any conflict which includes space as a theater of operations, regardless of the intended target. For example, a rapid delivery system in which troops are deployed from orbit might be described as "space warfare," even though the military uses the term as described above.

A film was produced by the U.S. Military in the early 1960s called *Space and National Security*which depicted space warfare. From 1985 to 2002 there was a United States Space Command, which in 2002 merged with the United States Strategic Command. There is a Russian Space Force, which was established on August 10, 1992, and which became an independent section of theRussian military on December 1, 2001.

Only a few incidents of space warfare have occurred in world history, and all were training missions, as opposed to actions against real opposing forces. In the mid-1980s a USAF pilot in an F-15 successfully shot down the P78-1, a communications satellite in a 345-mile (555 km) orbit.

In 2007 the People's Republic of China used a missile system to destroy one of its obsolete satellites, and in 2008 the United States similarly destroyed its malfunctioning satellite USA 193. To date, there have been no human casualties resulting from conflict in space, nor has any ground target been successfully neutralised from orbit.

International treaties governing space limit or regulate conflicts in space and limit the installation of weapon systems, especially nuclear weapons.

MILITARY TECHNOLOGY IN SPACE WEAPONS

On Tuesday April 24 at 7pm Global Network (GN, Global Network against Weapons and Nuclear Power in Space) members and supporters gathered at the Continuing Education Building of the University of New Mexico to protest. Just a few days previously the campus paper had announced the award of a 'defence' grant to its Electrical and Computer Engineering department for work on a super laser weapon project. Also, just a few blocks away at UNM's Institute for Space and Nuclear Studies, work is being carried out on nuclear power supplies for space vehicles and platforms. What have these two projects in common? The answer lies in the Space-Based Laser Integrated Flight Experiment, which forms what George Bush calls the "next generation weaponry" and is at the heart of our campaign against "weapons and nuclear power in space". Part of the 'experiment' is to build a Space-Based Laser Readiness Demonstrator - this is a scaled down version (at an estimated cost of $1. billion) of the proposed weapon system which would eventually be deployed for theater ballistic missile defense and as an anti-satellite weapon.

If the SBL IFX is successful, the US Department of Defense will decide whether to deploy a fully operational network of 20-30 laser battle stations giving global coverage. The first launch of an operational system could occur in 2020 and it could take several years to launch the full constellation of spacecraft around Earth. The Pentagon estimates that the total SBL program will cost $30 billion.

Why the nuclear connection? Any pace-based laser will require tremendous amounts of power and, as a study commissioned by the US Congress notes "nuclear reactors thus remain the only known long-lived, compact source able to supply military space forces with electric power"... nuclear reactors "could meet multimegawatt needs of space-based lasers, neutral particle beams, mass drivers, and railguns."

Also - New World Vistas: Air And Space Power For The 21st Century, states: "In the next two decades, new technologies will allow the fielding of space-based weapons of devastating effectiveness... These advances will enable lasers with reasonable mass and cost to effect very many kills." But "power limitations... currently make large space-based radars and space-based weapons relatively unfeasible... A natural technology to enable high power is nuclear power in space." This is the reason why nuclear power is being developed for use in outer space. So - the development of a SBL is already well underway - and forms a major part of the US Space Command plans to "dominate" and "master" space. As international weapons expert John Pike has said:

> *"Whoever controls space has control of Earth... the United States is unable to resist it. If the U.S. is in a position to control Earth from outer space, there's nothing to stop us. Of course we're going to do it."*

In January this year US Defense Secretary Donald Rumsfeld spoke of a "space Pearl Harbor" and a commission he formerly headed unveiled a report calling for tighter security for American space systems. "The US... needs to take seriously the possibility of an attack on US space systems," said the report "... The US is more dependent on space than any other nation" and the report called for a 'technological push' to foil threats from foreign nations or terrorists.

However, as reported in the Spring 2001 GN Newsletter, the environmental assessment for the SBL refers to the possibility of a catastrophic explosion that could result in a sudden release of a large quantity of toxic materials and/or destruction of surrounding structures with additional environmental consequences - although no reason for such an assessment of risk is given. Just another reason why the SBL is nicknamed "Death Star". It is a frighteningly ambitious component of Star Wars to be used as a boost-phase missile interceptor and satellite destroyer

Boost-Phase Missile Interception

Lasers are very attractive to the military because they travel so fast - at the speed of light. Therefore they are being seriously considered for intercepting missiles during their boost-phase. Apart from the SBL, two other methods of achieving this with lasers are currently being funded - airborne and ground based High Energy Laser systems. Of course, one major difficulty with this approach (apart from the fact that it might be technically difficult - if not impossible - and extremely expensive) is that boost-phase defences would break the ABM Treaty (if it still exists at the time of this presentation!). However - as we know - a number of influential US generals and politicians believe that the laser weapon provides such a valuable defense that it is worth abrogating the treaty.

The stated advantages of a boost-phase system for Ballistic Missile Defence Systems are that it would:

- provide another tier of missile defence;
- remove the problem of debris falling over the target area (as occurs with "terminal intercept");
- prevent the deployment of multiple warheads;
- does not require the ability to differentiate between war-heads and decoys;
- would deter the use of payloads through threat of "country of origin impact of debris".

It also, of course, enhances the US first strike capability and its ability to knock out other nation's space hardware. The SBL can also be used for NMD as well as TMD - in fact strategic missiles would be more vulnerable to laser attack in boost phase than theatre missiles because of their longer boost times. They also have higher burn-out altitudes which reduces the atmospheric effects that would interfere with laser beam propagation from space.

An alternative space based system would incorporate fewer SBL platforms (perhaps 3) with a number of orbiting relay mirrors (perhaps 24) to direct the beams. A number of configurations are possible and this type of configuration is favoured by many military.

Military Lasers

The Air Force, Army and Navy all started working on lasers in the mid-1960s, and the idea of a SBL has been around since 1977. Initial tests involve a megawatt-class chemical laser with a large, multi-segmented mirror that unfurls and locks into place to create a 13-foot (4-meter) diameter reflecting surface. The entire spacecraft would weigh between 45,000 and 50,000 pounds (20,455 and 22,700 kilograms). The competing lasers are hydrogen fluoride (HF), deuterium fluoride (DF), and chemical oxygen iodine (COIL).

The HF laser uses atomic fluorine and molecular hydrogen to produce excited hydrogen fluorine molecules producing several simultaneous wavelengths in the range of 2. - 2. microns. At these wavelengths the beam is mostly absorbed by the earth's atmosphere and can only be used above the earth's atmosphere e.g. for the SBL. A HF laser has been test fired at the TRW San Juan Capistrano test facility in California.

The DF laser uses deuterium (an isotope of hydrogen) and atomic fluorine. Longer wavelength laser light than for HF lasers is produced (3. - 4 microns), giving better transmission through the atmosphere but requiring larger optical surfaces to shape and focus the beam. The Chemical Oxygen Iodine Laser (COIL) was developed at the Air Force Research Laboratory in Albuquerque in 1977. It is the basis of the $1. billion Air Force Airborne Laser Attack Aircraft - scheduled for anti-missile tests in 2003.

On October 1997 the Pentagon conducted a "laser dazzler" test against one of its satellites using the Army's MIRACL DF laser (Mid-Infrared Advanced Chemical Laser) based at White Sands Missile Range, N.M. In 1996 a MIRACL laser shot down a rocket at the same site.

A new, lightweight, "all gas" Iodine Laser, or AGIL has also been developed by the Air Force Research Lab. This laser uses nitrogen chloride and iodine which are mixed in a vacuum chamber. AGIL has a better atmospheric transmission, which is important for a laser weapon required to reach targets in the atmosphere or even near the surface of the Earth. A basic weapon-size AGIL laser will take at least until 2003 to develop, demonstrate and test.

The Army's Tactical High Energy Laser (THEL) system is designed by a team led by TRW Corp. After the war in Lebanon in April 1996, Israel was promised by the Clinton administration that the U.S. would help develop a laser-based anti-missile system capable of destroying incoming Katyusha rockets. The US Army and the Israeli Ministry of Defense paid weapons contractor TRW $200 million to build a HF laser to generate a powerful infrared beam that can pass through the atmosphere.

On 6 June 2000 the THEL intercepted and destroyed an armed Russian made Katyusha rocket at White Sands Missile Range, N.M. and on Aug. 28 and Sept 14 the demonstrator shot down two rockets launched in succession. The system detected the 10 foot long, 5 inch diameter rocket with its radar before shooting it down. THEL has a range of about 12 miles and costs about $3,000 per destroyed rocket to use.

The U.S. military's first high energy weapon is likely to be the Airborne Laser mounted on a Boeing 747, it is being designed to acquire, track, and destroy theatre ballistic missiles. The system is expected to be deployed in 10 years. The Air Force has proposed spending $11 billion to develop a fleet of seven airborne lasers that could be used for battlefield anti-missile defense at a cost of about $10,000 per shot, based on the price of the laser fuel.

Last month Raytheon Electronic Systems, a subcontractor to Lockheed Martin Space Systems, carried out a 'first light' test of the Track Illuminator Laser (TILL) at the High Energy Laser Centre in El Segundo in California. The TILL is part of the Beam Control/Fire Control system for the US Air Force's Airborne Laser (ABL) programme, which will aim and fire a high-energy laser at a target missile in its boost phase.

However, also last month Nathan Kopeika of Ben-Gurion University told a conference in Florida that he believes engineers working on the Airborne Laser (ABL) project have overlooked the effect of tiny dust particles in the atmosphere, called aerosols.

These could scatter and weaken the laser beam, making it incapable of destroying incoming missiles. "We found that, after a propagation of 100 kilometres, aerosols can widen a laser beam up to a cross section one kilometre wide—several orders of magnitude worse than optical turbulence," he said.

The Space Based Laser represents the ultimate in current military thinking about space weaponry and demonstrates the extent to which the US Space Command is prepared to go to realize their vision of domination. We must continue to bring these issues to the attention of the citizens of the world - this is no way to spend our limited resources, no way to increase global security, no way to take our first steps outside our own planet. We must strive to keep space for peace.

On 21 December, 2000, the Stennis Space Center, Mississippi, was selected as the site of the SBL performance test facility. Local people will be holding a vigil at the site on 12 May and on 13 October there will be an action at Stennis as part of the GN International Day of Action.

SPACEPLANE

A spaceplane is an aerospace vehicle that operates as an aircraft in Earth's atmosphere, as well as a spacecraft when it is in space. It combines features of an aircraft and a spacecraft, which can be thought of as an aircraft that can endure and maneuver in the vacuum of space or likewise a spacecraft that can fly like an airplane.

Typically, it takes the form of a spacecraft equipped with wings, although lifting bodieshave been designed and tested as well. The propulsion to reach space may be purely rocket based or may use the assistance of airbreathing jet engines. The spaceflight is then followed by an unpowered glide return to landing.

Only five spaceplanes have successfully flown to date, having reentered Earth's atmosphere, returned to Earth, and safely landed — the North American X-15, Space Shuttle, Buran, SpaceShipOne, and Boeing X-37. All five are considered gliders. As of 2015, only these aircraft and rockets have succeeded in reaching space. Two of these five (X-15 and SpaceShipOne) are rocket-powered aircraft, having been carried up to an altitude of several tens of thousands of feet by an atmospheric mother ship before being released, and then flying beyond the boundaries of the earth's atmosphere under their own power. Three (Space Shuttle, Buran, and X-37) are vertical takeoff horizontal landing (VTHL) vehicles relying upon rocket lift for the ascent phase in reaching space and atmospheric lift forreentry, descent and landing. The three VTHL spaceplanes flew much further than the aircraft launched ones, not merely leaving the earth's atmosphere but also entering orbit around it, which requires at least 50 times more energy on the way up and heavy heat shielding for the trip back. Also, of the 5 vehicles, three have been piloted by astronauts, with the Buran and X-37 flying unmanned missions.

Description

Significant features distinguish spaceplanes from spacecraft.

Aerodynamic lift

All aircraft utilize aerodynamic surfaces in order to generate lift. For spaceplanes a variety of wing shapes can be used. Delta wings are common, but straight wings, lifting bodies and even rotorcraft have been proposed. Typically the force of lift generated by these surfaces is many times that of the drag that they induce.

Atmospheric Reentry

Because suborbital spaceplanes are designed for trajectories that do not reach orbital speed, they do not need the kinds of thermal protection orbital spacecraft required during the hypersonic phase of atmospheric reentry. The Space Shuttle thermal protection system, for example, protects the orbiter from surface temperatures that could otherwise reach as high as 1,650 °C (3,000 °F), well above the melting point of steel.

Aircraft landing

A spaceplane operates as an aircraft in Earth's atmosphere. Aircraft may land on firm runways, helicopter landing pads, or even water(amphibious aircraft), snow or ice. To land, the airspeed and the rate of descent are reduced such that the aircraft descends at a slow enough rate to allow for a gentle touch down. Landing is accomplished by slowing down and descending. This speed reduction is accomplished by reducing thrust and/or inducing a greater amount of drag using flaps, landing gear or speed brakes.

Splashdown is an easier technical feat to accomplish, requiring only the deployment of a parachute (or parachutes), rather than successfully aviating theatmosphere. Project Gemini's original concept design was as a spaceplane, with paraglider and wheels (or skis) attached. However, this concept was abandoned in favor of parachute splashdowns, because of expensive technical failures during testing and development. Whereas Project Gemini's splashdown parachutes took only 5 months to develop in 1963, Gemini's spaceplane concept failed to materialize even after nearly 3 years of continued development.

SPACE WARFARE AND WEAPONRY

Space warfare or space combatwas the use of armed starships and other spacecraft for the purposes of military actions across star systemsand the galaxy. Along with ground warfare and starfighter combat, by 0 BBY space warfare was one of three most significant branches of warfighting. Evolving from water navyengagements and in turn the earliest orbital battles, space warfare became a high technology affair that often defined the outcome of the galaxy's most important conflicts.

Technological innovation determined the design of warships and naval doctrine and the outcome of battles. While the sizes and capabilities of starships varied, four main technologies drove and were advanced by space warfare: weapon systems, shield technology, sublight propulsion, and hyperdrive technology.

There were two basic types of space weaponry: energy and conventional. Energy weapons began withmicrowave lasers for offense and were typically secondary to conventional, physical weapons. From 4000 BBY however, energy weapons were the dominant form of weaponry in space combat, dominated by theturbolaser and the laser cannon, outgrowths of blaster technology that had matured at the same time. On capital ships, energy weapons were normally grouped into batteries based upon the weapon type and its placement upon the hull.

For example, on an *Imperial*-class Star Destroyer the heavy turbolasers on the portside of the hull's dorsal surface would be grouped into one battery, while those on the starboard dorsal surface would be grouped into a second battery. Targeting computers in capital ships were usually shared between the weapons of each battery, allowing the gunners to concentrate their fire on particular targets. Other designs of energy weapon included the charric, a Chiss advancement of early microwave lasers; the ion cannon, an electromagnetic weapon used to non-destructively disable electronic systems; and the superlaser, a Clone Wars development that was an immensely more-powerful design of laser that could cause planetary-scale damage.

Conventional weapons were the first weapons used in space combat. Although the first conventional space weaponry included projectiles such as slugs, technology further progressed and came to encompass guided missiles and torpedo launchers. Conventional weapons could be guided, as in the case of missiles, or unguided, as in the case of bombs. Conventional weapons came to include thenuclear bomb, the proton bomb, proton torpedo, and the concussion missile.

Shield technology

Deflector shields were a critical component in starship design and were used to mitigate damage from impacts. They included ray shields, which protected against energy weapons, and particle shields, which repelled physical objects. Both types consumed large amounts of energy and for a long period in galactic history, were reserved for only the largest warships with the greatest power-generating capability. Early warship captains therefore thought in terms of armor for defense. Other early defenses included charged particle clouds to diffuse energy weapons and hulls treated with kiirium to reflect beams.

A refinement of the squintpipe process in the 7500s BBY produced shields that were stronger and quicker to regenerate, and also reduced the effective size of deflector shield generators. From then on, reliable deflector shields could be fitted to ships of all sizes. Other defenses included point-defense laser cannons, which were designed to destroy incoming threats like torpedoes before they could hit the ship.

In spite of the necessary elements of deflector shields in starship designs, not all ships incorporate them. A notable example of ships lacking deflector shields are the TIE-series starfighters, in particular the TIE/LN starfighter, which was not included alongside life-support systems because Imperial doctrine dictated that their usage among fighter pilots was a sign of cowardice.

Propulsion technology

Sublight drives propelled ships below the speed of light and were best represented by ion drives: powered by fusion generators, these engines expelled particles at a very high speed to provide propulsive force. Sublight engines determined speed and maneuverability and could prove decisive: theGalactic Empire's TIE/LN starfighter used an extremely efficient twin ion engine design and stripped-down spaceframe to improve its mobility. The Alliance to Restore the Republic countered this with the faster and more maneuverable RZ-1 A-wing interceptor, which the Empire countered in turn with the even fasterTIE/IN interceptor.

Hyperdrive technology was an enormous influence on strategy in space warfare: fleets travelling faster-than-light in hyperspace had to traverse known hyperlanes to avoid dangerous mass shadows. For much of galactic history, starships lacked the computing power to calculate safe routes between systems and were confined to jumps within networks of jump beacons. In war this allowed navies to effectively pin ships at a certain point by disabling its beacon. By 4100 BBY, navigation computers had advanced to the point that jump beacons were no longer needed, making control of routes more difficult, as blockading one route merely pushed ships to one of many alternative ones. However, statistically speaking, only a few of these route could be traversed quickly, and a military force that controlled the fast routes could rapidly redeploy to intercept an adversary using the slow ones. Hyperlanes thus determined the strategic geography of space warfare, and fleets repeatedly battled over the same planets on significant hyperspace routes, such as Chazwa, or planets at hyperlane junctions such as Yag'Dhul or Brentaal IV. Militaries might also maintain secret hyperlanes to get the drop on their enemies: during the Clone Wars,General Grievous made use of a secret route through the Deep Core to directly attack Coruscant, while the Galactic Republic and the CIS negotiated with the Hutts for control of the Nexus Route connecting each other's core territories. The Rebel Alliance also made use of secret Claatuvac Guild routes supplied to them by Chewbacca for hit-and-hype raiding against the Empire.

Ship classes

Ships designed for war were typically split into two broad classes: starfighters and capital ships.

Starfighters

Starfighters were small craft typically piloted by one or two beings. Their operations and role encompassed an entire doctrine and form of warfare in its own right, known asstarfighter combat. Types included *space superiority fighters,bombers*, and *snubfighters*.

Space superiority fighters were stripped-down ships, usually minimally armed and armored, and were used to combat enemy bombers but typically could not attack capital ships.

Bombers were more heavily-armed starfighters and were usually equipped with bombs, torpedoes and missiles so that they could makebombing runs on enemy warships. They were typically less-maneuverable than space superiority fighters and usually required their own fighter escort to avoid being shot down.

Snubfighters sat between space superiority fighters and bombers in size and armament and were designed to both dogfight with other fighters and attack capital ships.

Though snubfighters like the RebelX-wing and Y-wing became famous, for the majority of galactic history snubfighters were not heavily used in deep-space combat: commanders considered it better to operate snubfighters from planet-based surface airfields to strike through cloud cover and launch torpedo strikes and strafing runs against attacking ships and troop transports.

However, the advantages of snubfighters tended to disappear in the great ranges between opposing fleets and their payloads were not as great as dedicated bombers.

It was only after the success of N-1 starfighters against Trade Federation battleships at the Battle of Naboo in32 BBY, an experience confirmed by the role of Y-wings against the *Malevolence* at the Battle of the Kaliida Nebula during the Clone Wars, that the snubfighter began to be taken seriously as a deep-space battleship killer.

Starfighters may or may not have had a hyperdrive; if not, they were often launched from a carrier or other larger craft. Some, like Imperial TIE/LN starfighters, were armed only for fighter-on-fighter combat; more versatile ones, like the Rebel X-wing and Y-wing snubfighters, were also capable of anti-ship and anti-surface attacks. Bombers like the TIE/sa bomber and the A/SF-01 B-wing starfighters were typically poor dogfighters and relied on heavy shielding or escorts to push through fighter screens and attack warships.

By nature, a starfighter was intended to be small, fast and agile, designed to operate either on its own or as part of a squadron or a fighter wing on a variety of mission profiles, ranging from escort duty to reconnaissance missions and full-scale assault. Due to their size, starfighters could not engage in self-sufficient operations for any long period of time, needing a base of operations to provide fuel, repairs and supplies for the pilot, given as these cannot be carried aboard in any large quantity.

Capital ships

A dizzying variety of capital ship classifications existed throughout galactic history. However, all agreed that a capital ship was a military starship that was at least one hundred meters in length. After the Clone Wars, the most common classification system was the Anaxes War College System, which replaced the system instituted after theRuusan Reformation. The largest class recognised by that system was the cruiser, reflecting the Ruusan Reformation's restriction on transgalactic warships larger than six hundred meters.

By the time theClone Wars broke out, many rich sectors had commissioned much larger warships with local-range hyperdrives for their defense, with lengths of several kilometers and making the cruiser an increasingly-meaningless class.

Under the Anaxes War College System, ships smaller than one hundred meters were classified as either *starfighters*, or if they were unarmed, *space transports*. Mindful of what had happened to the cruiser class, the Anaxes architects extended their classification system to account for the possibility of truly gigantic warships.

Corvettes were fast, light attack ships which were used in a variety of roles, including blockade running, anti-starfighter missions, or escort and support for larger ships. *Frigates* sat between two hundred and four hundred meters and served the purpose of eliminating smaller vessels of an enemy fleet and often carried their own starfighter squadrons.

*Cruisers*were from four hundred to six hundred meters in length and were heavily armed relative to their size and could often trade blows with much larger ships. *Heavy cruisers* were from six hundred to one thousand meters in length and were typically the backbone of any fleet engagement. *Star Destroyers* were between one and two kilometers in length and were typically the most numerous large starship, specializing in heavy ship-to-ship combat.

Battlecruisers were from two to five kilometers in length and were heavily armed, designed for long-range, independent operations hunting down other capital ships Finally, *dreadnoughts* were ships over five kilometers in length and so powerful that the mere threat of their deployment could pacify multiple sectors.

Additionally, the Anaxes War College System carried a shorthand for use during engagements, one that lumped warships of different classes based on their size and capability.

Corvettes, space transports and starships acting as warships in-theater were designated as *gunships*, small, fast, heavily-armed ships that specialized in destroying the maximum number of small enemy ships in a space battle and relied on evasion far more than their shields to escape damage. Frigates and lighter cruisers - the workhorses of most military engagements - were identified as *cruisers*. Big ships of the line whose mere presence could change the course of a battle were referred to as *battleships*.

6

Radical New Strategy for Information Warfare and Military Space

Krutskikh's comments are important because they may help explain the radical strategic doctrine that underlies Russia's hacking and attempted manipulation of the 2016 presidential campaign in America, as well as Russian political subversion in Europe. His title is "special representative of the president for international cooperation in the field of information security."

A senior Obama administration official described Krutskikh as a "senior-level adviser" to President Vladimir Putin and "a long-standing player in cyber issues" at the foreign ministry. The official said he couldn't confirm the details of Krutskikh's remarks, but that "they sound like something Andrey would say."

According to notes of Krutskikh's speech, he told his Russian audience: "You think we are living in 2016. No, we are living in 1948. And do you know why? Because in 1949, the Soviet Union had its first atomic bomb test. And if until that moment, the Soviet Union was trying to reach agreement with [President Harry] Truman to ban nuclear weapons, and the Americans were not taking us seriously, in 1949 everything changed and they started talking to us on an equal footing."

Krutskikh continued, "I'm warning you: We are at the verge of having 'something' in the information arena, which will allow us to talk to the Americans as equals." Putin's cyber adviser stressed to the Moscow audience the importance for Russia of having a strong hand in this new domain. If Russia is weak, he explained, "it must behave hypocritically and search for compromises. But once it becomes strong, it will dictate to the Western partners [the United States and its allies] from the position of power."

Krutskikh's comments may have been a precursor of a new doctrine for information operations announced publicly by the Kremlin in December. The senior administration official described the Russian strategy: "They think of information space as a domain of warfare. In the U.S, we tend to have a binary view of conflict — we're at peace or at war. The Russian doctrine is more of a continuum. You can be at different levels of conflict, along a sliding scale."

Russian hacking during the 2016 presidential campaign, as outlined in the unclassified report released this month by U.S. intelligence agencies, is an example of Russia's use of new tools in this continuum of conflict, the U.S. official said. "Certainly, I believe the Russians are working to increase their capabilities in cyberspace, because they've realized they can use cyberspace to pursue their foreign policy goals," he said.

In Russia's view, America is pushing just as aggressively in the information space, but denies it. "Things we perceive as free speech, they perceive as aggressive behavior from the West," noted the senior U.S. official.

Putin, for example, saw Hillary Clinton's support for anti-Putin dissidents as an attempt to foment a "color revolution." Russians also claim (without public evidence) that the U.S. orchestrated last year's disclosure of the "Panama Papers," which included allegations of Russian money laundering, and last year's allegations by the World Anti-Doping Agency of drug use by Russian athletes.

In Putin's mind, the United States attacked first in the information war. Russia is now strong enough to retaliate, as Krutskikh signaled in his February 2016 speech.

Krutskikh and other Russian cyber experts don't appear to have been deterred by public warnings or sanctions. Krutskikh was quoted by the Russian Information Agency Dec. 29 describing U.S. sanctions announced that day as "the agony of the ruling elite," reflecting "the personal hatred" of President Obama, and "an attempt to prevent future cooperation."

"We don't exclude the lifting of the sanctions after Trump enters office," Krutskikh said.

Krutskikh's comments highlight the emerging world of information warfare, where "fake news" and hacking are tools for covert warriors in many nations. The senior administration official warns: "The Russians are particularly advanced — in technology, organization and doctrine. They're at the head of the pack. But there will be others."

IMPORTANCE OF INFORMATION WARFARE

Given the above context, one can get an insight into evolution of Chinese theories and concepts on Information Warfare (IW). As with all its military theories and strategic perspectives, Chinese traditional wisdom and strategic thought is applied to all new concepts and precepts originating from the US, Russia or elsewhere. The first wave of Chinese writings on IW appeared in the mid-1990s following the success of US information technologies in the first Gulf War of 1991. Though this war was a defining event for all militaries of the world, its impact on the PLA was greater because of the aspirations of the Chinese political and military leadership towards acquiring comprehensive national strength. The PLA was first off the block in developing theories of IW and adapting Western concepts to suit local conditions. A PLA General, writing on challenges and importance of IW, observed: In near future, Information warfare will control the form and future of war. We recognise this developmental trend of information warfare and see it as a driving force in China's military and combat readiness. This trend will be highly critical to achieve victory in future wars. The General further emphasised that China must use a practical combination of IW and Maoist and Marxist military thought to guide IW issues under military construction. The military must study ways of using inferior equipment to achieve victory over the enemy's superior equipment. He advocated study on how to conduct 'People's war in IW domain'. The underlying theme of Chinese concepts on IW has been emphasis on devising ways and means to attack an enemy's weaknesses and vulnerabilities, and on exploiting own strengths. The other fundamental assumption is that superior tactics can compensate for inferior technology.

People's Warfare in Information Warfare Context

According to some Chinese military analysts, because of the increasing relevance of information technology (IT) to people's lives, individuals who take part in IW are not all soldiers and that anybody who understands computers may become a fighter. IW is inexpensive as the targeted party can be delivered a paralysing blow through the net and it may be difficult for the latter to discern where the attack originated. Large amount of useless information can be created to block or stop the functioning of an adversary's information system.

Thus, a People's War in context of IW can be carried out by hundreds of millions of people, using open-type modern information systems. Even political mobilisation for war can be achieved via the internet, by sending patriotic e-mail messages and by setting up databases for education.

This finds further support from another Chinese author, who observes that "even as ... government mobilised troops, the numbers and roles of traditional warriors will be sharply less than those of technical experts...since thousand of personal computers can be linked up to perform a common operation, to perform many tasks in place of a large-scale military computer, an IW victory will very likely be determined by which country can mobilise the most computer experts and part-time fans... That will be a real People's War."

Preparing for people's war is a recurring theme in Chinese writing, as IW will be carried out by the PLA and society as a whole. This concept has found practical expression in turning some of the 1.5 million reserve forces into mini-IW regiments. The People's Armed Forces Department (PAFD) has reportedly organised militia/ reserve IW regiments at district levels in many provinces.For instance, in Echeng district of Hubei province, the PAFD has a network warfare battalion as well as electronic warfare, intelligence and psychological warfare battalions, and also a training base for IW activities. The PAFD has also carried out 'Informaticised People's Warfare Network Simulation Exercise'. A version of this concept was also put into practice following the bombing of the Chinese embassy in Belgrade on May 8, 1999, during 'Operation Allied Force'. The Chinese hacked a number of US political, military and diplomatic web sites, and also carried out a network battle by mobilising thousands of net users for sending emails and viruses. This caused servers to crash, paralysing a large number of web sites.

Cyber Warfare

Concerns about China's net force were heightened after the aforementioned attacks on US computer systems and after the Chinese militia carried out IW exercises, which included India, the US, Taiwan and Japan as target countries.

The aim of such training was to disrupt critical infrastructure like banking, power supply and telecommunication networks in the target country as part of China's strategy of asymmetric approach to warfare. In the cyber domain, the Chinese have adopted three methods for targetting such networks; the first is the use of e-mails for planting viruses; then phishing and lastly, the introduction of 'intelligent trojans' and 'vacuum trojans'. Diverse routes of planting trojans and viruses have been used to attack critical PCs, which in turn send out files or cause Chinese Concepts and Capabilities of Information Warfare 785 malfunction. Hackers' tools are becoming more robotic and simple; for instance, a vacuum trojan will extract information from a pen drive automatically when connected to a USB port. It is also believed that the next step could be planting the targeted sites with the more difficult to detect fake data or partially fake data.

In Nanjing, the PLA has developed more than 250 trojans and similar tools. Here, it needs to be remembered that foreign companies like Network Solutions, were made to hand over 300 computer viruses by the Ministry of Public Security's lab in an effort to speed up the certification of antivirus products.

Further, the Chinese Academy of Sciences, which provides suggestions about national information security policy and law, has established the State Lab for Information Security. The lab has 'National Attack Project' as one of its research programmes.

Also, select professionals have been inducted into militia organisations to boost combat capabilities in future wars. Thus, China has been paying much attention to offensive strategies in cyberspace even as it concentrates on defensive IW.

Definition and Goals of Information Warfare

The Chinese understanding of IW, which was initially based on western concepts, has increasingly moved towards evolving its own orientation.

Chinese experts believe that IW's essence is the sum of information capabilities capable of breaking the will to resist by attacking an enemy's cognitive understanding and convictions, forcing it to give up all resistance and terminate the war. The goal is to "force enemy to regard their goal as our goal, to force the opponent to give up the will to resist and end confrontation and stop fight by attacking enemy's perceptions and belief via information energy." Xie Guang, the then Vice Minister of Science and Technology and Industry for National Defence, defined IW in December 1999 thus: "IW in military sense means overall use of various types (of) information technologies, equipment and systems, particularly his command systems, to shake determination of enemy's policy makers and at the same time, the use of all the means possible to ensure that one's own systems are not damaged or disturbed." This definition apparently includes the aspects of IW's goals at the larger national level. A further elaboration was done by two senior PLA colonels, who described IW as consisting of five major elements and two general areas. The five elements are:

- Substantive destruction, the use of hard weapons to destroy enemy headquarters, command posts, and command and control (C2) information centres
- Electronic warfare, the use of electronic means of jamming or the use of anti-radiation [electromagnetic] weapons to attack enemy information and intelligence collection systems such as communications and radar
- Military deception, the use of operations such as tactical feints [simulated attacks] to shield or deceive enemy intelligence collection systems
- Operational secrecy, the use of all means to maintain secrecy and keep the enemy from collecting intelligence on our operations.
- Psychological warfare, the use of TV, radio, and leaflets to undermine the enemy's military morale.

The two general areas are information protection (defence) and information attack (offence). Information defence means preventing the destruction of one's own information systems, ensuring that these systems can perform their normal functions. In future wars, key information and information systems will become "combat priorities", the key targets of enemy attack. It also includes many other manifestations of IW like computer virus warfare, precision warfare and stealth warfare, all dependent in some manner on information and software programmes.

Information Operations

Information Operations (IO) are specific operations and are considered to be at the core of IW, in the same manner as IW is considered to be at the core of informationalisation. In fact, IO is a manifestation of IW on the battlefield. It can be both of the defensive and offensive types, and can be conducted at the strategic, operational, campaign and tactical levels at times of peace, wars and crises. Principles of IO have been defined by Chinese military authors to include centralised command, decentralised control (multi-level power delegation), multi-dimension inspection and testing, timely decision-making and integration of military and civil actions with focus on key links. Major General Dai Qingmin, Director of PLA's General Staff responsible for IW and IO (and also ex-Commander of PLA's IW Centre in Wuhan) observes that integrated and joint information operations give more scope and purpose to people's war. (In fact, jointness and integration is a major theme of the 2004 White Paper).

He defines IO as a series of operations with an informationalised environment as the basic battlefield condition, with military information and information systems as the direct operational targets and electronic warfare (EW) and computer networks as the principal form. He has outlined various IO strategies because, as mentioned earlier, according to the traditional Chinese approach strategies can compensate for inferior equipment and technologies and, in the case of IO, it may also compensate for gaps in information or poor information about the enemy. Some of the IO strategies are:

- Jamming or sabotaging an enemy's information or information system.
- Sabotaging an enemy's overall information operational structure.
- Weakening an enemy's information fighting capacity.
- Dispersing enemy forces, arms and fires while concentrating own forces, arms and fire.
- Confusing or diverting an enemy and creating an excellent combat opportunity for on self.
- Diverting an enemy's reconnaissance attempt and making sufficient preparations for it.
- Giving the enemy a false impression and launching surprise information attack on him at the same time.
- Blinding or deafening an enemy with false impressions.
- Confusing an enemy or disrupting his thinking.
- Making an enemy believe that what is true is false and what is false is true.
- Causing an enemy to make a wrong judgement or take wrong action.

In the IW exercises conducted by PAFD, 10 methods of IO were practised and these can be viewed as tactics in the electronic battlefield. These are:

- Planting information mines
- Conducting information reconnaissance
- Changing network data
- Releasing information bombs
- Dumping information garbage
- Disseminating propaganda
- Applying information deception
- Releasing clone information
- Organising information defence
- Establishing network spy stations.

Computer Network Operations

In Chinese writings on Information Warfare, networking has also been the focus of discussions. The recent emphasis on jointness and integration apply equally to integrating various military networks. A critique by Timothy Thomas notes that the Chinese feel it necessary to prepare for a "network people's war". Computer network warfare has been included by Dai Qing as one of the six forms of IW (i.e. operational security, military deception, psychological warfare, electronic warfare, computer network warfare and physical destruction). Though there is no evidence of a formal Chinese doctrine, Chinese theorists have coined the term "Integrated Network Electronic Warfare" (INEW) and this has also been referred to by Timothy Thomas as a half cousin, given its similarities and points of divergences to the US approach.

INEW has been described as a series of combat operations that integrate electronic warfare and computer network warfare measures to disrupt the normal operation of an enemy's battlefield systems while protecting one's own with the objective of attaining information superiority. The essence of computer network warfare (CNW) is "to disrupt layers in which information is processed, by seizing and maintaining control of network space". EW is targeted at networked information systems and informationalised weapon systems in order to increase combat effectiveness. According to Dai, INEW is necessary for system to system confrontation on the informationalised battlefield, as systems are centres of gravity. Any disruption in system will lead to a disconnect between the people and weapons.

Thus, INEW lays stress on coordinating and integrating all aspects of C4ISR and weapon platforms and weapon systems to produce the desired effects at the target end. The effectiveness of weapon platforms and network systems is directly proportional to its levels of integration. As in other spheres, integration produces a combat capability greater than the sum of its parts and, this is true for information operations as well.

China's computer network operations (CNO) comprise network attacks, defence, and exploitation. According to the Pentagon's Annual Report for 2005 to the Congress on China's military power, the PLA views CNO as critical to seize the initiative and "electromagnetic dominance" early in a conflict, and as a force multiplier. This concept outlines the integrated use of electronic warfare, CNO and limited physical strikes against key C4ISR nodes to disrupt an enemy's battlefield network information systems. It is believed that the PLA has established information warfare units to develop viruses to attack enemy computer systems and networks, and tactics to protect friendly computer systems and networks. The PLA has increased the role of CNO in its military exercises. Although initial training efforts focused on increasing the PLA's proficiency in defensive measures, recent exercises have incorporated offensive operations, primarily as first strikes against enemy networks.

The main area of weakness that the Chinese espy, especially with regard to US forces, is the deployment phase. US forces are largely dependent upon computer and communication systems, both military and nonmilitary, and the particularly weak links in the logistics network systems make them susceptible to computer network attacks. Logistics network systems may be relatively easy to penetrate compared to other C4 systems though it will be more useful to penetrate command and information links. However, the priority of Chinese CNW seems to be to prevent the force from deploying at the first place and thereafter breaking the linkages between decision-makers and weapon platforms. This approach rhymes with the oft-stated Chinese strategy of attacking weaknesses and avoiding strengths of the enemy. As observed by James Mulvenon, Chinese strategists theorise that:

- Computer network attack is the most effective means for a weak adversary to fight a strong one.
- It can be used as a means to deter the enemy.
- It has longer range than the conventional power projection assets, as long distance surveillance and precise powerful and long distance attacks are available to the military.

Psychological Operations and Information Warfare

Another important component of information Warfare with Chinese characteristics is psychological warfare. Chinese doctrine has traditionally focused more attention on the psychological dimensions of IW, including deception, though of late they have also been paying equal, if not more, attention to the technological dimensions. The target in psychological operations is always the people and decision-makers, so that their will and perceptions are attacked to alter their beliefs, goals and behaviour. This is aimed at both military and civil components of an adversary's populace. Psychological operations comprise of manipulation of media to support military efforts and include conventional methods of propaganda like distribution of leaflets, radio and TV broadcasts, and other means of communication. Like most of the components of IW, psychological operations are a continuum of actions in peacetime, crisis time and war time.

In August 2005, the PLA conducted a joint exercise, involving not only all its services but also troops from Russia. The exercise involved distribution of leaflets over the opponent, electronic warfare to confuse incoming missiles and adoption of electronic counter measures. These exercises involved the use of live missiles and ammunition, and showcased precision warfare capabilities as well as the latest military equipment. These exercises could also be said to have had a psychological dimension for deterring Taiwan or those aiding it in its political objectives.

Here, it can be argued that the Chinese appear to have taken a leaf out of the US forces' tom-tomming of the awesome power of their arsenal and military capabilities before the start of 'Operation Iraqi Freedom', which had the effect of lowering the morale of the Iraqi military. The US forces also air dropped over 31 million leaflets for propaganda purposes besides physically attacking Iraqi forces' command and control networks based on fibre optic lines and radio and computer servers. US forces had been issued cyber-guidance as early as February 2003 for operations in Iraq. The PLA has thus been quick to absorb lessons on IW from 'Operation Iraqi Freedom'.

The Chinese also observed the power of media when CNN's broadcast of a US soldier's body being dragged through the streets of Mogadishu transformed perceptions of victory into defeat. Authors of the Chinese book titled Unrestricted Warfare reflected on the incident thus: Did CNN's broadcast of an exposed corpse of a US soldier in the streets of Mogadishu shake the determination of the Americans to act as the world's policeman, thereby altering the world's strategic situation? And should an assessment of wartime actions look at the means or the results?

PLA's IW/EW Capabilities

The 2004 White Paper shows that the Chinese military has understood that there is a large and expanding technology gap between it and modern militaries, especially that of the US. China's leaders, including President Hu Jintao, have ordered the PLA to pursue "leap ahead" technologies and "informationalised" capabilities to increase weapons' mobility, firepower and precision. This perspective applies to IW also.

The Central Military Commission's (CMC) Third or Technical Department of General Service Headquarters is responsible for strategic SIGINT and has established a number of monitoring stations to intercept signals from countries like India, Taiwan, Japan, South Korea and others. The PRC also established a Fourth Armed Forces Department in 1990 to look after offensive and defensive IW activities. It has also built "an information warfare simulation centre" for training its corps of network warriors. The centre uses high technology simulation skills and equipment to simulate information warfare and its environment. The Fourth Department has special detachments and units that manage and direct SIGINT and EW operations for the PLA at all levels and includes operations of the Air Force and the Navy.

The PRC has completed one million km of fibre optics line and communication infrastructure called "Eight Horizontal Grids and Eight Vertical Grids" supported by satellite, ground mobile receiving stations and ground to air data links. With technologies obtained from Western countries and by exploiting its booming commercial IT and telecommunications sector, it has improved the quality of its military programmes. The PLA has acquired and deployed a wide variety of air, sea and land-based intelligence, surveillance and reconnaissance (ISR) systems to enhance its ability to detect monitor and target military activities in Asia and West Pacific Ocean. Some of the latest programmes include electro-optics, synthetic aperture radar, over the horizon radars, and surveillance systems that can detect stealth aircraft.

EW is a key element in the PLA's 'Three Attacks and Three Defences' strategy (attack stealth aircraft, cruise missiles and helicopters; defend against precision strikes, electronic warfare, and enemy reconnaissance) to meet the requirements of 'local war under high tech conditions' which has now progressed to 'local war under informationalised conditions'. Both military and civil sectors are actively exploring IW concepts which could lead to developing a corps of network warriors to defend China's telecommunication, command and information networks while uncovering vulnerabilities of adversaries' networks.

At the national level, China has a C3I system based on fibre optic cables, satellite communications, micro-wave links, tropo-scatter communications and automated command and control systems. The PLA has both secured and non-secured telecommunications and has an army wide data communication network and integrated field operations communication system. Its WAN is capable of supporting peacetime operations within Chinese borders and limited pre-planned operations along China's periphery but is inadequate for large-scale joint operations.

The Chinese Army has a family of battlefield ELINT systems like DZ 9002 that detect, intercept, analyse and record an adversary's signal emissions. DZ 9001 has been developed both for defensive and offensive electronic counter measures (ECM). DZ 9300 is a man-packed radar reconnaissance system meant for special operations forces and rapid reaction forces. A bodyguard laser countermeasures system has also been developed to counter precision-guided munitions guided by laser emissions. There are also a variety of jamming systems with the ground forces.

The PLA Air Force is developing capabilities in airborne warning and control systems (AWACS), airborne early warning, and ECM aircraft and UAVs. Shaanxi Y-8 has been designed for special EW, ELINT and ECM missions. This aircraft was first observed in operation in the summer of 2004 and it is believed that some of its equipment may be from the US Navy's EP-3 ELINT aircraft that made an emergency landing in Hainan in April 2001. Another version of the Y-8 aircraft is 'Balance Beam' airborne early warning aircraft meant for tactical ISR, EW and ELINT missions. It made its maiden flight in 2001 and its finalised version Y-8 F600 flew in January 2005. The PLA Air Force is planning for 4-6 AWACS and has about 20 other dedicated ELINT aircraft like HD-5, TU-154M and HZ-6. HD-5, an older version, is being replaced by HZ-6 which has improved capabilities. UAV's configured for ELINT and EW missions are also in use. In July 2002, the PLA inducted the Israeli anti-radar hunter killer HARPY UAV. The Chinese Navy also has over a dozen ships and several trawlers for various electronic warfare missions. Four Yuan Wang and Shiyan class ships monitor space events and are capable of collecting and monitoring missile and satellite telemetry data and communications. Chinese industry has developed three types of systems, based on Soviet-era systems, which have been further upgraded and modernised.

Space is another area where the Chinese have been making rapid advances, especially in the field of ISR and anti-satellite technologies. China considers space as a 'commanding height' and it plans to control space and win the information war after having built up an informationalised PLA. In 2003, the PLA had six dual-use dedicated satellites for military purposes. In 2004, China placed 10 satellites into orbit and has a similar schedule through 2006. It hopes to have more than 100 satellites in orbit by 2010, and launch an additional 100 satellites by 2020. In the next decade, Beijing will most likely field radar, ocean surveillance, and improved filmbased photo-reconnaissance satellites. China will eventually deploy advanced imagery, reconnaissance, and Earth resource systems with military applications. China's ZY-2 payloads have digital imagery reconnaissance capabilities and have worldwide coverage. Beijing also tested new film-based imagery satellites and small digital imagery satellites in 2003 and 2004. It is also developing its own GPS navigation system based on the Beidou series of navigational satellites. The PLA possesses anti-GPS jammers obtained from Russia, which however may not be very effective against the NAVSAT satellite system of the US.

China is also developing electronic intelligence (ELINT) and signals intelligence (SIGINT) reconnaissance satellites. These digital data systems will be able to transmit directly to ground sites, and China may be developing a system of data relay satellites to support global coverage. Furthermore, Beijing has acquired mobile data reception equipment that can support more rapid data transmission to deployed military forces and units. China is developing micro satellites for remote sensing as well as for putting into place networks of electro-optical and radar satellites. In April 2004, Beijing launched a micro satellite with a probable imagery mission. China is also conducting research to develop ground-based laser ASAT Weapons. All these capabilities will contribute to China's prowess in the field of information warfare.

Implications for India

Attaining information superiority has become one of the most important objectives to be achieved in the era of knowledge age warfare. The concept of information superiority is somewhat analogous to similar concepts of air, sea or space superiority. This is because proper use of information is as lethal as other kinds of power. Further, the concept of information superiority leads us to attainment of decision superiority. Information operations are increasingly being considered as important as sea, land and air operations. Information operations can vary from physical destruction to psychological operations to computer network defence. Wellconducted joint information operations with new RMA technologies, improved organisations and doctrine will greatly contribute to a successful and decisive outcome.

It is in this context that a Defence Information Warfare Agency (DIWA) under the Integrated Defence Staff Headquarters has been formed to coordinate efforts of the three services and certain other agencies to handle all aspects of information warfare. The Indian concepts of IW are generally based on Western concepts and according to the 2004 Army Doctrine, IW encompasses the elements of command and control warfare, intelligencebased warfare, electronic warfare, cyber warfare, psychological warfare and network centric warfare, military deception and secrecy as well as media support. Though the three Services have different set ups for IW activity, DIWA is the nodal and apex policy-making body to formulate joint and integrated responses to IW challenges. Therefore, an IW doctrine needs to be formulated, which it is believed, is under the process of being evolved by DIWA. However, it is at operational levels that weaknesses in our IW efforts exist. There is a need for joint linkages and joint planning to synchronise our response to all elements of information warfare.

The Indian armed forces have made considerable progress in establishing C4ISR networks. But given that these are service wise, there is a need for establishing a Joint Inter-Services Network. The other areas that need attention are:

- In the era of cyber warfare, information warfare and net wars, information systems, both civil and military networks, should have adequate redundancy, survivability and electronic security.
- For optimisation, the strengths of our IT infrastructure and industry and advancements in satellites and radio-based systems should be jointly exploited by the military and civil sectors.
- Joint network and individual services networks should be able to function in all environments including nuclear. For instance, they should be hardened against or be resistant to an EMP attack.
- We need to induct a wide variety of military satellites for upgrading our strategic ISR, SIGINT, ELINT, COMMINT, imagery and navigation capabilities.
- We need to reflect on the Chinese model of net force based on their militia and examine whether there is a need to adopt a similar model in our Territorial Army units. Even though Computer Emergency Response Teams (CERT) at national and lower levels have been formed to respond to cyber attacks on civilian infrastructure, the concept is more defensive in nature. A pro-active concept like that of net force may be more appropriate.

THE AMERICAN AGE & MILITARY SPACE FORCE

Imagine that you were alive in the summer of 1900, living in London, then the capital of the world. Europe ruled the Eastern Hemisphere. There was hardly a place that, if not ruled directly, was not indirectly controlled from a European capital. Europe was at peace and enjoying unprecedented prosperity. Indeed, European interdependence due to trade and investment was so great that serious people were claiming that war had become impossible—and if not impossible, would end within weeks of beginning—because global financial markets couldn't withstand the strain. The future seemed fixed: a peaceful, prosperous Europe would rule the world.

Imagine yourself now in the summer of 1920. Europe had been torn apart by an agonizing war. The continent was in tatters. The Austro-Hungarian, Russian, German, and Ottoman empires were gone and millions had died in a war that lasted for years.

The war ended when an American army of a million men intervened—an army that came and then just as quickly left. Communism dominated Russia, but it was not clear that it could survive. Countries that had been on the periphery of European power, like the United States and Japan, suddenly emerged as great powers. But one thing was certain—the peace treaty that had been imposed on Germany guaranteed that it would not soon reemerge.

Imagine the summer of 1940. Germany had not only reemerged but conquered France and dominated Europe. Communism had survived and the Soviet Union now was allied with Nazi Germany. Great Britain alone stood against Germany, and from the point of view of most reasonable people, the war was over. If there was not to be a thousand-year Reich, then certainly Europe's fate had been decided for a century. Germany would dominate Europe and inherit its empire.

Imagine now the summer of 1960. Germany had been crushed in the war, defeated less than five years later. Europe was occupied, split down the middle by the United States and the Soviet Union. The European empires were collapsing, and the United States and Soviet Union were competing over who would be their heir. The United States had the Soviet Union surrounded and, with an overwhelming arsenal of nuclear weapons, could annihilate it in hours.

The United States had emerged as the global superpower. It dominated all of the world's oceans, and with its nuclear force could dictate terms to anyone in the world. Stalemate was the best the Soviets could hope for—unless the Soviets invaded Germany and conquered Europe. That was the war everyone was preparing for. And in the back of everyone's mind, the Maoist Chinese, seen as fanatical, were the other danger.

Now imagine the summer of 1980. The United States had been defeated in a seven-year war—not by the Soviet Union, but by communist North Vietnam. The nation was seen, and saw itself, as being in retreat. Expelled from Vietnam, it was then expelled from Iran as well, where the oil fields, which it no longer controlled, seemed about to fall into the hands of the Soviet Union. To contain the Soviet Union, the United States had formed an alliance with Maoist China—the American president and the Chinese chairman holding an amiable meeting in Beijing. Only this alliance seemed able to contain the powerful Soviet Union, which appeared to be surging.

Imagine now the summer of 2000. The Soviet Union had completely collapsed. China was still communist in name but had become capitalist in practice. NATO had advanced into Eastern Europe and even into the former Soviet Union. The world was prosperous and peaceful. Everyone knew that geopolitical considerations had become secondary to economic considerations, and the only problems were regional ones in basket cases like Haiti or Kosovo.

Then came September 11, 2001, and the world turned on its head again. At a certain level, when it comes to the future, the only thing one can be sure of is that common sense will be wrong.

There is no magic twenty-year cycle; there is no simplistic force governing this pattern. It is simply that the things that appear to be so permanent and dominant at any given moment in history can change with stunning rapidity. Eras come and go.

In international relations, the way the world looks right now is not at all how it will look in twenty years... or even less.

The fall of the Soviet Union was hard to imagine, and that is exactly the point. Conventional political analysis suffers from a profound failure of imagination. It imagines passing clouds to be permanent and is blind to powerful, long- term shifts taking place in full view of the world.

If we were at the beginning of the twentieth century, it would be impossible to forecast the particular events I've just listed. But there are some things that could have been—and, in fact, were—forecast. For example, it was obvious that Germany, having united in 1871, was a major power in an insecure position (trapped between Russia and France) and wanted to redefine the European and global systems. Most of the conflicts in the first half of the twentieth century were about Germany's status in Europe. While the times and places of wars couldn't be forecast, the probability that there would be a war could be and was forecast by many Europeans.

The harder part of this equation would be forecasting that the wars would be so devastating and that after the first and second world wars were over, Europe would lose its empire. But there were those, particularly after the invention of dynamite, who predicted that war would now be catastrophic. If the forecasting on technology had been combined with the forecasting on geopolitics, the shattering of Europe might well have been predicted.

Certainly the rise of the United States and Russia was predicted in the nineteenth century. Both Alexis de Tocqueville and Friedrich Nietzsche forecast the preeminence of these two countries. So, standing at the beginning of the twentieth century, it would have been possible to forecast its general outlines, with discipline and some luck. the twenty-first century

Standing at the beginning of the twenty-first century, we need to identify the single pivotal event for this century, the equivalent of German unification for the twentieth century. After the debris of the European empire is cleared away, as well as what's left of the Soviet Union, one power remains standing and overwhelmingly powerful. That power is the United States. Certainly, as is usually the case, the United

States currently appears to be making a mess of things around the world. But it's important not to be confused by the passing chaos. The United States is economically, militarily, and politically the most powerful country in the world, and there is no real challenger to that power.

Like the Spanish-American War, a hundred years from now the war between the United States and the radical Islamists will be little remembered regardless of the prevailing sentiment of this time.

Ever since the Civil War, the United States has been on an extraordinary economic surge. It has turned from a marginal developing nation into an economy bigger than the next four countries combined. Militarily, it has gone from being an insignificant force to dominating the globe. Politically, the United States touches virtually everything, sometimes intentionally and sometimes simply because of its presence. As you read this book, it will seem that it is America- centric, written from an American point of view. That may be true, but the argument I'm making is that the world does, in fact, pivot around the United States.

This is not only due to American power. It also has to do with a fundamental shift in the way the world works. For the past five hundred years, Europe was the center of the international system, its empires creating a single global system for the first time in human history. The main highway to Europe was the North Atlantic. Whoever controlled the North Atlantic controlled access to Europe—and Europe's access to the world. The basic geography of global politics was locked into place.

Then, in the early 1980s, something remarkable happened. For the first time in history, transpacific trade equaled transatlantic trade. With Europe reduced to a collection of secondary powers after World War II, and the shift in trade patterns, the North Atlantic was no longer the single key to anything. Now whatever country controlled both the North Atlantic and the Pacific could control, if it wished, the world's trading system, and therefore the global economy. In the twenty-first century, any nation located on both oceans has a tremendous advantage.

Given the cost of building naval power and the huge cost of deploying it around the world, the power native to both oceans became the preeminent actor in the international system for the same reason that Britain dominated the nineteenth century: it lived on the sea it had to control. In this way, North America has replaced Europe as the center of gravity in the world, and whoever dominates North America is virtually assured of being the dominant global power. For the twenty-first century at least, that will be the United States.

The inherent power of the United States coupled with its geographic position makes the United States the pivotal actor of the twenty-first century. That certainly doesn't make it loved. On the contrary, its power makes it feared. The history of the twenty-first century, therefore, particularly the first half, will revolve around two opposing struggles. One will be secondary powers forming coalitions to try to contain and control the United States. The second will be the United States acting preemptively to prevent an effective coalition from forming.

If we view the beginning of the twenty-first century as the dawn of the American Age (superseding the European Age), we see that it began with a group of Muslims seeking to re- create the Caliphate—the great Islamic empire that once ran from the Atlantic to the Pacific. Inevitably, they had to strike at the United States in an attempt to draw the world's primary power into war, trying to demonstrate its weakness in order to trigger an Islamic uprising. The United States responded by invading the Islamic world. But its goal wasn't victory. It wasn't even clear what victory would mean. Its goal was simply to disrupt the Islamic world and set it against itself, so that an Islamic empire could not emerge.

The United States doesn't need to win wars. It needs to simply disrupt things so the other side can't build up sufficient strength to challenge it. On one level, the twenty-first century will see a series of confrontations involving lesser powers trying to build coalitions to control American behavior and the United

States' mounting military operations to disrupt them. The twenty-first century will see even more war than the twentieth century, but the wars will be much less catastrophic, because of both technological changes and the nature of the geopolitical challenge.

As we've seen, the changes that lead to the next era are always shockingly unexpected, and the first twenty years of this new century will be no exception. The U.S.–Islamist war is already ending and the next conflict is in sight. Russia is re-creating its old sphere of influence, and that sphere of influence will inevitably challenge the United States. The Russians will be moving westward on the great northern European plain. As Russia reconstructs its power, it will encounter the U.S.-dominated NATO in the three Baltic countries—Estonia, Latvia, and Lithuania—as well as in Poland. There will be other points of friction in the early twenty-first century, but this new cold war will supply the flash points after the U.S.–Islamist war dies down.

The Russians can't avoid trying to reassert power, and the United States can't avoid trying to resist. But in the end Russia can't win. Its deep internal problems, massively declining population, and poor infrastructure ultimately make Russia's long- term survival prospects bleak. And the second cold war, less frightening and much less global than the first, will end as the first did, with the collapse of Russia.

There are many who predict that China is the next challenger to the United States, not Russia. I don't agree with that view for three reasons. First, when you look at a map of China closely, you see that it is really a very isolated country physically. With Siberia in the north, the Himalayas and jungles to the south, and most of China's population in the eastern part of the country, the Chinese aren't going to easily expand. Second, China has not been a major naval power for centuries, and building a navy requires a long time not only to build ships but to create well-trained and experienced sailors.

Third, there is a deeper reason for not worrying about China. China is inherently unstable. Whenever it opens its borders to the outside world, the coastal region becomes prosperous, but the vast majority of Chinese in the interior remain impoverished. This leads to tension, conflict, and instability. It also leads to economic decisions made for political reasons, resulting in inefficiency and corruption. This is not the first time that China has opened itself to foreign trade, and it will not be the last time that it becomes unstable as a result. Nor will it be the last time that a figure like Mao emerges to close the country off from the outside, equalize the wealth—or poverty—and begin the cycle anew. There are some who believe that the trends of the last thirty years will continue indefinitely. I believe the Chinese cycle will move to its next and inevitable phase in the coming decade. Far from being a challenger, China is a country the United States will be trying to bolster and hold together as a counterweight to the Russians. Current Chinese economic dynamism does not translate into long-term success.

In the middle of the century, other powers will emerge, countries that aren't thought of as great powers today, but that I expect will become more powerful and assertive over the next few decades. Three stand out in particular. The first is Japan. It's the second- largest economy in the world and the most vulnerable, being highly dependent on the importation of raw materials, since it has almost none of its own. With a history of militarism, Japan will not remain the marginal pacifistic power it has been. It cannot. Its own deep population problems and abhorrence of large- scale immigration will force it to look for new workers in other countries. Japan's vulnerabilities, which I've written about in the past and which the Japanese have managed better than I've expected up until this point, in the end will force a shift in policy.

Then there is Turkey, currently the seventeenth-largest economy in the world. Historically, when a major Islamic empire has emerged, it has been dominated by the Turks. The Ottomans collapsed at the end of World War I, leaving modern Turkey in its wake. But Turkey is a stable platform in the midst of chaos. The Balkans, the Caucasus, and the Arab world to the south are all unstable. As Turkey's power grows—and its economy and military are already the most powerful in the region—so will Turkish influence.

Finally there is Poland. Poland hasn't been a great power since the sixteenth century. But it once was—and, I think, will be again. Two factors make this possible. First will be the decline of Germany. Its economy is large and still growing, but it has lost the dynamism it has had for two centuries. In addition, its population is going to fall dramatically in the next fifty years, further undermining its economic power. Second, as the Russians press on the Poles from the east, the Germans won't have an appetite for a third war with Russia. The United States, however, will back Poland, providing it with massive economic and technical support. Wars—when your country isn't destroyed—stimulate economic growth, and Poland will become the leading power in a coalition of states facing the Russians.

Japan, Turkey, and Poland will each be facing a United States even more confident than it was after the second fall of the Soviet Union. That will be an explosive situation. As we will see during the course of this book, the relationships among these four countries will greatly affect the twenty-first century, leading, ultimately, to the next global war. This war will be fought differently from any in history—with weapons that are today in the realm of science fiction. But as I will try to outline, this mid-twenty-first century conflict will grow out of the dynamic forces born in the early part of the new century.

Tremendous technical advances will come out of this war, as they did out of World War II, and one of them will be especially critical. All sides will be looking for new forms of energy to substitute for hydrocarbons, for many obvious reasons. Solar power is theoretically the most efficient energy source on earth, but solar power requires massive arrays of receivers. Those receivers take up a lot of space on the earth's surface and have many negative environmental impacts—not to mention being subject to the disruptive cycles of night and day. During the coming global war, however, concepts developed prior to the war for space- based electrical generation, beamed to earth in the form of microwave radiation, will be rapidly translated from prototype to reality. Getting a free ride on the back of military space launch capability, the new energy source will be underwritten in much the same way as the Internet or the railroads were, by government support. And that will kick off a massive economic boom.

But underlying all of this will be the single most important fact of the twenty-first century: the end of the population explosion. By 2050, advanced industrial countries will be losing population at a dramatic rate. By 2100, even the most underdeveloped countries will have reached birthrates that will stabilize their populations. The entire global system has been built since 1750 on the expectation of continually expanding populations. More workers, more consumers, more soldiers—this was always the expectation. In the twenty-first century, however, that will cease to be true. The entire system of production will shift. The shift will force the world into a greater dependence on technology—particularly robots that will substitute for human labor, and intensified genetic research (not so much for the purpose of extending life but to make people productive longer).

What will be the more immediate result of a shrinking world population? Quite simply, in the first half of the century, the population bust will create a major labor shortage in advanced industrial countries. Today, developed countries see the problem as keeping immigrants out. Later in the first half of the twenty-first century, the problem will be persuading them to come. Countries will go so far as to pay people to move there. This will include the United States, which will be competing for increasingly scarce immigrants and will be doing everything it can to induce Mexicans to come to the United States—an ironic but inevitable shift.

These changes will lead to the final crisis of the twenty-first century. Mexico currently is the fifteenth-largest economy in the world. As the Europeans slip out, the Mexicans, like the Turks, will rise in the rankings until by the late twenty-first century they will be one of the major economic powers in the world. During the great migration north encouraged by the United States, the population balance in the old Mexican Cession (that is, the areas of the United States taken from Mexico in the nineteenth century) will shift dramatically until much of the region is predominantly Mexican. The social reality will be viewed by the Mexican government simply as rectification of historical defeats. By 2080 I expect there to be a serious confrontation between the United States and an increasingly powerful and assertive Mexico. That confrontation may well have unforeseen consequences for the United States, and will likely not end by 2100.

Much of what I've said here may seem pretty hard to fathom. The idea that the twenty-first century will culminate in a confrontation between Mexico and the United States is certainly hard to imagine in 2009, as is a powerful Turkey or Poland. But go back to the beginning of this chapter, when I described how the world looked at twenty-year intervals during the twentieth century, and you can see what I'm driving at: common sense is the one thing that will certainly be wrong. Obviously, the more granular the description, the less reliable it gets. It is impossible to forecast precise details of a coming century—apart from the fact that I'll be long dead by then and won't know what mistakes I made.

But it's my contention that it is indeed possible to see the broad outlines of what is going to happen, and to try to give it some definition, however speculative that definition might be. That's what this book is about.

Before I delve into any details of global wars, population trends, or technological shifts, it is important that I address my method—that is, precisely how I can forecast what I do. I don't intend to be taken seriously on the details of the war in 2050 that I forecast. But I do want to be taken seriously in terms of how wars will be fought then, about the centrality of American power, about the likelihood of other countries challenging that power, and about some of the countries I think will—and won't—challenge that power.

And doing that takes some justification. The idea of a U.S.–Mexican confrontation and even war will leave most reasonable people dubious, but I would like to demonstrate why and how these assertions can be made. One point I've already made is that reasonable people are incapable of anticipating the future. The old New Left slogan "Be Practical, Demand the Impossible" needs to be changed: "Be Practical, Expect the Impossible." This idea is at the heart of my method. From another, more substantial perspective, this is called geopolitics.

Geopolitics is not simply a pretentious way of saying "international relations." It is a method for thinking about the world and forecasting what will happen down the road. Economists talk about an invisible hand, in which the self-interested, short-term activities of people lead to what Adam Smith called "the wealth of nations." Geopolitics applies the concept of the invisible hand to the behavior of nations and other international actors. The pursuit of short-term self-interest by nations and by their leaders leads, if not to the wealth of nations, then at least to predictable behavior and, therefore, the ability to forecast the shape of the future international system.

Geopolitics and economics both assume that the players are rational, at least in the sense of knowing their own short-term self-interest. As rational actors, reality provides them with limited choices. It is assumed that, on the whole, people and nations will pursue their self-interest, if not flawlessly, then at least not randomly. Think of a chess game. On the surface, it appears that each player has twenty potential opening moves. In fact, there are many fewer because most of these moves are so bad that they quickly lead to defeat. The better you are at chess, the more clearly you see your options, and the fewer moves there actually are available. The better the player, the more predictable the moves. The grandmaster plays with absolute predictable precision—until that one brilliant, unexpected stroke.

Nations behave the same way. The millions or hundreds of millions of people who make up a nation are constrained by reality. They generate leaders who would not become leaders if they were irrational. Climbing to the top of millions of people is not something fools often do. Leaders understand their menu of next moves and execute them, if not flawlessly, then at least pretty well. An occasional master will come along with a stunningly unexpected and successful move, but for the most part, the act of governance is simply executing the necessary and logical next step. When politicians run a country's foreign policy, they operate the same way. If a leader dies and is replaced, another emerges and more likely than not continues what the first one was doing.

I am not arguing that political leaders are geniuses, scholars, or even gentlemen and ladies. Simply, political leaders know how to be leaders or they wouldn't have emerged as such. It is the delight of all societies to belittle their political leaders, and leaders surely do make mistakes.

But the mistakes they make, when carefully examined, are rarely stupid. More likely, mistakes are forced on them by circumstance. We would all like to believe that we— or our favorite candidate—would never have acted so stupidly. It is rarely true. Geopolitics therefore does not take the individual leader very seriously, any more than economics takes the individual businessman too seriously. Both are players who know how to manage a process but are not free to break the very rigid rules of their professions. Politicians are therefore rarely free actors. Their actions are determined by circumstances, and public policy is a response to reality. Within narrow margins, political decisions can matter. But the most brilliant leader of Iceland will never turn it into a world power, while the stupidest leader of Rome at its height could not undermine Rome's fundamental power.

Geopolitics is not about the right and wrong of things, it is not about the virtues or vices of politicians, and it is not about foreign policy debates. Geopolitics is about broad impersonal forces that constrain nations and human beings and compel them to act in certain ways. The key to understanding economics is accepting that there are always unintended consequences.

Actions people take for their own good reasons have results they don't envision or intend. The same is true with geopolitics.

It is doubtful that the village of Rome, when it started its expansion in the seventh century BC, had a master plan for conquering the Mediterranean world five hundred years later. But the first action its inhabitants took against neighboring villages set in motion a process that was both constrained by reality and filled with unintended consequences. Rome wasn't planned, and neither did it just happen.

Geopolitical forecasting, therefore, doesn't assume that everything is predetermined. It does mean that what people think they are doing, what they hope to achieve, and what the final outcome is are not the same things.

Nations and politicians pursue their immediate ends, as constrained by reality as a grandmaster is constrained by the chessboard, the pieces, and the rules. Sometimes they increase the power of the nation. Sometimes they lead the nation to catastrophe. It is rare that the final outcome will be what they initially intended to achieve.

Geopolitics assumes two things. First, it assumes that humans organize themselves into units larger than families, and that by doing this, they must engage in politics. It also assumes that humans have a natural loyalty to the things they were born into, the people and the places.

Loyalty to a tribe, a city, or a nation is natural to people. In our time, national identity matters a great deal. Geopolitics teaches that the relationship between these nations is a vital dimension of human life, and that means that war is ubiquitous. Second, geopolitics assumes that the character of a nation is determined to a great extent by geography, as is the relationship between nations. We use the term geography broadly. It includes the physical characteristics of a location, but it goes beyond that to look at the effects of a place on individuals and communities. In antiquity, the difference between Sparta and Athens was the difference between a landlocked city and a maritime empire. Athens was wealthy and cosmopolitan, while Sparta was poor, provincial, and very tough. A Spartan was very different from an Athenian in both culture and politics.

If you understand those assumptions, then it is possible to think about large numbers of human beings, linked together through natural human bonds, constrained by geography, acting in certain ways. The United States is the United States and therefore must behave in a certain way. The same goes for Japan or Turkey or Mexico. When you drill down and see the forces that are shaping nations, you can see that the menu from which they choose is limited.

The twenty-first century will be like all other centuries. There will be wars, there will be poverty, there will be triumphs and defeats. There will be tragedy and good luck. People will go to work, make money, have children, fall in love, and come to hate. That is the one thing that is not cyclical. It is the permanent human condition.

But the twenty-first century will be extraordinary in two senses: it will be the beginning of a new age, and it will see a new global power astride the world. That doesn't happen very often. We are now in an America-centric age.

To understand this age, we must understand the United States, not only because it is so powerful but because its culture will permeate the world and define it. Just as French culture and British culture were definitive during their times of power, so American culture, as young and barbaric as it is, will define the way the world thinks and lives. So studying the twenty-first century means studying the United States.

If there were only one argument I could make about the twenty-first century, it would be that the European Age has ended and that the North American Age has begun, and that North America will be dominated by the United States for the next hundred years.

The events of the twenty-first century will pivot around the United States. That doesn't guarantee that the United States is necessarily a just or moral regime. It certainly does not mean that America has yet developed a mature civilization. It does mean that in many ways the history of the United States will be the history of the twenty-first century.

Top to bottom overhaul replaces hodgepodge of systems with state-of-the-art, coordinated technology plan Unity and simplicity are moving to the Pentagon. After more than 50 years of accumulating individual communications technologies to meet information distribution needs, the military headquarters is following the lead of its individual services and is well on its way, on time and on budget, to creating a joint and integrated information technology system.

The renovation effort, while incorporating today's most current technologies, is also leaving avenues open for technologies yet to be developed. The design, which initially features separate systems for voice, data and video, will ultimately be collapsed into a single backbone. New network administration technologies will reduce the time required to monitor and repair systems.

But plans call for more than just capabilities to be combined. When the transformation is complete, the current individual U.S. Army, Navy, Air Force and Marine Corps systems will operate as a joint system, and advances in technology could bring the existing four security backbones into a single environment with separation taking place at the faceplate instead of the backbone.

Mindful of the rapid pace of technology change as well as personal preferences, planners view flexibility as crucial to systems being designed to fulfill the needs of Pentagon residents well into the next century.

Asynchronous transfer mode (ATM) is at the core of the architecture, but edge devices will allow users to employ their own preferences including token ring, fiber distributed data interface, transmission control protocol/Internet protocol or even ATM.

Multiple local area networks (LANs), both classified and unclassified, will be replaced by a single backbone for each security level. The current 22 red secure and black general-purpose switches will be reduced to eight. Two cable television systems will be combined into a single system.

The 11 general-purpose and three command and control automated data processing centers will be consolidated into two general-purpose centers and one command and control center. Work now conducted in two radio rooms will be managed in one room, and a consolidated message support center will replace three message centers now in place. Command and operations centers will be collocated in the Pentagon basement. Videoconferencing capabilities will be designed and implemented on one set of standards so they are uniform throughout the building for both desktop and large conferencing functions.

The Army's information management and telecommunications (IM&T) project management office is spearheading the effort. GTE Government Systems, Arlington, Virginia, is the primary contractor for the renovation on the above-ground telecommunications backbone. The firm leads a team of 11 subcontractors and two electronic equipment suppliers, under a contract valued at approximately $110 million for work to be conducted during the next 10 years.

Col. Robert A. Kirsch II, USA, IM&T project manager, says that, while the team is exploring emergent technologies, at this point only well-established techniques are being incorporated into the plan.

"The only experimentation we are willing to do is outside of the implementation of the renovation. We're doing a lot of that. We are looking at technology that is coming down the pipe. But we're interested in doing state-of-the-art [technology] that we know is mature enough to provide the user capabilities that are required, but it is not so state-of-the-art that there are potential pitfalls that we might encounter because it hadn't been fully tested," Col. Kirsch notes.

"As time goes by, we have the ability to upgrade the active components. The passive infrastructure we're installing is being implemented in such a way that allows us to implement for the next 50 years, because we use both multimode and single-mode fiber as the sole path for the backbone and twisted pairs going out from the edge device to the users for telecommunications," he adds.

Although the information technology renovation is a current focus, the monumental task of updating the Pentagon's top five floors actually began several years ago. The project was divided into five wedges.

Temporary quarters have been set up in three buildings in nearby Rosslyn and Crystal City and in nonrenovation areas of the Pentagon to act as swing space. Each location is equipped with information technology systems that allow personnel from the section undergoing renovations to continue to communicate with workers not affected by the construction.

Consolidation of the numerous systems that have arisen over the years is at the center of the work. Much of the existing twisted pair wire, fiber optic and coaxial cables are unstructured and unmapped, with only the individual agencies being aware of the layout of their own wires.

Col. Kirsch estimates that as much as 50 percent are not being used, and many times active wiring is not identified until repairs are required. After the renovation is complete, this will no longer be the case, he adds.

Administration of the systems is also being consolidated. Information technology management now conducted in seven technical control facilities will be accomplished in one primary location, and multiple network management centers will be replaced with a single center.

In addition, to address the problem of accumulated wiring systems that have been installed for additional capabilities in the last several decades, a highly structured implementation system has been put in place.

The Pentagon's physical construction of poured concrete has so far been an advantage in this part of the effort. The structure can be gutted down to the concrete, whereby new conduit and cable trays will be installed. Contractors will place new fiber and twisted pair cables as required. The well-documented installation will enable future capabilities to be added either by employing existing infrastructure that is not in use or by putting new wiring in place as needed, the colonel explains. Initial plans call for four physically separate networks, one for each security level of unclassified, secret, top secret and sensitive compartmented information. Each backbone is designed using a synchronous optical network, or SONET, ring, ATM switches and frame switches. The equipment will be centrally located in communications equipment rooms and telecommunications closets.

ATM technology was chosen because the renovation team believes it will enable additional capabilities as technologies evolve. "The objective is to integrate voice, data and video onto a single backbone as technology becomes available," Sajeel Ahmed, IM&T senior systems engineer, explains.

"On the user side, this could mean telephones integrated with computers—one device instead of two—and desktop video from the same network, running through one pipe. The technology is not there just yet, but that's what we're shooting for." Some of these technologies are still being developed in laboratories; they are not economical to install at this time or the quality of service is currently not at the level required, he adds.

Dependability and life-cycle costs were also substantial considerations in designing the new systems. They are two of the reasons commercial off-the-shelf technologies are being used. "We want to put something in that is mature," Robert W. Morris, IM&T product manager for information technology systems, explains. "We want the U.S. commercial world to be using this before we go to it.

"When we designed the backbone, we looked at concerns and design considerations, laid it out over the life cycle, and tried to figure out which ones were most important and had the most lasting effects.

We determined that the most important consideration was adequate, powered, conditioned space. The next thing was the pathways to connect those spaces, then the media itself in terms of what kinds of fiber. The next piece was the hardware, the switches themselves, then finally the software that rides those switches. Each one has a shorter and shorter life cycle. Technology changes every 18 months. We can just change the switch or modify software," Morris relates.

The nature of Pentagon operations influenced these choices. "In the building, users move around a lot, or new groups form quickly for crises," Ahmed explains.

"We had to implement something so that we can reconfigure the backbone or a piece of the backbone quickly so it is all part of the infrastructure instead of running more cables. Instead of building four separate infrastructures, we have one physical infrastructure, but we are using virtual LAN technology to keep traffic separate between organizations. This also allows us to reconfigure the network quickly as requirements change." "From the data backbone perspective, it is the ultimate purple system," Col. Kirsch adds. "Security is a concern. Current technology does not allow us to collapse all levels of classification into a single backbone.

We are headed in that direction and the ability will be there in the future using things like fast-lane technology, which provides ATM encryption." Under current design plans, equipment from each security level shares physical space with a separate fiber path for each of them down to the faceplate.

If technology advances occur during the renovation period that would allow a single backbone to be used for all security levels, it would be incorporated into the system; however, separation would still be necessary at the faceplate level, the colonel says. Continued interoperability between currently available and future technology has been key in the overall design of the renovation program. GTE's contract includes wedge-one work with options for wedges two through five.

The company has been given total latitude in providing the solutions for requirements that the IM&T team has identified as part of the architecture. "In wedge two, when [GTE] resubmits its architecture and wedge design, if it chooses to go to different subcontractors for hardware, it would be responsible for demonstrating interoperability and integration between those devices," Morris says. "If new technology comes up in the next 10 years, we will look at that," Col. Kirsch adds. "If it causes us to change the architecture, we would change and GTE would implement active components that would allow us to move to that technology."

The company is required to update and resubmit infrastructure and design plans every two years, taking into account any changes in technology, reviewing systems already installed, and forecasting future advances.

"From the user's perspective, there won't be anything unique that you can't or won't be able to do then. The renovation is not designed to provide a Cadillac for a solid Ford. We are providing state-of-the-art capability that is well structured, well defined, well architected and well implemented," the colonel maintains.

"If the user has three data drops and a telephone now, that's what he or she will get. This individual won't get more. We're not providing additional capability; we're meeting users' current requirements. But we are building infrastructure for the next 50 years, so if a user's requirements go from three to five, we will be able to provide additional drops," he adds. To ensure room for growth, 50 percent spare capacity was included in the initial assessment. The renovation program team also conducts industry forums to receive expert input about architecture.

THE SOVIET UNION AND OUTER SPACE

In spite of the non-weapon character of American satellite systems and efforts to demonstrate that the United States space program is purely peaceful in nature, the Soviets have maintained a persistent and intense political attack against American activities in space. American reconnaissance satellites came to be widely discussed as the possible successors to the U-2, and in June, 1960, Khrushchev told a Bucharest audience that Russia would "paralyze" other American espionage activities, apparently referring to the so-called "spy in the sky" satellites. Since that time there has been nothing in Soviet behavior to suggest that the Kremlin has grown less sensitive to American reconnaissance efforts. Even the Tiros weather satellites and other civilian programs have called forth Russian condemnation of American espionage and militarism.

At the United Nations the controversy over permissible and impermissible activities in space has come to focus on United States reconnaissance satellites. Western nations have consistently defended space reconnaissance and surveillance activities, while the Soviet bloc has bitterly denounced them as intolerable violations of the sovereign right of secrecy.

Communist representatives have also raised the specter of accidental war by stressing the danger that a false alarm by an early-warning satellite could trigger an American attack. Delegates from the Soviet bloc have further demanded that navigational satellites be used solely to guide merchant vessels and not to assist military ships or planes. Regardless of the American contention that our space program is peaceful and does not threaten any nation, the Russians clearly do not see it that way. While castigating the United States for its alleged devotion to militarizing outer space, the Soviet Union has persistently sought to convince the world that its own space efforts are purely peaceful and dedicated to the good of all mankind. At the same time, the Russians have very successfully exploited their accomplishments in space to build an image of military might on earth.

Apprehension about the military implications of Soviet activities in space centers essentially in two areas: are the Russians developing an antisatellite capability, and are they working on bombardment satellites? The consistent threats to paralyze United States reconnaissance and surveillance satellites suggest that the Soviets may indeed be seriously engaged in devising a satellite interceptor and that they are very likely to use it. Although Soviet warnings are generally vague, and although the Russians also have expressed interest in frustrating American intelligence efforts by camouflaging potential targets and by constructing sham installations to deceive photography from space, they may prefer direct action against the offending satellites.

The threats gain additional credence from reported Soviet progress in related areas of military technology. In October, 1961, Marshal Rodion Malinovsky, the Russian Defense Minister, claimed that "the problem of destroying rockets in flight has been successfully solved." Some months later Premier Khrushchev boasted that his rocket forces could hit a fly in space. Commenting on this claim recently, President Kennedy seemed to concede that the Russians might be able to hit one fly, but he questioned whether they could counter a whole swarm of flies coming from many directions simultaneously. The implication was that the United States government credits the Soviets with considerable success in destroying discrete targets but doubts that they could meet a full-scale missile barrage.

It seems reasonable to deduce that Soviet progress in anti-missile technology is applicable in several respects to satellite interception, at least in the case of low-altitude targets. Moreover, since there are relatively few satellites and satellite orbits are more predictable than missile trajectories, the task of killing a satellite appears on the surface to be considerably more tractable than that of destroying a flock of incoming warheads.

Some commentators have seen another approach to satellite interception in the near rendezvous of the Vostoks III and IV last summer. The spacecraft are thought to have come within about three miles of one another, a range at which even a relatively simple weapon would probably have been effective. A co-orbital approach to satellite interception would, of course, be extremely expensive, and few authorities believe this to be a likely technique for Soviet anti-satellite operations. The Soviets might, however, want to rendezvous with an American satellite in order to capture the device. Once the satellite was returned to earth, Russian technicians could gain detailed knowledge of American satellite technology and learn how effective the satellites really are. For instance, the Kremlin would no doubt pay dearly to know just what sort of pictures U.S. reconnaissance satellites are capable of obtaining.

At any rate, the unclassified evidence about possible Soviet anti-satellite efforts, though slight, is susceptible of ominous interpretations. The Russians have left no doubt that they find a number of American satellites highly offensive, and they may soon have the technical capability to do something about these annoying devices. But what about the possibility that the Russians will perfect and deploy some sort of bombardment satellite?

The paramount fact is that the Soviets already have placed in orbit several enormous payloads, the Vostok satellites, which seem large enough to serve as space bombers. These vehicles are said to weigh well over 10,000 pounds, and some press reports have cited Russian payloads of up to 14,000 pounds. By comparison, the American Mercury capsules for manned space flight weigh roughly 3000 pounds. In addition, recent months have seen the Soviets explore a variety of new orbits, including some which provide maximum satellite coverage of the United States.

Not only is the awesome size of the Vostoks the subject of much speculation; the satellites have been surrounded by a number of quite explicit Soviet claims of their military significance. In the wake of cosmonaut Titov's flight in Vostok II during August, 1961, Premier Khrushchev said, "We placed Gagarin and Titov in space, and we can replace them with bombs that can be diverted to any place on earth." In the midst of the Cuban crisis of last October, the Soviet Premier pointedly listed spaceships among the "deadly weapons" whose existence made a peaceful solution of the dispute imperative. And Marshal Malinovsky underlined the military implications of Vostoks III and IV when, in a message to the twin cosmonauts he added, "Let our enemies know what techniques and what soldiers our Soviet power disposes of." Most recently, the commander in chief of Soviet strategic rocket forces, Marshal Biryuzov, injected a new degree of explicitness into the crescendo of threats. declaring, "It has now become possible at a command from earth to launch rockets from satellites at any desirable time and at any point in the satellite's trajectory." It is known that the Russians have indeed fired rockets from satellites to launch space probes, but the deliberate ambiguity of the marshal's statement was no doubt intended to suggest that targets on earth could also be reached by such rockets.

Do these declarations mean that the Vostoks are actually prototypes of orbital bombers? Too little is known of the satellites to offer a firm conclusion on that issue, but Western defense experts have generally agreed that space bombers are feasible. The main question has been whether bombardment satellites offer sufficient advantages to justify the great expense of developing and deploying them, particularly when effective and cheaper alternatives are available. In this country the Department of Defense has felt that existing or planned delivery systems are adequate to the nation's strategic needs and that there is no "clear and urgent military requirement" to work on bombardment satellites. This seems a sensible conclusion for a country with overwhelming strategic superiority, but does the situation look the same from the Russian point of view? On our answer to that question hinge some critical decisions which will have a grave influence on the security of the free world.

We are now reasonably confident that, in spite of their early achievements in testing intercontinental ballistic missiles, the Soviets have not deployed operational missiles as rapidly as the United States. In terms of strategic missiles, the Soviets must concede a long period of inferiority to the West. Since they have no prospect of overtaking the United States in the numbers of deployed missiles, additions to the Russian missile inventory offer only marginal political and strategic advantage.

But a breakthrough into space-based strategic weapons might give the Soviets phenomenal returns on their investment, especially since the basic technology for such a deployment already has been provided by their research on large rockets and space vehicles. The Soviets could count on the novelty of bombardment satellites to shape the popular perception of the strategic balance and to inspire still greater respect for Russian military prowess. In terms of technological and military prestige, space bombers might well appear more attractive to the Kremlin than mere increments to Soviet missile forces. With their keen appreciation of the political utility of novel weapons, the Soviets could view bombardment satellites as promising tools of blackmail, even if they did not fundamentally alter the balance of strategic power.

In military terms alone, the development of orbital bombers might appeal to the Soviets. First of all, warheads de-orbited from satellites could reach their targets so quickly that a defending nation would lose the precious minutes of warning for which the United States has purchased such costly facilities as the Ballistic Missile Early Warning System. Still more threatening in this respect would be systems which did not require that warheads be delivered to a specific target on earth. Donald Brennan has suggested that devices of several hundred megatons in yield could be detonated in orbit at altitudes comparable to those at which the Vostoks fly. Depending on weather conditions, such a weapon might set fire to much of a continent, approaching the ultimate in instantaneous devastation.

If the Soviets could bypass BMEWS and other warning systems, soft targets like airfields and naval installations would become even more vulnerable to thermonuclear attack than they are at present. Civil defense efforts would be rendered futile. Among other psychological effects, the Russians could hope that the appearance of bombardment satellites would seriously undermine Western morale. The special political and military advantages of bombardment satellites, even if rather more costly than other forces, could prove decisive to Soviet strategic planners. One factor in the surprisingly slow growth of Russian missile strength may be the progress of Soviet technology toward an operational bombardment satellite.

AMERICAN SPACE STRATEGY

There is a strong American consensus in support of the basic elements of national space policy. The world will be a much safer place if we can succeed in maintaining space as a sanctuary for purely peaceful activities. But how do we keep the arms race from spreading to this new arena?

Presently the United States hopes to accomplish this noble purpose by a declared policy of abstaining from developing space weapons. While pressing for international agreement on the peaceful use of space, we promise the Soviets that we will refrain from orbiting weapons of mass destruction so long as they do not station such devices in space. At the same time, our emphasis is on unimpeded free access to space for non-weapon satellites, including some to which the Soviets strenuously object. But, sad to say, our dedication to peaceful activities in space, together with our repeated assurances to the Soviets that the United States will never begin a space arms race, may frustrate our search for a satisfactory understanding on permissible activities in space.

By voluntarily and unilaterally forgoing precautionary development of space weapons, especially anti-satellite systems and bombardment satellites, we remove the major incentive for the Soviets to come to terms on an arms-control treaty for space. Since the United States is abstaining from serious research on space weapons anyway, the Russians do not face a threat from that quarter, except insofar as they consider themselves menaced by American reconnaissance and surveillance satellites. So long as there is no inspection agreement and the United States refrains from substantial research on the military uses of space, the Soviets are free to test and possibly to deploy various military space systems at minimum risk.

In negotiations regarding space the United States has already given the Russians the very prize for which we propose to negotiate. The Soviets enjoy adequate security that the United States will not use space for deployment of weapons, while the United States has no comparable guarantees from the Soviets. From Moscow's point of view, there is no need to negotiate in earnest for arms control in space. This seems to be a recurring pattern in Soviet-American relations. In its eagerness to demonstrate its good faith, the United States has time and again foolishly squandered its diplomatic capital. In Korea a hint of Communist willingness to discuss armistice terms led the United States to suspend its increasingly successful military operations, the principal factor which had brought the Chinese and North Koreans to the armistice table. With the pressure off, the Communists were able to regroup their forces and to drag out the negotiations interminably. In order to promote a nuclear-test-ban treaty, the United States entered into the test moratorium. Since the Western powers were not testing anyway, the Soviets had no need for a formal agreement; instead they were encouraged to prolong the discussions indefinitely while secret research and test preparations wiped out the Western lead in nuclear weapons technology. The United States has yet to comprehend that most painful paradox of the cold war: concessions may sometimes be fatal to the success of negotiations, especially when those concessions involve the substance of the issue at stake.

A vital question for American policy makers in the months ahead is whether we are committing the same mistake in negotiations concerning space. There is no assurance that American restraint in the development of space weapons will evoke similar behavior on the part of the Soviets. Indeed, current political and technical trends make it seem more likely that the Russians will regard space weapons as highly advantageous, both politically and militarily.

It may be that in order to protect American satellites from Soviet anti-satellite operations, which seem only too probable in the case of American reconnaissance satellites, the United States must also possess satellite interceptors with which to threaten reprisals against Soviet satellites. Similarly, should Soviet bombardment satellites materialize as a threat, the United States may urgently need an effective anti-satellite system or possibly bombardment satellites of its own with which to bargain for mutual withdrawal of strategic forces from space. It has even been suggested that some space-based systems might be able to neutralize ground-based missiles. If so, the

United States may yet require space-based weapons itself in order to maintain its deterrent posture.

It is a truism that successful negotiation requires a mutuality of interest among the parties. In efforts to achieve preventive arms control in space or elsewhere, the mutuality must reside in a recognition of common danger. The swelling chorus of demands for an increased military space effort by the United States stems not from repudiation of the worthy American goal of a demilitarized space but from a feeling that the potential dangers of military exploitation of space technology are much too one-sided in the present circumstances. A serious and substantial military space program by the United States may be necessary to induce the Soviets to enter into adequately verifiable agreements reserving space for peaceful activities. Only by making sure that the dangers of hostile use of space are mutual can we be confident of ensuring reciprocal restraint in the deployment of space weapons and of preserving a stable strategic balance on earth.

FRANCE AND THE EUROPEAN SPACE AGENCY

France worked on the Hermes manned spaceplane launched by Ariane rocket in the late 20th century, and proposed in January 1985 to go through with Hermes development under the auspices of the ESA. Hopper was one of several proposals for a European reusable launch vehicle (RLV) planned to cheaply ferry satellites into orbit by 2015. One of those was 'Phoenix', a German project which is a one-seventh scale model of the Hopper concept vehicle. The suborbital Hopper was a FESTIP (Future European Space Transportation Investigations Programme) system study designA test project, the Intermediate eXperimental Vehicle (IXV), has demonstrated lifting reentry technologies and will be extended under the PRIDE programme.

Japan

HOPE was a Japanese experimental spaceplane project designed by a partnership between NASDA and NAL (both now part of JAXA), started in the 1980s. It was positioned for most of its lifetime as one of the main Japanese contributions to the International Space Station, the other being the Japanese Experiment Module. The project was eventually cancelled in 2003, by which point test flights of a sub-scale testbed had flown successfully.

Germany

After the German Sänger-Bredt RaBo and Silbervogel of the 1930s and 1940s, Eugen Sänger worked for time on various space plane projects, coming up with several designs for Messerschmitt-Bölkow-Blohm such as the MBB Raumtransporter-8. In the 1980s, West Germany funded design work on the MBB Sänger II with the Hypersonic Technology Program. Development continued on MBB/Deutsche Aerospace Sänger II/HORUS until the late 1980s when it was canceled. Germany went on to participate in the Ariane rocket, Columbus space station and Hermes spaceplane of ESA, Spacelab of ESA-NASA and *Deutschland* missions (non-U.S. funded Space Shuttle flights with Spacelab). The Sänger II had predicted cost savings of up to 30 percent over expendable rockets. The Daimler-Chrysler Aerospace RLV was a much later small reusable spaceplane prototype for ESA FLPP/FLTP program.

India

AVATAR is an early-2000s concept of a mannedsingle-stage reusable spaceplane capable of horizontal takeoff and landing, by India's Defense Research and Development Organization, the Indian Space Research Organization (ISRO) and other research institutions, intended for both military and civilian satellite launches. The ISRO plans to test the concept with a scaled-down suborbital Reusable Launch Vehicle-Technology Demonstrator (RLV-TD) spaceplane in 2015, and aims to fly the full prototype by 2025.

China

Shenlong is a proposed Chinese robotic space plane that is similar to the American Boeing X-37. Only a few images have been released since late 2007.

7

Global Cybersecurity Challenges

CYBERSECURITY AWARENESS IN INDIA

The Internet connects approximately 2.7 billion people around the world. Spread of Internet of things could result in 75 billion devices connected to the web by 2020i. India is recording the fastest growth for internet usage. It is the third largest user of the Internet and the numbers are likely to increase exponentially with the implementation of the Digital India Programme. Indians are believed to be generally aware of the need for security of their assets and invest in multiple types of antivirus softwares. The government as well as private organisations have evolved several measures. In addition, the Digital India Programme is likely to create a better eco system for cybersecurity in India.

Manifested Cybersecurity Challenges

Cybersecurity is a major concern, as attackers require a small investment and operate under a cover of anonymity. It offers an easy method to potentially cripple industry, academia, government, as well as the military in the domains of air, land, maritime, and space. It is hence emerging as an important tool in both irregular and conventional conflicts. Adversaries include both state and non-state actors, ranging from amateur to highly trained professional hackers. Cybersecurity concerns have reached such dimensions that in September 2015, in a summit meeting, US and China signed an agreement stating that neither government will conduct or knowingly support cyber-enabled theft of intellectual property, including trade secrets or other confidential business information for commercial advantageii.

In the recent past, the US had planned to carry out a massive cyberattack on Iran's nuclear and infrastructure facilities in case of failure of the nuclear deal negotiationsiii. The plan codenamed Nitro Zeus was intended as a follow-up to Olympic Games, the code name of a cyberattack carried out jointly by the US and Israel that destroyed 1,000 centrifuges and temporarily disrupted production at Iran's uranium enrichment facility at Natanz. Iran on its part had employed its Revolutionary Guards for siphoning off several million dollars from 50 US banks from 2011 to 2013 and had gained access to the SCADA system of a dam in Manhattan, which could have imperiled public safetyiv. Seven Iranian firms were indicted in the US on 24 Mar 2016 for cyber crimes.

A recently published report by data-mining experts from the University of Maryland and Virginia Tech ranks India among the nations most vulnerable to serious cyberattacksv. Denmark, Norway and Finland were ranked among the best protected and the US was ranked the 11th safest of the 44 nations studied. Cyberattacks on India have increased from about 13,000 in 2011 to more than 70,000 by the end of 2015. Most attacks are reported to be originating from countries such as China, Pakistan, Bangladesh, Turkey, Algeria, UAE, Brazil, US, and Europe. A high-profile cyberattack on 12 July 2012 breached the email accounts of about 12,000 people, including officials from the Ministry of External Affairs (MEA) and Ministry of Home Affairs (MHA)vi.

POTENTIAL GLOBAL CYBERSECURITY CHALLENGES

Deepweb

The deepweb, deepnet, invisible web or hidden web is a part of the World Wide Web whose contents are not indexed by standard search engines for different reasons. The portion of the web that is indexed by standard search engines is known as the surface web. The deep web also includes many common uses such as web mail, online banking and video on demand. The first conflation of the terms deepweb and darkweb came about in 2009. Early estimates suggested that the deepweb is 400 to 550 times larger than the surface web. Deepweb is growing exponentially. Most of the web's information is inaccessible. Traditional search engines cannot see or retrieve contents in the deepweb due to several technical reasons.

Inabilities of Traditional Search Enginesvii

Contextual Web: Pages with content varying for different access contexts e.g., ranges of client IP addresses or previous navigation sequence.

Dynamic content: Dynamic pages which are returned in response to a submitted query or accessed only through a form, especially if open-domain input elements such as text fields are used; such fields are hard to navigate without domain knowledge.

Limited access content: Sites that limit access to their pages in a technical way e.g., using the Robots Exclusion Standard or CAPTCHAs, or no-store directive which prohibit search engines from browsing them and creating cached copies.

Non-HTML/text content: Textual content encoded in multimedia image or video files or specific file formats not handled by search engines.

Private Web: Sites that require registration and login, i.e. password-protected resources.

Scripted content: Pages that are only accessible through links produced by JavaScript as well as content dynamically downloaded from Web servers via Flash or Ajax solutions.

Software: Certain content is intentionally hidden from the regular Internet, accessible only with special software.

Unlinked content: Pages which are not linked to by other pages, which may prevent web crawling programmes from accessing the content.

Deepweb Search Engines

Some of the Deepweb search engines are: The WWW Virtual Library, Deep Web Research Tools, Surfwax, IceRocket, Stumpedia, Freebase and TechDeepWeb.

Darkweb

The darkweb forms a small part of the deep web, the part of the web not indexed by search engines, although sometimes the term deepweb is confusingly used to refer specifically to the darkweb. The darknet which constitute the darkweb include small, friend-to-friend peer-to-peer networks, as well as large, popular networks like Freenet, I2P, and Tor, operated by public organizations and individuals. Users of the darkweb refer to the regular web as the Clearnet due to its unencrypted nature. The Tor darkweb is often referred to as onionland, a reference to the network's top level domain suffix.onion and the traffic anonymisation technique of onion routing.

Internet Corporation for Assigned Names and Numbers (ICANN)

The Internet Corporation for Assigned Names and Numbers (ICANN) is a nonprofit organization that is responsible for coordinating the maintenance and methodologies of several databases, with unique identifiers, related to the namespaces of the Internet - and thereby, ensuring the network's stable and secure operation. Much of its work pertains to the Internet's global Domain Name System (DNS). The numbering facilities ICANN manages include the Internet Protocol address spaces for IPv4 and IPv6, and assignment of address blocks to regional Internet registries. ICANN also maintains registries of Internet protocol identifiers and performs the actual technical maintenance work of the central Internet address pools and DNS Root registries.

ICANN was incorporated on September 30, 1998 in the State of California. It is headquartered in the Playa Vista section of Los Angeles, California. Reportedly, there are criticisms from ICANN constituencies including the

Noncommercial Users Constituency (NCUC) and the At-Large Advisory Committee (ALAC) that there is not enough public disclosure and that too many discussions and decisions take place out of the public sight.

Proposal for Internet Governance by the UN

During a summit meeting of India, Brazil, and South Africa (IBSA) held in September 2011, it was sought to move Internet governance into a UN Committee on Internet-Related Policy (UN-CIRP)x. The move was a reaction to a perception that the principles of the 2005 Tunis Agenda for the Information Society have not been met. The statement called for the creation of a new political organization operating under the auspices of the United Nations to provide policy recommendations for the consideration of technical organizations such as ICANN and international bodies such as the ITU.

Multi Stakeholder Approach

The Multi Stakeholder Approach is a plan for international governance of the Internet that was first proposed at the Global Multi stakeholder Meeting on the Future of Internet Governance (GMMFIG) conference (23–24 April 2014) and later developed into the NetMundial Initiative by the ICANN CEO along with representatives of the World Economic Forum (WEF) and the Brazilian Internet Steering Committeexi. The meeting produced a nonbinding statement in favor of consensus-based decision-making by the stake holders.

Multilateral Management

A few governments, including Russia, China, Iran and India, were unhappy with the final resolution and wanted multi-lateral management for the Internet, rather than broader multi-stakeholder management. But the Panel on Global Internet Cooperation and Governance Mechanisms (convened by the ICANN and the World Economic Forum (WEF), supported and included the NetMundial statement in its own report. In June 2014, France strongly opposed ICANN, stating that ICANN is not a fit venue for Internet governance and that alternatives should be soughtxii.

CYBER WARFARE AND CAPABILITIES

Cyber Warfare Defined

Cyberwarfare is defined as actions by a nation-state to penetrate another nation's computers or networks for the purpose of causing damage or disruption. Other definitions also include non-state actors, such as terrorist groups, companies, political or ideological extremist groups, and transnational criminal organizations. Cyberwarfare utilises techniques of defending and attacking information and computer networks connected to cyberspace, often through a prolonged cyber campaign or a series of related campaigns. It denies an opponent's ability to do the same, while employing technological instruments of war to attack his critical computer systems. Many countries have made Cyberwarfare capability development an integral part of their overall military strategy.

China

China is believed to be using Microsoft source code to build its offensive and defensive capabilities. It is also believed to use a network of its students, businessmen, scientists, diplomats, and engineers from within the Chinese diaspora. China is generally considered responsible for a number of cyber-attacks on a number of public and private institutions in the US, India, Russia, Canada, and France, but the Chinese government denies any involvement in these activities. The PLA is reportedly using information warfare units to develop viruses to attack enemy computer systems and networks. These units include civilian computer professionals.

On 23 Mar 2016, Chinese national Su Bin, 50, pleaded guilty in a California federal court for conspiring with two unnamed persons in China from October 2008 to March 2014 to gain unauthorized access to the computer networks of defense firms to obtain sensitive military information and to export that information illegally from the US to China. Mr. Bin had earlier been charged in a 2014 indictment with hacking into the computer networks of Boeing and other contractors, as part of a scheme to steal plans for the F-22 and F-35 fighter aircraft and C-17 transport aircraft.

A report by the cybersecurity firm Mandiant has estimated the PLA Cyber Command to have 130,000 personnel divided between its various operational divisions. On 1 February 2016, China announced its biggest military reform since the 1950s, including the creation of a Strategic Support Force. According to observers, the SSF will form the core of China's information warfare force and its specific missions will include target tracking and reconnaissance, daily operation of satellite navigation, operating Beidou satellites, managing space-based reconnaissance assets, and attack and defence in the cyber and electromagnetic spaces.

USA

Cyberwarfare is a part of the US's military strategy of proactive cyber defence and the use of cyberwarfare as a platform for attack. In 2009, President Barack Obama declared the US digital infrastructure to be a strategic national asset, and in May 2010 the Pentagon set up its new US Cyber Command (CYBERCOM), to defend their military networks and attack other countries' systems. CYBERCOM is reportedly building a Cyber Mission Force of 133 teams, selected from 6,200 personnel from across the military departments and defence establishments. The Cyber Mission Force, which is expected to be fully operational in 2018, is believed to be employing capabilities across the spectrum of cyber operationsxiii. The Pentagon is likely to spend a total of $6.7 billion on cyberwarfare capability building in 2017. In all, the Pentagon is projected to spend $34.6 billion over the next five years for this purpose.

During the last week of February 2016, Secretary of Defence Ashton Carter told a House subcommittee that CYBERCOM was conducting offensive operations against the Islamic State. This signaled a shift in the fight against the Islamic State and acknowledged the undertaking of cyberattacks during armed conflict by the US.

Russia

It has been claimed that Russian security services organized a number of denial of service attacks as a part of their cyberwarfare against other countries. Most notably, the 2007 cyberattacks on Estonia and the 2008 cyberattacks on South Ossetia, Georgia, and Azerbaijan caused a major disruption. In March 2014, a Russian cyberweapon called Snake or "Ouroboros" is reported to have created havoc on Ukrainian government systems.

Cyber Security Policy of India

The cybersecurity policy of India, issued in 2013, outlines a mission to protect information and infrastructure in the cyberspace, build capabilities to prevent and respond to cyber-threats, reduce vulnerabilities and minimise damage from cyber-incidents through a combination of institutional structures, people, processes, technology and cooperationxiv.

The amended IT Act, 2008 describes the Indian Computer Emergency Response Team (CERT In) as the designated national agency to perform all important functions in the area of Cyber Securityxv. Rendering advice on proactive cyber activities also forms a part of the charter of the CERT In. Important virus alerts are issued by this organization: on 25 Feb 2016, the CERT In issued a notification regarding the existence and modus operandi of a virus named Ransomeware Locky which is injected through spam mails. It encrypts the files of the victim, and demands payment through Bitcoins for their de-cryption.

In 2011, the Indian Government created a new subdivision, the National Critical Information Infrastructure Protection Centre (NCIIPC) to protect energy, transport, banking, telecom, defence, space and other sensitive areas. India now has its first National Cyber-Security Coordinator (NCSC), a position created to coordinate among all cyber agencies in the country. Experts are being recruited for cybersecurity research and development work. A few IITs could also become Centers of Excellence for cybersecurity technology development.

Cybersecurity Organisations

The important national cybersecurity organizations in India are: National Information Board, National Security Council Secretariat (NSCS), National Crisis Management Committee, National Cyber Response Centre, National Technical Research Organisation (NTRO) (includes the National Critical Information Infrastructure Protection Centre), National Disaster Management Authority (NDMA), National Cyber Security and Coordination Centre and National Intelligence Grid (NATGRID).

Governance function is also carried out by the Ministries of Home Affairs, External Affairs, Defence and Communications & Information Technology. A Joint Working Group has been created among these ministries to coordinate internet governance policies. The NSCS is the nodal agency for cyber security and internet governance in India.

Prime Minister Narendra Modi on 01 March 2015 advised the National Association of Software and Services Companies (NASSCOM) to create a Cyber Security Task Force (CSTF), with the aim to develop and provide cyber security solutions to the Indian and global markets. Consequently, NASSCOM along with the Data Security Council of India (DSCI) created a task force comprising of leaders from the IT industry, security product companies, and enterprises like banking, telecom, energy sector and senior officers from the government. The vision of the task force is to build the cybersecurity industry up from the current one percent to ten percent by 2025, build a trained base of one million certified and skilled cybersecurity professionals and come up with more than a hundred successful security product companies from India, thus making it a global leader in the cybersecurity space by 2025. Several other private initiatives and blogs such as Perry4Law are also contributing to cybersecurity in India.

Cyber-Security Agency/Command of India

Cybersecurity is given a high priority in the Defence Forces. Personnel are sensitised periodically about the development in this field. An air gap is maintained between the computers hosting sensitive information and the internet connected computers. Procedural controls for keeping pen drives etc away from the sensitive areas are exercised. Breaches in cyber security are treated very seriously. However, despite the heightened cybersecurity awareness, there are growing concerns that our military establishments could be breached by organised cyberespionage.

The Indian Defence Forces are steadily moving towards Network Enabled Operations, and cyberspace forms the backbone of the system. A dedicated cybersecurity ecosystem is essential for unhindered operations in this architecture. There is an urgent need for further tightening of the cybersecurity network mechanism in the country to obviate the security threat inherent in cyberattacks.

In 2012, the Chiefs of Staff committee recommended the urgent formation of a Cyber Command along with Space and Special Forces Commands. India is now in the process of creating the Defence Cyber Agency (DCA) which could be a precursor to the creation of the Defence Cyber Command, like the one in the US. The DCA is likely to be headed by a two star general. Reportedly, the plan is to upgrade and expand the existing Defence Information Assurance and Research Agency (DIARA) into the DCA. Since the stakes are high, India is required to invest more in enhancing cybersecurity awareness, training and ecosystem improvements. It is essential to build our cyberwarfare capabilities, and to have a Defence Cyber Agency/ Defence Cyber Command in place on priority for this purpose.

Recommended Approach for India

Enhanced Awareness: Cybersecurity issues affect computers and networks in a stealthy manner. A well informed user can help in early detection and mitigation of a threat. A periodic awareness campaign by the government and other big players-something like road safety week or fire safety week campaigns, should be extended for cybersecurity awareness also.

Cyber Security Training: Cybersecurity training would enhance awareness and provide deterrence. Training capsules at all levels- schools, colleges, workplaces should be periodically conducted.

Eco-System Improvements: These improvements will create a better and safer environment for internet and social media functioning. Indian efforts for freeing ICANN from vested interests could contribute to a better ecosystem. Safe and secure gateways and networks at the national level are essential. Encryption will further help secure the system.

Cyber Warfare Capability: India has centres of excellence in various cybersecurity related areas. There is a plethora of organisations dealing with various aspects of cybersecurity. None of these organisations however, seems to be dealing with aspects of cyber warfare. Concerted efforts at the national level are needed for building up the cyber warfare capability in India.

Defence Cyber Agency/Command: A central organization; oriented, equipped, manned and trained towards cyber war fighting is needed to ensure that all aspects of cybersecurity are adequately addressed. A Defence Cyber Agency/Command can serve this purpose and should be raised without further delay.

INTELLIGENCE FOR CYBER-SPACE

Although many of the intelligence methodologies and principles remain the same, new ways of thinking appropriate to the cyber-domain are essential. The lack of borders in cyber-space is a critical difference from the more familiar domains of intelligence. Indeed, geography and political borders often aided traditional military intelligence analysis-it is a simple thing to develop threat scenarios if the potential enemy can only use certain terrain or sea lines of communication and then, only at certain times of the year-while simple factors of physics such as time and distance also provided opportunities for warning. Within the Internet, however, these limiting factors are absent, (although other limiting factors, such as geometry of network connectivity, might exist in a form useful to be incorporated into intelligence analysis), contributing to what can appear to be "instantaneous threats".

Assessment of cyber-space threats requires not only a merger of old methodologies and new modes of thinking but also analysts willing and able to approach the art of threat assessment and warning from new perspectives. Only with a distinctive blend of the traditional and the new will it be possible to obtain real understanding of threats and vulnerabilities, to differentiate among types of intrusions and to forecast or anticipate specific incidents or clusters of incidents in ways that lengthen warning time.

Enhancing the ability to identify perpetrators is also highly desirable: removing the cloak of anonymity would make perpetrators more concerned about the potential costs and risks of their actions and could have an important deterrent effect. In short, there are several fundamental questions at the heart of the intelligence process. They consist of variations on the who, what, when, where, why and how questions that are familiar parts of most research and analysis.

Security Challenging

Efforts to identify intruders are critical both to the assessment of the challenge and the nature of the response. Potential intruders run the gamut from young hobbyists engaged in the equivalent of joy riding to terrorist organizations and nations that are intent on maximizing damage to the target. The problem of identification is particularly difficult in a domain where maintaining anonymity is easy and there are sometimes time lapses between the intruder action, the intrusion itself, and the actual disruptive effects. Moreover, the consequences are not always commensurate with the objectives, in some cases falling short of what the intruders hoped to achieve, and in others going well beyond what they had envisaged.

There is a broad spectrum of potential intruders on the Internet and an almost equal number of motives for intrusions against organizations. Not surprisingly, this includes perpetrators conducting operations against other perpetrators. As enticing as this prospect is, it does not mitigate the effects of such internecine rivalry. New and more sophisticated tools are often the result of such interplay. This sort of jousting can also provide valuable insights to analysts once it is recognized, but does not simplify the analytic task and puts an incredible strain on limited analytic/warning resources. With the continuing proliferation of sophisticated computer technologies into the mainstream population, attribution for an intrusion becomes more difficult by the day.

The dynamism of the intruder population is itself a problem. On the one hand, success breeds imitation and the sophistication of readily available tools means that even those with limited skills can become intruders.

On the one hand, there is a certain degree of attrition in the intruder community. Indeed, there are many reasons why intruders might cease their activity, including increased maturity, a need to find gainful employment, and a perception of the rewards of working to increase network security rather than attack it. The implication, of course, is that the mix of agents threatening network security is changing as the nature of the Internet changes.

The vast majority of the intrusions are probably being conducted by nuisance hackers or "ankle-biters" who have limited objectives and are usually satisfied with the actual penetration of the system or conduct relatively harmless cyber-vandalism such as the defacement or alteration of web-sites. While aggravating to the target, no significant or lasting damage occurs. The more serious problem occurs when an intrusion is carried out by a more sophisticated intruder (either an individual or a group) whose objective is better defined and involves malicious intent. Motives for these sorts of intrusions are also as varied as the persons carrying them out. They range from greed to defined military strategy and doctrine, and all that falls in between. Four of the more dangerous, and less well defined categories of intruder are governments conducting operations against other sovereign states, the organized terrorist group, insurgency or revolutionary groups, and organized crime.

All these entities are beginning to appreciate the potential power, anonymity, and effectiveness of the Internet. There are myriad examples of governments instituting programmes for Computer Network Warfare. In the case of Russia, policy-makers consider the security of their information infrastructure so critical that–rhetorically at least-they equate an attack against it with a strategic nuclear strike (and have promised an appropriate response). As a result of the realization of the criticality of information infrastructures, computer warfare is now a part of the formal Russian Military Strategy and Doctrine. The same is true of organized terrorist groups. In fact, "most of the 30 top terrorist organizations identified by the U.S. government have web pages and use e-mail, and are ``fairly well developed" at using the Internet."[Casciano] In many cases, dependence on technology is viewed as an Achilles Heel to be exploited by terrorist organizations.

Within the U.S., many of the more militant indigenous groups have discovered the power of the Internet and have well designed and effective Web sites. Indeed, militia and supremacist groups have had significant increases in membership since developing their Web pages. It is a natural progression from using the Internet for propaganda and recruiting to exploiting its potential as a weapon. There is also growing evidence that some of the active insurgency groups around the world are discovering the potential of the computer. It is just a matter of time until they discover the effect of a computer-generated attack against the infrastructure of the government they are fighting. Once that realization is made, cyber-attacks will likely become a weapon of choice for organizations intent on overthrowing an existing government. Disturbingly, Aum Shinrikyo, the group responsible for the Sarin gas attack on the Japanese subway, has increasingly been involved in the Japanese software industry!

Organized crime probably was the first of the sophisticated intruder threats to realize the power and value of the computer. In 1995, it was discovered that the Cali cartel had sophisticated state-of-the-art equipment for electronic eavesdropping, while smaller drug trafficking organizations in Colombia are using the Internet to pressure the Colombian government to change the policy of extraditing traffickers to the United States. Furthermore, the use of computers by organized crime organizations to garner illicit profits is well documented. However, some criminal efforts have gone beyond simple siphoning of funds and money laundering. Extortion of money from financial institutions by threatening to destroy or modify their computer databases is also evident. It is probable that at least some of these extortion operations are conducted by transnational criminal groups. Some of the extortion efforts go wrong–as did the effort to extort Bloomberg. In other cases, however, large payoffs are almost certainly made to the extortionist. It seems likely, therefore, that larger and potentially more dangerous operations should be anticipated.

The obvious challenge is to develop a capacity to identify and track the activities of these potential intruders with the goal of being able to provide predictive analysis and warning of intrusions. Some of the traditional intelligence techniques should apply to these threats, but new methodologies and the ability to contemplate new and complex concepts have to be developed concurrently. This will become even more important (and difficult) as perpetrators of increasing sophistication operate on the Internet. As motivations vary, so will the efforts of the individuals behind malicious operations to either conceal or reveal their responsibility. All of this complicates efforts to track responsible parties determine attribution. Nations and transnational criminal organizations, by their nature, will be diligent in their efforts to maintain anonymity. In some of these cases, identifying the intended victim may give valuable insight into tracking the intruder. Sometimes the target of an intrusion allows the analyst to rule out certain possible perpetrators. A multi-million dollar extortion plot against a major financial institution is probably not the work of a 13-year-old hacker working out of his bedroom. At the same time, however, many victims, especially within government or sensitive industries such as banking or insurance, often complicate the effort to track intruders because of their reluctance to report the incident. In other cases, such as politically motivated attacks, the perpetrators may want their identity known, but not their location. As such operations become more sophisticated, tracking the attack back to its point of origin will be a major challenge to the intelligence analysts involved. What is clear from all of this is that tracking intruders and gaining attribution is much more than just a technical challenge.

One difficulty, of course, is that there are legal constraints on intelligence collection, especially by the military and the national security establishment. Traditionally the focus of intelligence has been on foreign threats, and there are restrictions on intelligence activities directed against individuals or groups that are domestic in nature. Insofar as these groups are the focus of government attention, it is from the law enforcement community. This points to yet another problem: that of coordination and information sharing between the traditional national security agencies and the law enforcement community. Generally law enforcement focuses on individual cases and wants evidence that stands up in court; intelligence agencies in contrast are concerned with protecting the sources of their information so that they can continue to use them. The problem with cyber-threats is that they fall in the gray area where crime and national security merge into one another.

Forms of Intrusion are Occurring

It is tempting to see intrusions in terms of a pyramid that goes from transient vulnerability probing and defacing web-sites at the base to large scale efforts to undermine the critical missions of an organization or the critical functions of a nation at the top-and to suggest that there is an inverse relationship between frequency and significance, with many trivial incidents and comparatively few of the more serious incidents. There are several difficulties with this however. The first is that probes that appear relatively insignificant could be a harbinger of more serious intrusions. The second is that there is sometimes a gap between intent and consequences–the effects and impact of an incident can either fall far short of what was intended, or far exceed what the perpetrator initially envisaged. This lack of congruence between limited intent and far-reaching consequences stems from the capacity of worms and viruses for infinite replication and multiplication combined with the seamless inter-connectivity of systems. Incidents such as the Love Bug cross the public-private divide and have an indiscriminate impact on corporations, governments, and private individuals irrespective of the initial target. In cases such as this, the consequences have less to do with targeting than with the ubiquity of a particular programme such as Microsoft Outlook that is used as the vector of transmission. In effect, the incident takes on its own momentum.

When the consequences are widespread, of course, the incident becomes very public and is the subject of much media and official commentary. In many other cases, however, there is far greater reticence about the scale, type and targets of attack. The analytic effort must successfully build a trust relationship for the collection of data across a broad variety of organizations. This trust relationship allows for observation of incidents from early probing and experimentation through widespread deployment of automated forms of intrusion. For example, in recent months (June and July 2000) CERTÒ/CC has received reports of intrusions involving a wide variety of automated tools, ranging from simple viruses and system corruption toolkits through complex viruses designed to attack relatively hardened sites with low probability of detection and distributed tools designed to crash network infrastructure. Roughly 10%-25% of the CERT/CC reports involve viruses. Roughly 20%-40% are intrusions where the victim site cannot discern the type of the intrusion from available data. The remaining intrusions are a large number of other forms of intrusion, including compromise of system administration accounts, web defacements, reconnaissance attempts and misuse of computing resources.

Being intruded Upon

Determining who are the victims of intrusions is, in some respects, an enormously significant part of the intelligence process. It is important-at least in those cases where attacks are not indiscriminate-to differentiate between public and private targets, to distinguish infrastructure targets from individual targets, to distinguish between intrusions that focus on targets of convenience and those that are much more precise and calculated. For example, existing analysis has shown a link between port scanning and certain types of later intrusions, but this needs to be more fully explored to provide for effective warnings.

Profiling victims can sometimes play a critical role in determining the nature of the intrusion and the nature of the intruders. For this to be done, understanding is needed of the level of "background noise", probes and intrusion attempts occurring across the Internet. Once understood, it may be possible to isolate this activity from the more significant activity directed at a particular victim.

Victim profiles will be just as important, in terms of strategic intelligence analysis of the Internet, as profiling potential intruders. The more serious the intrusion, the more critical this sort of profiling will be. One of the potential hurdles to this effort, however, will be the natural tendency of the victim, whether private or public, to withhold sensitive or proprietary information. A few examples of this kind of reticence would be financial institutions withholding information about loses due to intrusions; companies failing to divulge the nature of an intrusion due to proprietary corporate data; or a government agency protecting information that is sensitive or even classified. Beyond simply protecting proprietary or sensitive data, there are also serious legal questions that have not yet been resolved in the courts or in the legislature. These include constitutional guarantees of privacy; contradictory national laws (or lack of laws) as perpetrators use the global network; laws limiting various governmental agency's efforts to track down the source of an intrusion, and the need to determine what is domestic and what is foreign.

If these barriers can be overcome, critical information will become available. Details of the victim's infrastructure, the nature of the intrusion, identity clues left by the intruder, network traffic flow as observed by the victim site, and intrusion tools left as artifacts on the victim hosts can all provide indispensable clues. Without such information, motivation becomes more difficult to define and profiling efforts will be seriously flawed. Some work has already been accomplished in this area by organizations involved in incident monitoring, including the members of the Forum of Incident Response and Security Teams (FIRST) community.

Much more remains to be accomplished, however, as new cooperative agreements are forged and additional analytic efforts and methodologies are developed. Furthermore, while it is true that some of the legal restrictions are avoided by the voluntary nature of the cooperative relationships, they are by no means completely overcome. The keys to success seem to be twofold. First, the analytic organization has to prove itself to be a highly secure confidant, never disclosing victim identities while working to assist victims in recovering from intrusions. Second, it must return information that is of value to the victims, including information that might place the intrusion in a larger context as well as providing assistance in dealing with vendors or other sites. More simply put, the exchange of information must be in both directions. Experience with other organizations has shown that neither trustworthiness nor returned value alone is sufficient, but both appear to be required for effective information gathering with victims.

Beyond their reticence, victim organizations are often unaware of critical parts of their security stance. Available data suggests that victims are often not aware that their networks have been intruded upon. The effectiveness of installed security measures is often overestimated. Levels of trust given to users by computing practices are often unwarranted. All of this hampers both analysis and defence.

One of the reasons that profiling the victims is so critical is that it provides insights in to motivations that can greatly assist analysts in predicting future intrusions under similar circumstances. This insight will need to incorporate identification of circumstances that facilitate or hamper intrusion. For example, K-12 educational institutions might offer a significant opportunity for intruders to stage their attacks, since many such institutions lack knowledgeable system administrators. However, such hosts may be removed from the network during summer break and other times when school is not in session. During the Year 2000 rollover, conditions for system intrusion were relatively poor not only because of the active presence of a large number of system administrators, carefully monitoring their systems, but also the significant number of alternative activities available to potential intruders. These examples serve to identify that there exist time-varying circumstances; further analysis is required to delineate these factors more fully.

CHALLENGES TO NATIONAL SECURITY SPACE INVESTMENTS

U.S. national security space investments, as outlined and proposed in Part Two, must contend with a number of challenges abroad and at home. If the investments outlined in this study are to be effective and provide U.S. warfighters the capabilities they need, the challenges outlined below must be confronted. Some of these challenges will require further investments not yet identified, while others will require significant legislative, policy, organizational, and cultural changes in order to make the U.S. national security space establishment the world's leading provider of national security space effects.

A2/AD Capabilities and U.S. National Security Space Requirements. U.S. national security space systems underpin the American way of warfare that is the sine qua non of enduring U.S. tactical and operational success over the past few decades.

Success, however, can sow the seeds for future failure, and adversaries of the United States—actual and potential—have assiduously looked for vulnerabilities that might be successfully exploited, should conflict with the U.S. arise.

These adversaries, real and potential, have identified the critical role that space systems play in the American way of warfare and are developing capabilities designed to degrade, deny, and destroy U.S. satellites. These counter-space systems are part of a broad range of anti-access (A2) and area denial (AD) capabilities that seek to thwart U.S. air, sea, and space superiority by denying U.S. forces the strategic advantages they have enjoyed in these domains for many decades. In this regard, A2/AD counter-space capabilities include direct-ascent anti-satellite (ASAT) weapons; directed-energy weapons designed to dazzle the sensors on imaging satellites; jamming capabilities that disrupt the data-links between satellites and their terrestrial users; electromagnetic pulse (EMP) weapons that disable electronics within their blast radius; and the capabilities to ensure that these counter-space weapons can be used for effect, such as space situational awareness capabilities. Among the more prominent countries developing these counter-space A2/AD capabilities are the People's Republic of China and Iran, though others are also thought to be developing similar capabilities.

Since national security space systems are critically vital to the effective use of air, sea, and land forces, overcoming the A2/AD threat is among the biggest challenges and priorities facing the U.S today. In order to do so the United States needs to focus on the following areas:

- Space protection. Greater effort and funding must be devoted to space protection efforts that can prevent U.S. satellites from being dazzled and jammed by non-lethal A2/AD capabilities. This can be achieved through hardening against jamming attempts, and shutters and filters to protect imaging sensors. Space protection also involves defensive counter-space capabilities such as missile defense to counter direct-ascent ASAT weapons, offensive airpower against well-defended A2/AD targets, and special operations against critical A2/AD targets. Further research is also required for space propulsion technologies that can help critical space systems maneuver away from certain A2/AD counter-space threats, or at least complicate adversary attempts to track and target space assets. In order to ensure that commercially provided national security space capabilities can overcome the A2/AD threat, legislation and policy regulating commercial provision of these capabilities should stipulate that they feature the latest protective measures deemed necessary by the client (e.g., the U.S. Air Force). Similarly, the U.S. should carve out a leadership role in space protection technologies and methods, setting the standard for space protection among friends and allies. Indeed, among the criteria for deep collaboration among friends and allies in national security space should be minimum standards of space protection in foreign space systems before the U.S. engages.

- Responsive launch capability. Overcoming A2/AD threats also involves being able to expand space capability in a timely manner (meaning days, if not hours) in order to bolster capability already in orbit or to replace capability already lost. The U.S. has already demonstrated that the mass manufacturing of small yet capable satellites in a short period of time is possible through the Operationally Responsive Space (ORS) program or similar undertaking. What has not advanced is the ability to rapidly and responsively launch such capability on demand, and this is the second priority for investment in overcoming the counter-space A2/AD challenge. The United States must reinvigorate exploration of all possible methods for rapid and responsive launch, preferably developing a mix of capabilities between traditional launch vehicles launched from fixed sites, launch vehicles launched from mobile platforms, and air and sea launch.

- Off-the-shelf satellites. As already mentioned, the United States has demonstrated its ability to mass manufacture small but capable satellites in a short period of time. Yet the White House, in its FY 2013 budget request for national security space, proposed to shut the ORS program down. Parts of Congress have acted to save the program, while others have endorsed the President's decision. In the face of the A2/AD threat, shutting down the ORS program appears a retrograde step. Further gains in research and technology development, as well as enabling the entrenchment of the skill sets required for the development, acquisition, manufacturing, operation, and maintenance of small, mass-produced satellites, are a clear security priority. Whether through restoration of ORS or establishing the requirement in other programs, improving the speed to orbit is a recommended priority for national security space. To be clear, it is not argued here that all national security space functions can or should be carried out by small, mass-produced satellites. However, in overcoming the A2/AD threat, large numbers of small satellites (imaging and communications) launched rapidly can provide redundancy for U.S. space forces, and thwart adversary efforts to deny U.S. forces their space advantage.
- Commercial and allied space systems. Overcoming the A2/AD counter-space threat can also be achieved by employing commercial and allied space systems as appropriate. Commercial systems, especially foreign systems, and allied space systems can provide increased capacity as part of a surge in space capability, and as a measure of redundancy. The importance of engaging friends and allies in national security space will be discussed further, though it should be stated here that engagement and collaboration with allies must be based on strict criteria and guided by concise strategic necessity.
- Terrestrial redundancy. Also critical to overcoming the counter-space A2/AD threat is the development and

sustainment of robust terrestrial communications and ISR networks that can decouple from the space-based component to provide a measure of continuity for U.S. forces, even though a diminishment of capability would inevitably result.

- Mission assurance. Finally, overcoming the counter-space A2/AD threat requires that all U.S. forces—land, sea, air, space, and cyberspace—be able to achieve mission objectives in the face of degraded capabilities and compromised domain superiority. While every effort is required to ensure that U.S. forces receive critical space support through every phase of combat and post-combat operations, there is always the possibility that the adversary might succeed in its attempt to deny the U.S. its space superiority. In that case, all U.S. forces must be trained and equipped to achieve mission objectives in a severely degraded space environment. This training is already underway and should be further encouraged.

Confronting the counter-space A2/AD threat requires long-term preparation and development of technologies that will not appear and mature overnight. Long-term, sustained investments in the areas identified above are prerequisites to assuring U.S. superiority in every domain when confronted by any adversary.

Arms Control, Codes of Conduct, and U.S. National Security Space. Investments made by the Obama Administration in space protection and counter-space capabilities will most certainly run afoul of Chinese and Russian advocates of the proposed Treaty on Prevention of the Placement of Weapons in Outer Space and of the Threat or Use of Force Against Outer Space Objects (PPWT), and supporters of the International Code of Conduct (ICoC) for Outer Space Activities, formerly known as the European Union Code of Conduct (CoC) for Outer Space Activities.

The PPWT was first proposed by China and the Russian Federation in early 2008. It has been rejected outright by the Bush and Obama Administrations and will most certainly be rejected by a new Administration. On this topic, U.S. policy is abundantly and unambiguously clear since the draft treaty proposal was made by China and the Russian Federation. Given the outright rejection of the PPWT, as well as disquiet about its proposed provisions by other countries, the European Union proposed its voluntary and non-binding CoC late in 2008 as a compromise agreement. The Obama Administration has expressed its support for a revised and rebranded CoC (now called the ICoC) and is encouraging international discussion of its proposed provisions. While there is no prospect of any Administration agreeing to the proposed provisions of the PPWT, there is growing support in some circles in the United States for the ICoC. Such support fails to consider matters in which a CoC is not in the interests of the United States and can leave U.S. national security space capabilities needlessly vulnerable. Should the United States sign up to a renegotiated ICoC, it would doubtlessly take its obligations seriously, while other signatories would circumvent its provisions in order to gain a strategic advantage of the U.S. Should conflict occur between the U.S. and a country that has not lived up to the spirit and letter of the CoC, then U.S. space systems will be rendered needlessly vulnerable. Similarly, it is unclear how compatible the proposed provisions of the CoC are with the right of countries to act in self-defense of core interests if attacked. Many of the investments in programs associated with space protection and counter-space are likely to be at variance with the proposed provisions of the CoC.

Finally, while building a set of enduring norms of behavior in space operations is very much in the interests of the U.S. and other space-faring nations, it is far from clear how any CoC is better at establishing and instilling such norms than the widespread adoption of the norms already practiced by commercial satellite operators—norms established by experts (rather than diplomats) based on pragmatic need, enabling satellite operators to compete in the marketplace while at the same time engaging in mutual cooperation to avoid collisions, spectrum interference, and other mishaps.

Rejection of the PPWT is thoroughly justified and this sentiment should be reiterated to China and the Russian Federation. Similarly, the U.S. should eschew the draft CoC, given that it undermines U.S. interests and does not constrain countries of concern. Instead, the United States should complement the rejection of formal and semi-formal space arms control with a serious and concerted effort to bilaterally engage in space confidence-building measures with key space-faring nations, and support and encourage the establishment of meaningful norms of behavior in space operations as practiced by space operators every day.

Domestic Challenges and U.S. National Security Space. While the actions of adversaries and potential adversaries are almost impossible to control, and diplomatic initiatives by others can only be influenced, action—or lack of action—on the domestic front is very much within our control. An Administration looking to invest and revitalize U.S. national security space capabilities may not be able to directly control the actions of adversaries and international diplomats, but it can have a direct effect on domestic issues that can impede and undermine the overall effectiveness and readiness of U.S. national security space.

Continued support for export control reform already underway is warranted, especially reform of the International Trafficking in Arms Regulations (ITAR). Bipartisan support for ITAR reform appears to be strengthening even though the required legislation has yet to pass through the House and the Senate. To be clear, the problem is not the intent of ITAR, which is to prevent the unauthorized export of sensitive technologies that could undermine the U.S. advantage in key areas. The problem, rather, has been its implementation and the vast number of technologies that are subject to its strictures. It is now recognized that ITAR implementation stymies competitiveness and that many of the technologies subject to ITAR restrictions are in fact innocuous and freely and widely available on the open market abroad. ITAR reform is needed in order to help the U.S. space industry—especially second-tier and third-tier industry—compete in an increasingly competitive international market. Reform of ITAR not only allows American space companies to better compete in the international satellite market, it will also have the long-term effect of solidifying the overall technological superiority of the United States.

As currently implemented and interpreted, ITAR in fact impedes U.S. competitiveness and as a result acts as a disincentive to innovation over the long term. This is not to say that the technological "crown jewels" of the United States should be allowed to be sold to the highest bidder. There are technologies that offer the United States real advantages over the capabilities of other nations and these technologies should be protected with no expense spared. However, it is reasonable to speculate that the numbers of technologies that provide this kind of critical advantage are fewer than the total of the list, meaning that a preponderance of U.S.-developed satellite technology is safe enough to sell on the international market and that the list should evolve as technologies become diffused. Innovation is sustained through intense competition as well as through adequate research and development funding. Intense market competition without adequate research and development funding can result in missed opportunities; adequate research and development funding absent intense market competition results in fewer, if any, technological breakthroughs that might contribute to American technological superiority.

Along with the main challenges to revitalizing and investing in U.S. national security space, the study now identifies the capabilities in need of sustained investments in order for U.S. space superiority to endure over the coming decades, and as a result, ensure superior U.S. military effectiveness in the face of 21st-century challenges.

8

Military Space Systems: The Road Ahead

We want now to highlight several other military space systems that are in various stages of research and development. Systems under the umbrella of military space systems number in the dozens. There are nearly 50 different technologies in various stages of R&D across multiple programs—not including missile defense technologies that have direct connection to possible space weapons systems. Here I will focus on just four systems that, if successful, could radically alter the future military environment. I have highlighted these systems for various reasons ranging from probability of deployment to sheer entertainments sake.

First, there is the Multiple Kill Vehicle platform, or MKV. This best links missile defense technology with potential space weapons systems in the here and now. The MKV program is a product of the space and missile defense test center at Redstone Arsenal, whose stated mission is to manage advances missile defense and space technology research and development for the Army, the Missile Defense Agency (MDA), and other defense-related government organizations. Technology development areas include radar, optics, interceptors, lasers, information systems, space control, and space applications. The missile defense installation at Fort Greely is the first integration site for MKVs. The current interceptors at Ft. Greely are single-shot interceptors—one interceptor per rocket, meaning one chance to achieve a successful hit to kill against a ballistic missile. With MKVs integrated into the current ground-based midcourse (GMD) systems, that hit-to-kill capability will increase to seven shots per interceptor. The funding has been secured for this project. The systems will be integrated into the current ground based systems at Ft Greely—deployed on up to 7 interceptors—as early as FY07.

In March 2005 MDA Executive Director Lt. Gen. Henry A. "Trey" Obering III said: "MKV is a generational upgrade to ground-based midcourse interceptors to increase their effectiveness in the presence of countermeasures." Obering also stated that the MDA looks forward to the first intercept attempt using MKV by 2008. Various system comparisons suggest that this technology could be employed in future space-based defenses. Where the overlap into weaponizing space takes place is in regard to the carrier vehicle (CV), which for the MKV is the in-space deployment unit. The MKV/CV relationship is as follows: a ground-based platform launches the ground-based interceptor, which, when outside the atmosphere, releases the CV housing the MKVs; the CV then releases the MKVs to attempt their intercept. The possibility of a space-based CV with MKVs is theoretically possible, and one could assume that stationing a constellation of CVs in space for long periods could offer a mechanism not only for space asset protection and missile defense, but also for attacks on enemy spaced-based systems.

The second system I would like to highlight is a program which until recently was named the Common Aero Vehicle (CAV). This program called for a system to be developed by 2025 featuring a reusable hypersonic cruise vehicle that could take off from a conventional military runway and strike targets halfway around the world in less than two hours. The hypersonic cruise vehicle would carry a 5,000-kg payload comprising several CAVs: unpowered, maneuverable, hypersonic glide vehicles.

Each CAV would carry approximately 450 kg in munitions. In the near term DARPA and the Air Force propose developing, by 2010, a global strike capability that would launch CAVs using a low-cost, mission-responsive small launch vehicle, or on a traditional ballistic missiles.

This project is a significant part of the future Pentagon warfighting strategy and this has been mentioned by many military leaders, including Gen. Lance W. Lord, Commander of the Air Force Space Command, who stated to the House Armed Services Committee (HASC) in 2005: "This [CAV] is an incredible capability to provide the war fighter with a global reach capability against high payoff targets.

The Common Aero Vehicle matched to a responsive launch platform would provide a truly transformational capability to anywhere in the world regardless of the level of access.

The Common Aero Vehicle capability could be matched against an anti-access environment and still deliver a conventional payload precisely on target within minutes of a valid command and control release order. This is the type of Prompt Global Strike I have identified as a top priority for our space and missile force."

A future CAV launch platform based in space would have major diplomatic implications since there are no international treaties prohibiting the placement of conventional weapons in space. The Outer Space Treaty, for instance, only prohibits placing weapons on celestial bodies and placing weapons of mass destruction in orbit.

Another issue is the fact that such a space-based CAV system would not require overflight permission.

Such a system would also offer a means of dealing with both a continued lack of host nations for US military installations and the rapidly falling enlistment rate, since it could perform many of the functions of a forward-deployed force.

It would also permit very rapid attacks in areas that are difficult to reach from ground bases or aircraft carriers. Compared with air expeditionary forces, which require up to 48 hours or more to deploy, and carrier battle groups, which require over 96 hours to respond to a threat, a space-based CAV could respond within an hour or two. The most probable configuration for such a system would be a launch from a "responsive space lift vehicle," which, as mentioned earlier, is a rapidly advancing area with intense industry competition.

The overall capabilities of the CAV-responsive launch vehicle pairing include:

- Strike targets anywhere from the continental US (CONUS) in 120 minutes or less;
- Increase warfighting capability against hard and deeply buried targets;
- Minimize over flight and landing issues and concerns;
- Avoid risk to flight crews;
- Remain relatively invulnerable to anti-access threats;
- Cost competitive with other platforms

The requirements currently set for the system are:

- Precision strike
- Variety of conventional payloads
- In-flight target updates
- Worldwide all-weather range

Third, Brig. Gen. (Ret.) S. Pete Worden, formerly of US Strategic Command, brought to my attention Project Hot Eagle. The concept is space insertion and terrestrial extraction of ground troops. Marine Brig. Gen. Richard C. Zilmer describes this as the ability to "move a squad-sized unit of Marines to any place on Earth in less than two hours." Hot Eagle has key technology links to the Hypersonic Cruise Vehicle (HCV) and CAV programs. Though this system is far from being in a developmental phase—and that could be as far off as 2020—the CAV and HCV are already receiving funding and the CAV may be operable in just a few years.

Finally, another revolutionary technology under development involves the SMARTBus or "six-day satellite". This is a "plug, sense, and play" system, meaning that each component, once assembled, recognizes the others without the need for special programming or software drivers. It is a customizable off-the-shelf satellite system that will significantly reduce the cost, complexity, and the development time required to assemble a small satellite bus to meet a satellite developer's mission requirements. The SMARTBus program is funded by the Small Business Innovation Research (SBIR) program out of AFRL. Military applications might include asset replenishment in the event of an attack on our space assets and could require imaging, communications, and intelligence gathering abilities. Such a system might also be deployable in the theaters of military operations. Italian Air Force Lt. Col. Paolo Cesolari and Paolo Teofilatto released a study in April 2005 (reported by*Defense News*) stating that with the United States, NATO, and the European Union getting ready to dispatch military missions around on demand, setting up fast and temporary satellite intelligence and communications capabilities for those forces is becoming a headache. But as satellites get smaller, jets like a Eurofighter Typhoon could be used to launch microsatellites into orbit as quickly as forces deploy on the ground.

Conclusion

This presentation offers a snapshot of military space and dual-use technologies that are in various stages of research and development. Tax dollars are being spent, defense contractors are hard at work, and various branches of the military are awaiting results.

It is time for discussion nationally and internationally by concerned citizens, public policy analysts, and academics. With technological capabilities being researched, developed, close to deployment—and in some cases already deployed—is there an operable, deployed ASAT system on the horizon, without internationally-agreed, clearly-defined rules and limitations? The answer is certainly yes.

True, some of these systems may be "dream" technologies that will never reach the point of viability. For systems that are technically possible, however, we must ask, are they desirable? If deployed, will their impact on international security be positive or negative? If negative, what steps might be taken to prevent such developments?

Many people believe that a deployed anti-satellite capability and an ability to attack targets on or near the Earth's surface from space would create a global climate of insecurity both by enhancing current risks and by creating new problems. These new and increased risks would be the byproducts not only of systems to be deployed by the United States but also of the subsequent arms race in space which could be expected to result thanks to responses by China, Russia, the European Union, and perhaps Japan. Perhaps the most consequential impact would be increasing the probability of accidental nuclear war. Space-based weapons could shorten the road to armed conflict, whether nuclear or conventional. In the event that a space asset of one nation was attacked by another (on purpose or by accident), an immediate military response would be triggered, shortening the diplomatic process while escalating the armed conflict. Once employed regularly, anti-satellite systems and space weapons would litter LEO with debris, which in turn would permanently compromise our collective ability to explore the heavens and use space for constructive commercial purposes. The weaponization of space and the deployment of ASAT systems would undermine existing international arms control treaties that are already under stress. In addition, they would fly in the face of the collective will of the international community, which has demanded a ban on weapons in space for two decades and repeatedly been blocked by the United States. For those who share these concerns, one thing is certain: the time for international negotiations on a treaty to ban weapons in space is long overdue. Within a very few years, this potential development could become a reality.

SPACE FORCE OPERATIONS

Within the Department of Defense, the Air Force is the vanguard of space operations. The Air Force provides essential support and expertise for space activities to other military departments and the civil sector. Air Force space operations are based on the core competencies and missions outlined in *Air Force Basic Doctrine*.

Space force operations focus on controlling the space environment, applying force, conducting enabling and supporting operations for terrestrial forces, and supporting space forces. Gaining space superiority is a primary goal of a military campaign and must be gained early to ensure freedom of action.

Like air superiority, space superiority helps to provide the freedom to conduct operations without interference from an adversary. Although we have not yet had to fight for space superiority, in future conflicts adversaries may have imaging and other space systems capable of monitoring our operations. Hostile powers must not be permitted to freely use space systems against our national interests.

American military leaders cannot afford to have enemy commanders monitor our forces' activities, locate critical command nodes, identify maneuver elements as they deploy for combat, or witness the debarkation of forces and supplies. This information would substantially facilitate an adversary's war planning and execution, which could result in casualties for our forces. To ensure our forces maintain the ability to operate without being monitored from space, it is essential to gain and maintain space superiority and control the adversary's ability to exploit the space environment.

Space Control

Space control is the means by which we gain and maintain space superiority to assure friendly forces can use the space environment while denying its use to the enemy. To accomplish this, space forces must survey space, protect our ability to use space, prevent adversaries from interfering with that use, and negate the ability for adversaries to exploit their space forces. Counterspace is the mission carried out to achieve space control objectives by gaining and maintaining control of activities conducted in or through the space environment. Counterspace involves activities conducted by land, sea, air, space and/or special operations forces. Counterspace includes both offensive and defensive operations.

Offensive Counterspace

Offensive counterspace operations destroy or neutralize an adversary's space systems or the information they provide at a time and place of our choosing through attacks on the various elements of space systems. Although attacks could be carried out by space- or terrestrial-based forces, the principal means of conducting offensive counterspace operations is through the use of terrestrial-based forces such as air attacks against space system ground nodes or supporting infrastructure.

As the use of and investment in space increases, protection of our resources become critical. Because such protection introduces the possibility of earth-to-space, space-to-space, and space-to-earth operations, it is in our national interest to be prepared to develop the capability to support multipurpose operations in the space medium and employ such systems as national policy dictates. Offensive counterspace operations can involve the use of lethal or non-lethal means and are conducted to achieve five major purposes: deception, disruption, denial, degradation, and destruction of space assets or capabilities as required by the National Command Authorities (NCA) or Commander in Chief, United States Space Command (USCINCSPACE).

Deception consists of those measures designed to mislead the adversary by manipulation, distortion, or falsification of evidence to induce the adversary to react in a manner prejudicial to their interests.

Disruption is the temporary impairment of the utility of space systems, usually without physical damage to the space segments. These operations include delaying critical mission data support to an adversary. Given the perishability of information required to effectively command and control military operations, this disruption impedes the effective application or exploitation of that data. Examples of this type of operation include jamming or refusing or withholding data support or spare parts.

Denial is the temporary elimination of the utility of the space systems, usually without physical damage. This objective is accomplished by such measures as denying electrical power to the space ground nodes or computer centers where data and information are processed and stored.

Degradation is the permanent impairment of the utility of space systems, usually with physical damage. This option normally involves attacks against the terrestrial element of the space system.

Destruction is the permanent elimination of the utility of space systems, usually with physical damage. This last option includes special operations forces (SOF) missions to interdict critical ground nodes, airpower missions to bomb uplink/ downlink facilities, and attacks against mobile space elements.

Defensive Counterspace

Defensive counterspace operations reduce and preclude the effectiveness of an adversary's counterspace operations and preserve our ability to use friendly space systems. Missile defense operations to conduct national missile defense can be an element of defensive counterspace. Defensive counterspace operations consist of active and passive defense.

The objective of active defense is to detect, track, identify, intercept, and destroy or neutralize enemy space and missile forces. Active defense operations include maneuvering the spacecraft, deploying mobile ground links and terrestrial elements, and deploying decoys. It may also include the employment of lethal protection methods.

The objectives of passive defense are to reduce the vulnerabilities and to protect and increase the survivability of friendly space forces and the information they provide. Passive defense includes measures such as encryption, frequency hopping, and hardening. Space assets are also defended by camouflage, concealment, deception, redundancy, mobility, and dispersion.

Contributing Capabilities

The successful conduct of offensive and defensive counterspace operations relies upon the surveillance and reconnaissance of space and the ability to detect, track, and report on ballistic missile launches.

Surveillance and Reconnaissance of Space. Surveillance and reconnaissance of space detect and identify space systems and help characterize the space threat environment. Space surveillance (broad area coverage) provides information vital to the reconnaissance (close scrutiny) of an area or objects of specific interest. Space surveillance identifies alterations in the space environment, such as changes in the order of battle and deployment or retirement of space systems. Information derived from both surveillance and reconnaissance data allows planners to identify where force application or space control is required. This support is necessary for targeting and situational awareness and directly supports the counterspace mission as well as the terrestrial conflict.

Ballistic Missile Warning. Space-based systems and terrestrial sensors detect, track, and report on ballistic missile launches posing potential threats against North America, geographic theaters of operation, and space-based assets.

Ballistic missile warning provides critical information essential to the NCA decision process in determining an appropriate response to attack. Additionally, ballistic missile warning enhances the JFACC's counterair operations when conducting theater ballistic missile defense.

Application Of Force

The application of force consists of attacks against terrestrial targets carried out by military weapon systems operating in space. Currently, there are no force application assets operating in space, but technology and national policy could change so that force application missions can be performed from platforms operating in space.

For example, space systems such as the space-based laser could provide space-based attacks against terrestrial targets and provide the timely suppression of enemy defenses to improve the penetration effectiveness of air assets.

Space-based weapon systems that deliver this firepower may rely on other space-based systems for target acquisition, command and control, navigation, mid-course corrections, and terminal guidance. In addition to space-based systems, transatmospheric vehicles could also provide firepower to support future force application missions. Such space systems will be used when it is consistent with national policy and the best method to achieve the military objective.

Enhancing Operations

Force enhancement operations consist of those operations conducted from space with the objective of enabling or supporting terrestrial forces. Navigation, communications, reconnaissance, surveillance, ballistic missile warning, and environmental sensing help reduce uncertainty and friction at all three levels of war—strategic, operational, and tactical. Enabling and supporting space operations increase a force's ability to detect, plan, and react faster than an adversary's terrestrial forces operations. Force enhancement must include consideration of civil, commercial, and allied space support that can augment DOD space systems. These enhancements consist of data, data relay, analysis, or other enabling capabilities.

Supporting Space Forces

Space force support is carried out by terrestrial elements of military space forces to sustain, surge, and reconstitute elements of a military space system or capability. These activities deploy, sustain, or augment on-orbit spacecraft, direct missions, and support other government or civil organizations. Space force support involves spacelift and satellite operations.

Spacelift

Spacelift provides the Air Force with the ability to project power by delivering satellites, payloads, and material into or through space. The Air Force uses a combination of military, DOD civilian, and civilian contractor personnel to process, integrate, assemble, check out, and launch space vehicles. Civil and commercial contributions further expand the number of launch sites available to spacelift. During periods of increased tension or conflict, a spacelift objective is to launch and deploy new or replacement space assets and capabilities as necessary to achieve national security objectives. Air Force spacelift operations are conducted to deploy, sustain, or augment satellite constellations supporting US military operations.

Launch to deploy is a strategy defined as a launch, or series of launches, required to initially achieve a satellite systems' designed operational capability. This includes initial constellation deployments and research and development launches. This strategy uses a launch-on-schedule approach where launches are planned in the national mission model and space launch manifest and executed in accordance with the current launch schedule. Launch to sustain is a strategy to replace satellites predicted to fail or that fail abruptly. Launch to augment is a strategy to increase operational capability above the designed operational capability in response to war, crisis, or contingency. This strategy is considered in conjunction with non-space or non-launch alternatives.

Regardless of the launch strategy employed, planners must consider current satellite capabilities, residual assets possessing degraded utility, and reconstituted capabilities. Incorporating all of these capabilities helps ensure adequate force structure is available to satisfy operational requirements. The quality and capability of civil, commercial, and allied systems which augment military operations are a key determinant in the launch strategy adopted.

Satellite Operations

The Air Force Satellite Control Network (AFSCN) provides a means to maneuver, support, and sustain on-orbit forces. The AFSCN is a worldwide network of single-system and multiple-system facilities and sensors which provides telemetry, tracking, and commanding (TT&C) support, conducts network processes, and distributes mission data for virtually all DOD and United States civilian spacecraft and selected foreign space programs. AFSCN satellite support generally falls into three categories:

low-orbit vehicles which require high levels of support; medium-altitude vehicles which may require support only once every other revolution; and high-altitude vehicles which, depending on satellite requirements, need minutes to hours of support every day. The AFSCN also supports ballistic missile and suborbital launches.

THE MILITARY SPACE PROGRAM

As General Hamel mentioned, my job this morning is to provide a retrospective look at the past fifty years of military space and to present some future challenges as grist for our panel discussion. Spending some time reflecting on our past is wholly appropriate for a variety of reasons. First, as this audience knows well, 2007 is the fiftieth anniversary of Sputnik and the dawn of the Space Age. Secondly, understanding where we've been is useful as we think about the future. In that light, I think the philosopher; George Santayana had it right when he said, "Those who cannot remember the past are condemned to repeat it." Lastly, although the history of military space is relatively short; nevertheless, it has been a period of extraordinary accomplishments. As such, we should be mindful and proud of our history and celebrate those accomplishments.

This morning we will divide my presentation into five sections which are roughly in chronological order:

- The Early Years
- Creating the Force Structure
- Getting Organized
- Space Support to Contingency
- Conflict and Future Challenges

Obviously, I will only be able to scratch the surface on these subjects. Despite that disclaimer, I will try to highlight certain events that have special relevance today and for the future.

The Early Days

It is conventional wisdom to begin any discussion of military space with the Sputnik launch. However, I think it is important to note that there had been numerous studies dating back to 1946 which examined the feasibility of performing military missions from space to include reconnaissance, communications and weather.

Moreover, in the fifties prior to Sputnik, each service had established substantial and highly capable organizations to deal with space—the US Army Ballistic Missile Agency in Huntsville, Alabama, under the leadership of Wernher Von Braun and General John Medaris; the Navy at the Naval Research Lab and the Applied Physics Lab at John Hopkins; and the Air Force at the Western Development Division just north of here in Inglewood, California.

Over time and for a variety of reasons—not the least of which was Gen Schriever's and his team's work on the ICBM [Inter-Continental Ballistic Missile] program—the Air Force became the space service.

The launch of Sputnik was, of course, a shock to our national psyche and created a crisis atmosphere throughout the country. The US answer was the Explorer I launch in January 1958 and the Cold War space race was on. On the policy and organizational front, President Eisenhower signed into law the National Space Act in July 1958. The Space Act created NASA and split US space activities—civilian space would be a NASA responsibility while military space would be handled by the Defense Department. The third space sector was created when a covert organization, the National Reconnaissance Office, was established in January 1961—which incidentally was just five months after the first successful Corona launch which revolutionized imagery collection. While support agreements between these sectors were developed over time, the sectors, by policy and practice, were independent of each other.

I think it is also interesting to note that President Eisenhower established the precedent of White House interest and involvement in matters of space policy. This involvement is underscored by the fact that every President from Dwight D. Eisenhower to George W. Bush has published his administrations' space policy. Moreover, the broad policy tenets have, by and large, been consistent, and, in the case of military space policy, fairly permissive. For example, by policy, the US has always asserted the right to take any actions necessary to defend space capabilities and interests as well as deny an adversary's use of space that threaten our interests.

Creating the Force Structure

With that as background, the 1960s and early 1970s saw the rapid growth of military space technologies, infrastructure and programs.

The breadth of space capabilities developed during this time was indeed quite remarkable and in a word—breathtaking. In a little over a decade, the US went from reeling from the Sputnik launch to a full service space power with a range of satellites for communications, weather, warning, navigation and reconnaissance.

These satellites were supported by an extensive and highly capable infrastructure for launch and satellite control. Additionally, the military operated both a ground based space surveillance system to keep track of all the objects in space and an anti-satellite system.

Most everyone is familiar with the satellites, infrastructure and our spacetrack capabilities. What you may not know is that given the Soviet threat, developing an anti-satellite system was a high priority during the Cold War regardless of administration. The first program, SAINT, was a satellite interceptor—it was cancelled for political reasons and capability limitations. Program 437—a nuclear tipped THOR system—was deployed to Johnson Island in the Pacific and was operational from 1964 to 1975.

When the Soviets resumed testing of their co-orbital ASAT [Anti-Satellite] system in early 1976, the US had no comparable system having decommissioned Program 437 a year earlier. The Soviet action raised serious concerns about our satellite vulnerability and survivability. President Ford's response was the National Security Decision Memorandum 333 which resulted in the initiation of a new ASAT program—the F-15 Miniature

Homing Vehicle, a renewed emphasis on space surveillance and survivability through new technologies. The F-15 MHV was ultimately launched against a non-operational US satellite and successfully destroyed its target on Friday 13 Sept 1985—the program's only test against a satellite. Because of congressional restrictions on testing and budget constraints, the Air Force cancelled the program in 1988.

Getting Organized

The decade of the eighties can justifiably be called the space organization decade. For a number of reasons including the Soviet space threat; our increased dependence on space systems; the corresponding growth in the military space budget and a perceived need to change the orientation of space capabilities from technology push to operational pull—the Air Force created Air Force Space Command on Sept 1982. Coincidentally, the Command has just celebrated its twenty fifth anniversary.

A year later, the Naval Space Command was stood up at Dahlgren, Virginia. While the Air Force and Naval commands were responsible for organizing, training and equipping, there was a need for a combatant command for space. As such, the United States Space Command was created in 1985. Three years later, the Army Space Command was established.

US Space Command was disestablished in 2002 and its responsibilities transferred to US STRATCOM [Strategic Command]. As for the service space commands, they have continued to evolve with new missions. For example, the Army has combined space and missile defense into a single command. Naval Space Command has been transformed and is now part of Naval Network Warfare Command. The Air Force Space Command has added the ICBM mission and space and missile acquisition (SMC).

The mention of SMC's realignment under Air Force Space Command reminds me to mention that space organization and management has been a consistent topic of interest not only within the DoD [Department of Defense] but outside of the

Executive Department as well. In 2000, the Congress directed that a Space Commission be established to examine the organization and management of space activities that support national security interest. This Commission, under the then former Secretary of Defense Donald Rumsfeld, made a host of far reaching recommendations. Congress continues to be interested in how the military space sector is managed and accordingly has directed another space organizational review in the John Warner National Defense Authorization Act for FY 2008.

THOUGHTS FOR THE FUTURE

Since WWII, no one has even tried to challenge American airpower or that of our European allies. The Russians are mired in the aftereffects of the Cold War and a collapsed economy. Once-prominent aircraft manufacturers have been reduced to selling their inventories of fighter aircraft to foreign buyers, but there are few takers, and new systems are beyond their financial reach. The Japanese have been content to operate modified American systems.

The Chinese, whom some believe will be the greatest threat in the future, do not seem intent on demonstrating advanced aircraft systems. The Europeans are cooperatively building fighter aircraft systems with capabilities that will rival, but not exceed, the capabilities of the F-15 and F-16, not to mention the F/A-22. The newest fighter, the F-35 Joint Strike Fighter, is only marginally superior to the F-16, although it does have significant flexibilities, efficiencies, and some new capabilities, and it is being produced with advanced manufacturing techniques.

It is said that no American serviceman has been killed in battle by enemy air attack in the past 50 years. The Army now designs new systems based on the assumption that protection from above will almost always be provided by friendly air forces. Will our military aircraft fleet ever be challenged? If not, how do potential adversaries approach conflict with the United States? There are several possible scenarios.

The first scenario requires little analysis. In this scenario, there will be no technologically adept opponent of nearly equal capabilities for the foreseeable future. The grossly asymmetrical forces arrayed against us will not require improvement to our air forces. These dispersed, clandestine, and supranational enemies present few targets from the air, and the usefulness of airpower against these adversaries will continue to be marginal. Thus, our current force seems more than adequate.

In the second scenario, we assume that a technologically adept military competitor appears. In this case, we should be forewarned by intelligence agencies so that we can take the necessary steps to improve our systems. The current force, as modified, with the addition of the F/A-22 and the F-35 should be sufficient for at least the next 20 years. This scenario currently prevails among military planners.

A more worrisome scenario would be the nullification of U.S. military airpower by an unexpected technological advancement or breakthrough that cannot be countered quickly. Examples might include systems that negate stealth advantages coupled with weapons we cannot counteract or space-based systems that are out of our reach that could destroy our assets quickly. One can only hope that engineers somewhere are working on countering these eventualities.

With the advent of new unmanned aircraft systems, the risk to human beings may be greatly reduced. These systems are still in their infancy, probably comparable to aircraft in the 1950s, but the possibilities for their future application are endless, and new tactics are being developed every day.

But I do not believe the age of the fighter pilot is over, although the future will be very different. Unmanned machines under the control of fighter pilots flying in proximity may well represent the air power of the future- unmanned machines that can accomplish feats beyond the physical abilities of any man or woman, without the human risk.

Finally, we must consider space as a future battlefield, as well as systems that will allow its exploitation and will have some synergistic effects on the capabilities of air-breathing systems. In the 1960s, partial-orbit or fully orbital military systems were under consideration but were not implemented. Although the use of space for military power could be dreamed of, the underlying enabling knowledge and technologies did not yet exist. Everyone acknowledged that the first country to "own" space would "own" the planet, but the military did not have the technologies, budget, or the inclination to lead the nation to space.

Even the National Aeronautics and Space Administration (NASA), after visiting the moon, was content to fly the shuttle in low Earth orbit and develop unmanned systems to explore other planets. This attitude persists to the present day. In the late 1970s, the concept of an "aerospace plane" for space access emerged, but after the expenditure of more than a billion dollars, the project was shelved as technologically unachievable. The dream of flying to orbit in a hybrid, air-breathing/rocket system had to be abandoned. Later attempts were equally unsuccessful.

In various laboratories, experimentation is under way to develop ramjet and scramjet engines as the only way to achieve and sustain air-breathing flight above Mach 3 in the atmosphere. But after 50 years of effort, no production systems have emerged. In fact, it has only recently been verified that scramjet engines can actually fly and produce positive thrust; and this was accomplished in Australia.

In short, despite our ingenuity and engineering skill, we have not realized the benefits of greatly increased speed for commercial and military aircraft systems. Once Boeing dropped out of the supersonic airliner business, the Concorde was the only supersonic (Mach 2) commercial production aircraft to be operated successfully (but not economically).

In 1963, President Kennedy challenged Americans to land a man on the moon by the end of that decade and return him safely to Earth. Although in hindsight, this challenge seems foolhardy, it was met in 1969. Many now argue that the effort wore us out without delivering anything useful. I strongly disagree. Although many aspects of the project were premature, no one can dispute that the Herculean effort exemplified the best that our engineering talent could deliver. Grand plans need grand strategies, strategies that include a road map for what comes after the immediate challenge has been met. And there was no post-Apollo plan supported by the American public. This was not the fault of the engineering community but a failure of national leadership.

Three decades after Apollo, we still have no comparable vision for man in space. A plethora of unmanned systems have contributed collectively to our current standard of living and our nation's military capabilities. Communications satellites provide nearly instantaneous television pictures from halfway around the planet.

Weather satellites warn of impending disasters. Reconnaissance satellites keep the military informed of the activities of potential adversaries. Low, medium, and geosynchronous stationary orbits are filled with vehicles and systems, and new microsatellite arrays will soon be launched. The success of the global positioning system (GPS) satellite array has been phenomenal. But, with the exception of the space shuttle and temporarily manned orbiting systems, our space capability does not involve the presence of human beings and does little to satisfy our thirst for exploration. One can hope that the recently enunciated space vision of President Bush will lead to the development of a strategy for the moon and beyond that can be fully supported by the American people.

The challenges in materials science, thermal management, and many other technical areas to operate within the atmosphere at speeds above Mach 5 are too great, I believe, for an economical manned system (missile systems may be possible). Hybrid horizontal takeoff and landing systems, using both rocket and air-breathing propulsion for access to space, seem more likely. These systems could be useful for both military and commercial purposes and could avoid some of the extreme challenges of very high speed operations within the atmosphere. Military aircraft of the future will almost certainly operate in both air and space.

9

The Computer Technology and Cybernetic Warfare

As the intensity and breadth of the battlefield grew along with its logistical requirements, new communication technologies became necessary to achieve the required integration and coordination of increasingly large and intricate military systems.

The harnessing of electromagnetic forces for telecommunication purposes proceeded with telegraphy and telephony, simultaneously stimulating growing scientific interest in the concept of information. Cybernetics emerged from the unprecedented technological and industrial effort of the Second World War, in particular the work on the automation of anti-aircraft defences. The selfproclaimed 'science of communications and control' promised to manage chaos and disruption through self-regulating mechanisms of negative information feedback. By being defined in terms of negative entropy (negentropy), information became conceptualized as the source of all order. The computer, also developed during the war for the purposes of code-breaking and the computation of nuclear physics, emerged as the new dominant technology and abstract model through which the world came to be understood chiefly in terms of information processing.

The drive for complete predictability and centralized control over armed conflict was renewed under cybernetic warfare with the deployment of computers and automated control technologies, and the widespread application of the analytical tools of operations research and systems analysis.

The Cold War and the constant threat of nuclear annihilation required ever greater levels of automation and centralization of the war machine; and cybernetics, with its promise of stability in the face of perturbation, appeared best suited to the containment and management of a conflict of potentially apocalyptic proportions. Vast command and control architectures were established to organize the global projection of armed force and the rapid mobilization of military systems within the shrinking windows of opportunity afforded by nuclear weaponry. Scientific methodology was applied to warfare more systematically than ever, with operations research and systems analysis applied comprehensively to both tactical and strategic questions. The first two decades of the postwar era saw the rise of the defence intellectuals and their analytical tools in the United States, culminating in the nomination of Robert McNamara as Secretary of Defence.

In its most pristine form, cybernetic warfare fuelled wild yet enduring fantasies of omniscience and omnipotence on the battlefield. In 1969 General William Westmoreland, commander-in-chief of US forces in Vietnam, formulated his vision of the military's future, encapsulating this cybernetic ideal:

On the battlefield of the future, enemy forces will be located, tracked, and targeted almost instantaneously through the use of data links, computer assisted intelligence evaluation, and automated fire control. With first round kill probabilities approaching certainty, and with surveillance devices that can continually track the enemy, the need for large forces to fix the opponent becomes less important.

Towards Chaoplexic Warfare

Since the mid-1970s, the cybernetic mode of warfare has come under increasing challenge from the military reversal for US forces in Vietnam, geopolitical transformation following the end of the Cold War, and novel scientific developments growing out of the original corpus of cybernetics.

The increasing application of computers to the study of scientific problems, the exploration of non-linear mathematics, and an extension of the cybernetic analysis of systems to questions of self-organization opened the way for novel scientific approaches which eventually crystallized into the theories of chaos and complexity (here referred to together as *chaoplexity*). Information remains the central concept, and in this sense chaoplexity is an outgrowth of cybernetics; but the focus on change, evolution and positive feedback breaks with the cybernetic pioneers' concern for stability.

Chaos is seen no longer as simply a threat to order which must be averted at all costs, but as the very condition of possibility of order. The key notions here are those of non-linearity, self-organization and emergence, and the pivotal technological figure is that of the network, the distributed model of information exchange perhaps best embodied by the internet.

The Science of Chaoplexity

Although still firmly set in the informational paradigm, chaos theory and complexity science departed from cybernetics in shifting the focus away from the stabilizing self-regulation (or homeostasis) underlying the persistence of existing systems towards runaway processes of change leading to the emergence of new systems or patterns of behaviour.

Non-linear dynamics and positive feedback processes, whereby small causes can amplify into large effects, are crucial here. Chaos theorists have used computer simulations of non-linear systems to reveal how initially minute variations can ramp up into dramatic changes in the long-term behaviour of the system. The popular image invoked to illustrate this phenomenon is the 'butterfly effect': the notion that a butterfly flapping its wings in (say) Tokyo can cause a tornado in (say) California. While chaos theory has imposed serious limits on the ability to predict the long-term behaviour of systems, it has also provided new insights, uncovering a subtle order and structure to phenomena previously believed to be completely devoid of recognizable patterns, such as the turbulence of fluids or plate tectonics.

Building on the original insights of chaos theory, complexity scientists turned to the interactions of the different component parts of living systems, and particularly to the new properties and behaviours constituted through the networked selforganization of autonomous agents.

Self-organization is the process by which the autonomous interaction of individual entities results in the bottom-up emergence of complex systems, systems composed of many parts which are connected in a non-linear fashion.

The notion of the network is central to describing the patterns of interaction which are constituted by the interplay of entities in a complex system: 'The first and most obvious property of any network is its non-linearity— it goes in all directions. Thus the relationships in a network pattern are non-linear relationships. In particular, an influence, or message, may travel along a cyclical path, which may become a feedback loop. The concept of feedback is intimately connected with the network pattern.'

Of special interest are the 'complex adaptive systems' which display the ability to change and learn from experience. Complexity theorist John Holland defines a complex adaptive system as a dynamic network of many agents acting simultaneously, constantly both acting and reacting to what the other agents are doing. Since the control of a complex adaptive system tends to be highly dispersed and decentralized, any coherent behaviour in the system arises from competition and cooperation among the agents themselves. It is the accumulation of all the individual decisions taken by the multitude of agents which produces the overall behaviour of the system, which can thus be said to be emergent. Complex adaptive systems include living organisms, insect colonies, bird flocks, ecosystems, businesses, stock markets and other forms of social organization; the constituent agents may be cells, species, individuals, firms or nations. From the perspective of chaoplexity, the most successful systems are those that retain flexibility and openness in the interaction and organization of their parts within environments which elude complete predictability.

No longer is order to be sought in a natural tendency towards equilibrium. On the contrary, it is with non-equilibrium that order emerges from chaos, at the point where instability and creative mutation allow for the genesis of new forms and actions. As Ian King puts it, 'networking [is] a way of maintaining a low-level chaotic substrate so that—as in the brain—the chaos will from time to time give birth to an intellectual self-organizing structure'.

Decentralized self-organizing systems are inherently better equipped than centralized systems to deal with limited predictability and contingency. According to the biologist Christopher Langton, 'since it's effectively impossible to cover every conceivable situation, top-down systems are forever running into combinations of events they don't know how to handle. They tend to be touchy and fragile, and they all too often grind to a halt in a dither of indecision.' In contrast, decentralized systems of quasi-autonomous units can operate more effectively and with a greater degree of adaptability on the basis of the local calculations of the networked agents constituting them. For Stuart Kauffman, 'networks in the regime near the edge of chaos—this compromise between order and surprise—appear best able to coordinate complex activities and best able to evolve as well'.

Chaoplexity has challenged some of the most deeply held scientific convictions about the natural world and opened up whole new areas of research. It is now also increasingly weighing on the debates about military organization, heralding a new era in the scientific way of warfare.

The Dawn of Chaoplexic Warfare

Cybernetic warfare experienced its first serious reversal with the Vietnam War, where its analytical techniques and military systems foundered in the conditions of a low-intensity conflict. James Gibson has written persuasively about the failure in the jungles of South-East Asia of 'technowar', an approach to military conflict in which war was viewed as 'a production system that can be rationally managed and warfare as a kind of activity that can be scientifically determined by constructing computer models'.

The conduct of the war was blighted by the attempts of the military and political hierarchy to micro-manage the conflict and by an obsession with statistical evaluation and information-gathering which frequently created assessments of the war that were completely at variance with the reality on the ground.

Despite the deployment of an unprecedented telecommunications network in the field of operations, command and control technologies failed to perform as expected, with saturation and bottlenecks preventing information on Vietcong positions and movements from arriving in time to be actionable.

Perhaps most seriously, a misguided faith in the powers of technoscience to grant military omnipotence led policy-makers to embrace armed force more willingly as the means to solve complex strategic problems. Such hubris was perfectly encapsulated by Henry Kissinger's claim in 1968 that 'a scientific revolution has, for all practical purposes, removed technical limits from the exercise of power in foreign policy'.

The debacle in Vietnam provoked some soul-searching among strategists and military men but did not result in an immediate abandonment of the central principles of cybernetic warfare, which continued to dominate military thinking through the 1980s. All the early contributions to the debate on the revolution in military affairs were premised on the idea that computers, telecommunication links and precision-guided munitions would finally deliver the frictionless, automated battlefield promised by Westmoreland. However, new thinking drawing on the emerging non-linear sciences did begin to penetrate military theory, at first espoused only by isolated individuals but entering the mainstream at the turn of the century.

The late US air force colonel John Boyd is perhaps the most prominent pioneer of chaoplexic warfare, and increasingly is considered to be one of the most important military thinkers of recent times. Boyd is best known for his formulation of the OODA loop (observe–orient–decide–act), describing the decision-making process of the warfighter engaged in combat. Although this is at first sight reminiscent of a typical cybernetic feedback loop, whereby a system adjusts its behaviour to incoming information from its environment in order to meet a desired objective, Boyd was insistent on the need for the analytical frameworks used during the orientation phase to be continually challenged and reinvented through a perpetual process of 'destruction and creation'.

No predetermined automated response can prevail for long in a world that is 'uncertain, everchanging, unpredictable'. Boyd went on to contribute to US Marine Corps doctrine, which displays clear signs of the influence of chaoplexity in asserting that 'the best we can hope for is to impose a general framework of order on the disorder, to prescribe the general flow of action rather than to try to control each event', and that 'like a living organism, a military organization is never in a state of stable equilibrium but is instead in a continuous state of flux—continuously adjusting to its surroundings'.

If the earlier proclamations of an imminent revolution in military affairs remained firmly tributary to cybernetic conceptions, the ascent of network-centric warfare (NCW) marked the onset of a shift towards chaoplexic notions on the centre ground of debates over military doctrine. With its ideas couched in the language and concepts of the non-linear sciences, NCW first appeared on the scene within the US navy in the late 1990s before rapidly rising to become the new official Pentagon gospel under the agenda of 'Transformation' with the founding of the Office of Force Transformation in 2001 under the stewardship of its original formulator Vice Admiral Arthur Cebrowski.

According to Cebrowski, networkcentric warfare views war as a 'complex, adaptive system where non-linear variables continuously interact'. Since 'coordination from the top down inevitably results in delays and errors in force dispositions', the military should seek to acquire 'the ability of a well-informed force to organize and coordinate complex warfare activities from the bottom up'. For Cebrowski, what is being proposed is nothing less than a 'new theory of war'.

Such a new theory can emerge only by breaking with the command and control principles that governed cybernetic warfare during the Cold War, as suggested by Alberts and Hayes: Control Theory requires both prediction and the existence of an adequate set of levers of control ... [But] having effective, centrally managed levers that can control or even predictably influence a complex, adaptive system is far from guaranteed ... In the Information Age, control needs to be thought about and approached differently.

Control is not something that can be imposed on a complex adaptive system, particularly when there are many independent actors. Control, that is, ensuring that behavior stays within or moving to within acceptable bounds, can only be achieved indirectly.

The most promising approach involves establishing, to the extent possible, a set of initial conditions that will *result* in the desired behavior. In other words, control is not achieved by imposing a parallel process, but rather emerges from influencing the behaviors of independent agents. NCW theorists claim that through the distribution of information across the battlefield and the constitution of a common operational picture via an overarching 'Global Information Grid', command and control will be decentralized and individual troops will be freed to act on their own initiative, leading to self-synchronization, a clear nod to the chaoplexic notion of self-organization.

New tactical schemes denied to their hierarchical counterparts are seen as the emergent properties that will be unlocked by fully networked self-synchronizing forces. Drawing further from the writings of complexity theorists and deploying biological metaphors, military theorists appeal to the 'swarm', the networks of distributed intelligence that enable bees, ants and termites to evolve complex forms of collective behaviour on the basis of the simple rules of interaction of their individual members. Of particular interest are the resilience and flexibility of these swarms as amorphous ensembles whose continued existence and successful operation is not critically dependent on any single individual. Military swarms promise not only more adaptable and survivable forces but also new offensive and defensive tactics better suited to the contemporary battlespace. According to Alberts and Hayes, decentralization and information-sharing will permit military platforms to 'evolve from being networked entities to being nodes in the network, to organizing efforts resembling "packs" and "swarms"'. The ensembles of different entities making up fighting forces, whether human or robotic, will 'ultimately become dynamically reconfigurable packs, swarms, or other organizations of highly specialized components that work together like the cells of our bodies' and will be 'less mechanical and more organic, less engineered and more "grown"'.

Beyond the flexibility and evolutionary capability that are attributed to military swarms, it is also claimed that they will be able to bring force to bear in a new manner.

Rather than throwing themselves onto the enemy in 'waves', forces will be able to converge on their target from all directions in offensive bursts, thereby maximizing the shock effect.

For Arquilla and Ronfeldt, the full effects of swarming are achieved when the dispersed nodes of a network of small (and also perhaps some large) forces can converge on an enemy from multiple directions, through either fire or maneuver. The overall aim should be *sustainable pulsing*—swarm networks must be able to coalesce rapidly and stealthily on a target, then dissever and redisperse, immediately ready to recombine for a new pulse. A swarm network should have little to no mass as a rule (except perhaps during a pulse), but it should have a high energy potential—like a swarm of bees that can fell a mighty beast, or a network of antibodies that can attack a spreading virus.

Troops that can disperse swiftly after an attack or 'pulse' also have the advantage of being less vulnerable to enemy attacks, particularly in the context of the high lethality and precision characteristic of contemporary and future battlefields. The promises of network-centric warfare are bold and, for all its deployment of chaoplexic language, the doctrine suffers from a number of potentially critical weaknesses. In several respects it has not significantly broken with cybernetic warfare and therefore may not in fact implement all the features of a truly chaoplexic way of warfare.

While 'decentralization' is the order-word of the day, the networking of troops may in fact provide the technological infrastructure for greater micro-management than ever by a military brass which will have access to data feeds from anywhere in the battlespace.

Second, dependence on a unified 'Global Information Grid' could both create a critical vulnerability likely to be targeted by competent adversaries and deprive troops of the skills required to respond creatively to situations in which only limited local information is available (as most of the complex adaptive systems studied are found to do).

Furthermore, NCW advocates fall back all too often on impoverished conceptions of Boyd's OODA loop which substitute speed of execution of predetermined responses for creative thinking and adaptability to the unforeseen. Finally, there persists a tendency to see information technology as the panacea which will permanently lift the friction and fog of war which has plagued all past militaries, when in fact chaoplexity points to the irreducible contingency and unpredictability of war and the need to organize so as to tolerate and even take advantage of this uncertainty.

Ultimately chaoplexic warfare will depend more on doctrinal and organizational commitments than on any particular information technologies, which are liable to be employed to quite contrary purposes. The full arrival of chaoplexic warfare may therefore still lie ahead; but the debates around network-centric warfare clearly show an impetus towards greater decentralization and the use of the network form of organization within armed forces. NCW now has its counterparts in most major western militaries, including Network Enabled

Capabilities (NEC) in the United Kingdom, NATO Network Enabled Capabilities (NNEC), and Network Enabled Operations (NEOps) in Canada. Where such militaries have encountered recent setbacks, for example in Iraq, Afghanistan or Lebanon, it has been against opponents that have employed decentralized networks to good effect against better-equipped forces, thereby further stimulating discussion about their merits and underlining the limitations of established modes of operation. Just as the ideas of mechanism, thermodynamics and cybernetics inspired past military thought and practice in association with their respective paradigmatic technologies, a new set of scientific theories are now occupying a central role within the doctrinal and organizational changes of the armies of the early twenty-first century. Our network age is therefore also that of chaoplexity.

CYBER WARFARE CHALLENGE

Cyber warfare encompasses government and public and private domains. As clarified earlier, this must be coordinated by the NSCS (National Security Council Secretariat). In the USA it comes directly under the White House. Thus the need to create a Directorate or Special Wing in the NSCS for this. It would oversee and coordinate both defensive and offensive cyber operations. There is also a requirement for intimate involvement of the private sector, as they are equal, if not larger, stakeholders. Regular meetings must be held and, if needed, working groups created. Current organisations which could be tasked to take on the cyber warfare challenge include the NTRO, HQ IDS (Headquarter Integrated Defence Services), DRDO, RAW and IB. Representatives of CERT, NASSCOM, etc. will invariably be involved. Each would have to function under guidelines and through proxies. This includes:

Raising of Cyber Command

While cyber warfare is ongoing activity during peacetime, there is a dire need to develop this capacity for a warlike situation. Cyber warfare in a manner is NCW and will form an essential part of preparation of the battlefield in any future conflict. Such attacks may also precede the kinetic war. Building this capability will take time and must remain covert and ambiguous.

It could also form part of the strategic deception process. This should be the responsibility of the Armed Forces (HQIDS) along with the DRDO and other experts. Detailed discussions and consultations in this regard require to be initiated. India must raise a Cyber Command.

This will comprise not only the three services but personnel from the DRDO and scientific and technological community. It could work with the space command because many aspects overlap and would economise on resources.

It will oversee all activities undertaken during peacetime, as also plan for offensive cyber operations as required, to include preparation of the battlefield. It must work in close concert with the NTRO. To determine the structure it would be prudent to study the mission and objectives of USCYBERCOM (US Cyber Command) as a guide.

USCYBERCOM plans, coordinates, integrates, synchronises and conducts activities to: "direct the operations and defense of specified Department of Defense information NWs and; prepare to, and when directed, conduct full spectrum military cyberspace operations in order to enable actions in all domains, ensure US/Allied freedom of action in cyberspace and deny the same to our adversaries." The Command is charged with pulling together existing cyberspace resources, creating synergy and synchronising war-fighting effects to defend the information security environment.

It comes under the Strategic Command, which also has the Space Command as a constituent. A similar structure for India could be considered, especially as the US has evolved its structure based on experience and also because it functions as an open democracy. India already has the Strategic Forces Command, which could be augmented with both Space and Cyberspace Wings. These may be of smaller size to start with, and will develop in accordance with threats and needs. Each service has its own requirements. The structure therefore has to be need-based and flexible. The various elements of this could be:

Army, Navy and Air Force CERTs

These would monitor traffic, disseminate information, ensure remedial measures to ensure ongoing security to networks and systems. They would also in a manner be charged with protection of critical infrastructure of each service, i.e. communication backbone, power systems, high-priority networks. The structure thus envisages a Defence CERT which works in concert with each service CERT.

CYBER-WARFARE TACTICS

Other cyber tactics are less sophisticated. The attack that temporarily brought down Estonian networks began with a flood of bogus messages targeting government servers, called a "denial of service" attack. The approach harnesses "botnets"—massive networks of interconnected computers—to bombard targeted networks with information requests while masking the location of the primary attacker. James Lewis, a security expert with the Center for Strategic and International Studies (CSIS), says hackers in the Estonia example likely took control of tens of thousands of computers around the world without the knowledge of their owners and directed them at the government's servers. The result, he says, was a relatively minor attack that was nearly impossible to trace.

Another technique is the use of "malware," "spyware," and other malicious programs imbedded into computer systems to steal information without user knowledge. The software is designed to hide undetected and siphon information from its host—everything from secrets stored on personal computers to Pentagon military mainframes. A December 2007 analysis of U.S. Air Force cyber vulnerabilities notes much of the Pentagon's operating systems are off-the-shelf components manufactured overseas, due to cheaper costs. But pinching pennies has potentially opened U.S. military networks to intrusion. "Foreign countries could place hidden components inside the computers, making the computers vulnerable for attack and/or spying," the analysis concludes.

> *"Our ability to penetrate into enemy computer networks, our ability to exploit communication networks, to manipulate digital information, is real." –Defense Analyst William M. Arkin*

Less common but far more worrisome are cyber attacks aimed at critical infrastructure—like nuclear-power-plant control systems, banks, or subways. In March 2007 the Department of Energy's Idaho Lab conducted an experiment to determine whether a power plant could be compromised by hacking alone. The result—a smoking, self-combusting diesel generator incapacitated by nothing more than keystrokes—sent shivers (CNN) through the private sector. The worries were apparently well-founded.

In January 2008 a CIA analyst told U.S. utilities that hackers had succeeded in infiltrating electric companies in undisclosed locations outside the United States and, it at least one instance, shut off power to multiple cities. The hackers then demanded money (AP). "The [U.S.] government is scrambling to try and protect its own systems, to try and check the Chinese from reading government email," says economist Scott Borg, director of the U.S. Cyber Consequences Unit, a nonprofit research institute that studies cyber threats. "But the focus probably needs to be critical infrastructure. That's what we need to defend."

CASUALTIES OF CYBER WARFARE

That the United States and China have engaged in skirmishes in the cyber domain is no secret. Since the beginning of the 21st century, targeted cyberattacks, often with signs of Chinese origin, have attempted to penetrate the computer networks of U.S. corporations and government agencies in search of potentially valuable information. In response to this new strategic threat, the U.S. Military's Strategic Command commissioned the creation of a sub-unified Cyber Command in 2009, with one of its stated objectives being the "defense of specified Department of Defense information networks."

U.S. President Barack Obama very clearly defined the threat that cyberattacks pose to the economy, in both the public and private sectors, when he said that the "cyber threat is one of the most serious economic and national security challenges we face as a nation." Indeed, conflict in the cyber domain is still having some serious repercussions for the business world.

Civilian Involvement in Cyber Warfare

The characteristic of cyber warfare that makes it so uniquely dangerous to the corporate sector is that military power in the cyber domain must be extended through computer networks provided and maintained by non-governmental bodies. The use of these networks for cyberattacks or defense requires the conscription or cooperation of civilian resources. This creates extreme liabilities for the corporations that provide these networks, as they will quickly become the targets of suspicion and possible retaliation from the enemy state. In recent years, both Chinese and American companies have been caught in just this situation.

On October 8, 2012, the U.S. House of Representatives' intelligence committee released a report that warned of potential national security threats posed by Chinese telecommunication giants Huawei and ZTE. After conducting a year-long investigation of the suspect companies, the intelligence committee found serious vulnerabilities caused by hidden "backdoors" worked into the companies' technologies that would allow access to U.S. government and business networks.

The report advised against the purchase of products manufactured by Huawei or ZTE, and suggested that policymakers block any mergers between either of the two companies and U.S. telecommunication corporations.

These accusations have seriously hurt consumer confidence in the two companies, to the extent that in December of 2013, Huawei's executive vice president dramatically declared"we are not interested in the U.S. market anymore." While Huawei has managed to hold on to a small market share in America, the company's association with Chinese state-sponsored cyberattacks has devastated its ability to operate in the United States.

It became clear last year, though, that the United States was a perpetrator of cyberattacks as well as a victim. In June 2013, former U.S. National Security Agency contractor Edward Snowden provided the world with a look into the intelligence apparatus of the NSA, releasing thousands of classified documents to the media. The released documents revealed that the U.S., like China, was using domestic tech firms (in many cases without their knowledge or consent) as conduits for intelligence gathering cyberattacks. In May 2014, the Chinese government announced that it would no longer purchase or use two of Microsoft's main products, the Windows 8 operating system and the Microsoft Office 365 Suite. Then, in late July and early August, Chinese officials from the State Administration for Industry and Commerce (SAIC) raided multiple offices owned by Microsoft and its contractors in China. While vague statements about an anti-monopoly probe were made, the company's decision to end support for the Windows XP operating system – a move that would expose the many Chinese computers that use the operating system to security risks – was also cited as a factor in the raids.

While it is likely that the ban and subsequent raids were also intended to pave the way for new operating system technologies created in China, the Snowden revelations allowed potential U.S. espionage activities to be cited as a justification. Just as Huawei and ZTE suffered for their association with espionage activities of the Chinese government, Microsoft took a major hit because of the provocative actions of its government.

An Undefined Battlefield

On both sides of the Pacific, it is clear that both U.S. and Chinese tech firms are being caught in the crossfire of these cyber skirmishes between the two countries. Any escalation in tensions in the cyber domain could be disastrous to the private sector. Unfortunately, despite the risks that future cyberwars hold for multinational corporations, there is a marked absence of legislation, precedent, and international norms that could govern the relationships between private companies and the governments looking to use them as avenues through which cyberwar could be conducted.

For as long as these ambiguities exist, corporations that deal in the communication technology industry will exist in the gray area of an unregulated cyber battlefield devoid of any policies meant to protect the assets and infrastructures of civilian actors. It is in the interests of both countries to more clearly define, through domestic cooperation with corporate partners and with bilateral international discussion and agreement, the boundaries between civilians and the military in cyber warfare. Failure to do so could severely hamper the economic interaction that has been so lucrative for both countries and further destabilize an already fragile Sino-American relationship.

Government's Role in Domestic Cyber Security

While organizations have taken extensive measures to provide security against cybercrime, the challenges of a larger cyberwar against a capable and persistent foe require greater national organization and civilian-government cooperation. Unfortunately, in the United States, government responses to engagements in the cyber domain have been slow at best, but more often nonexistent. The cause of this is commonly the difficulty in identifying attackers and the lack of procedures in place for how a national response can and should be mobilized to address an attack on a civilian target. This lack of definition creates additional liability for the civilian counterpart because the opposing state (in this case China) does not know to what extent the civilian is involved with the defense and possible subsequent counterattacks. The lack of clarity directly increases the probability that the civilian will be the target of general suspicion and will suffer financial damage, as was seen with

Huawei, ZTE and Microsoft. In broad terms, foreign attacks on domestic civilian targets can be placed in one of two categories: those that pose a national security threat and those that cause potential financial harm to the recipient of the attack. These two types of attacks require specific responses that have not yet been clearly defined by the U.S. government and the business community.

A cyberattack that directly threatens the national security of the United States might require the temporary direct use, or even the partial or complete conscription, of a civilian network. Disruptions of public utilities, theft of sensitive information from a security contractor, or the sabotage of civilian networks necessary for the operation of the military are examples of intrusions that might necessitate such a response. However, the documents released by Edward Snowden revealed that civilian networks were commonly conscripted for foreign surveillance activities, often without the knowledge of their owners. One of the largest barriers that conscription faces to becoming a transparent counter-cyberattack strategy is the ambiguity surrounding the cyber domain in warfare. Because no legislation exists that explicitly defines cyberattacks as acts of war and because the Supreme Court has never ruled on the constitutionality of conscription in any form during peacetime, no precedent has ever been set that would instruct the government on how to publicly organize a defense in the case of a cyberattack against a civilian target that threatened national security. While this does not excuse the NSA of its secrecy, it does indicate the need for legal clarification on the matter of cyber warfare. A decisive answer to the question of the legality of government conscription of civilian network assets in the interests of national security would allow a transparent strategy that involved input from both civilian and government representatives to be formed.

Bibliography

Ahmad, Imtiaz: *State and Foreign Policy: India's Role in South Asia*, New Delhi, Vikas, 1993.

Alexander, J : *Military Technology and Equipment Technology*, Omega Pub, Delhi, 2008.

Burnes, Alexander: *Cabool; a Personal Narrative*, London, J. Murray, 1842.

Cole, Alan : *Mothers and Sons in Chinese Buddhism,* Stanford, CA: Stanford University Press, 1998.

Crichton, Michael: *Electronic Life, How to Think About Computers*, New York, Alfred A. Knopf, 1983.

David Post : *The Rise of Law in Cyberspace*, 48 Stan, L. Rev. 1367, 1996.

Dixit, Prabla: *Communalism: A Struggle for Power*, New Delhi, Orient Longman, 1981.

Dudeja, V. D. : *Crimes in Cyber Space-Scams and Frauds: Issues and Remedies*, Commonwealth, Delhi, 2003.

English, Barbara: *The War for a Persian Lady*, Boston, Houghton Mifflin, 1971.

Friedman, G.: *The Future of War: Power, Technology and American World Dominance in the 21st Century*, N.Y., Random House, 1996.

Garrelick, Renee. M.I.T. Beginnings: The Legacy of Nuclear Metals. Concord, MA: Nuclear Metals, Inc., 1995.

Gast, A. P. : *The impact of Restricting Information Access on Science and Technology* Retrieved October 1, 2008.

Gibson, James N. *Nuclear Weapons of the United States: An Illustrated History*. Atglen, PA: Schiffer Publishing Ltd., 1996.

Godwin, Mike: *Cyber Rights: Defending Free Speech in the Digital Age*. Times Books, 1998

Habberton, William: *Anglo-Russian Relations Concerning Afghanistan 1837-1907*, Urbana, University of Illinois, 1937.

Hahn, Harley: *Harley Hahn's Internet InSecurity*. Prentice Hall: Upper Saddle River, 2002.

Hittle, James D: *The Military Staff: Its History and Development*, The Stackpole Company, Harrisburg, 1961.

Hoffman, Bruce: *Inside Terrorism and Internet Crime*, New York: Columbia University Press, 1998.

Jones, W.H.: *Government and Politics of India Military*, London, Hutchinson, 1971.

Kala, G.K. : *Demystifying Military Leadership*, Manas Pub, Delhi, 2003.

Kaufmann, Albert R. *Nuclear Reactor Fuel Elements: Metallurgy and Fabrication*. New York: Interscience Publishers, Inc., 1962.

Kumar, Raj : *Weapons and Military Technology*, Sumit Enterprises, Delhi, 2009.

Laliberte, S. : *Security by Example Defend I.T.* New York, Addison Wesley, 2004.

Moseley, Philip E.: *Russian Diplomacy and the Opening of the Eastern Question*, Cambridge, Harvard University Press, 1934.

Norris, James A.: *The First Afghan War 1838-1842*, Cambridge, University Press, 1967.

Paul Buis : *Internet Security: Professional Reference*. New Riders: Indianapolis, 1996.

Radhakrishna: *Military Ethics: Guidelines for Peace and War*, Sumit Enterprises, Delhi, 2009.

Rosen, P.: *Societies and Military Power: India and its Armies*, Ithaca, Cornell University Press, 1996.

Shaun Narine, *Explaining ASEAN: Regionalism in Southeast Asia*, Boulder, CO: Lynne Rienner Publishers, 2002.

Singhal, D. P.: *India and Afghanistan: 1876-1907. A Study in Diplomatic Relations*, St. Lucia, University of Queensland, 1963.

Van Creveld, Martin: *The Art of War: War and Military Thought*, Smithsonian Books/Collins, Washington DC, 2005.

Verton, D. : *Black Ice: The invisible Threat of Cyber-terrorism*, New York: McGraw-Hill/Osborne, 2003.

William Aspray: *Computer, A History of the Information Machine*, New York, Basic Books, 1996.

Zanini, M.: *Countering the New Terrorism*, Santa Monica, CA: RAND, 1999.

Index

N

O

P

S

T

W

❑❑❑